DAY HIKES AROUND
Bozeman
MONTANA

INCLUDING THE GALLATIN
CANYON AND PARADISE VALLEY

Robert Stone

4th EDITION

Day Hike Books, Inc.

RED LODGE, MONTANA

Published by Day Hike Books, Inc.
P.O. Box 865
Red Lodge, Montana 59068
www.dayhikebooks.com

Distributed by The Globe Pequot Press
246 Goose Lane
P.O. Box 480
Guilford, CT 06437-0480
800-243-0495 (direct order) · 800-820-2329 (fax order)
www.globe-pequot.com

Cover photograph by Linda Stone
Design by Paula Doherty

The author has made every attempt to provide accurate information in this book. However, trail routes and features may change—please use common sense and forethought, and be mindful of your own capabilities. Let this book guide you, but be aware that each hiker assumes responsibility for their own safety. The author and publisher do not assume any responsibility for loss, damage, or injury caused through the use of this book.

Cover photo:
Hyalite Reservoir from the Hood Creek Trail, Hike 48

Back cover photo:
View from the Rock Creek Trail in Paradise Valley, Hike 92

Also by Robert Stone

Day Hikes In Yellowstone National Park

Day Hikes In Grand Teton National Park

Day Hikes In the Beartooth Mountains

Day Hikes Around Bozeman, Montana

Day Hikes Around Missoula, Montana

Day Hikes In Yosemite National Park

Day Hikes In Sequoia & Kings Canyon Nat'l. Parks

Day Hikes On the California Central Coast

Day Hikes On the California Southern Coast

Day Hikes Around Sonoma County

Day Hikes Around Big Sur

Day Hikes Around Monterey and Carmel

Day Hikes In San Luis Obispo County, California

Day Hikes Around Santa Barbara

Day Hikes Around Ventura County

Day Hikes Around Los Angeles

Day Hikes Around Orange County

Day Hikes In Sedona, Arizona

Day Hikes On Oahu

Day Hikes On Maui

Day Hikes On Kauai

Day Hikes In Hawaii

ACKNOWLEDGEMENTS

The author gratefully acknowledges
the following people for their assistance,
trail updates, and clarifications:

From the Gallatin National Forest ~ Livingston Ranger District:
Scott Laughlin
Jackie Riley
Wendi Urie

From the Gallatin National Forest ~ Bozeman Ranger District:
Jose Castro
Dan Kettman

Ted Lange at the Gallatin Valley Land Trust
for his assistance and dedication to the
expanding trail system in Bozeman.

Bill Olson for his hard work and devotion
in the development of the Big Sky trail system.

Hiking partner, Kofax

LINDA STONE

Table of Contents

THE HIKES

West Bridger Mountains

East Bridger Mountains • Bangtail Mountains

Bozeman Area
including "Main Street to the Mountains"

Hyalite Canyon

Madison River

Gallatin Canyon

Yellowstone National Park
from the Gallatin

Paradise Valley:
Gallatin Range on the West Side

Paradise Valley:
Absaroka Range on the East Side

West Boulder Valley

Regional Maps included:

p. 14 Overall map of all hikes
  16 Central Montana
  18 Bridger Mountains • Hikes 1–17
  60 City of Bozeman
  62 Bozeman and Vicinity • Hikes 18–43
128 Hyalite Reservoir
130 Hyalite Canyon • Hikes 44–55
162 Big Sky
164 Gallatin Canyon • Hikes 57–75
218 Yellowstone from the Gallatin • Hikes 76–84
238 Paradise Valley • Hikes 85–110
241 City of Livingston
274 North Paradise Valley to West Boulder

Suggested commercial maps for additional hiking:

U.S. Geological Survey topographic maps
U.S. Forest Service: Gallatin National Forest (East and West)
Beartooth Publishing: Bozeman–Big Sky–West Yellowstone
Bozeman: Bozeman Area Chamber of Commerce
Crystal Bench Maps: Bozeman
Rocky Mountain Surveys: Spanish Peaks

Hiking Bozeman

Bozeman, Montana is an active, thriving town dating back to the 1880s. It is rich in character, history, and landscape. There are eight historical districts, a wide variety of museums, art galleries, musical events, and the city is home to Montana State University. Surrounded by extraordinary wilderness, Bozeman is also a gateway city to the Gallatin National Forest and Yellowstone National Park.

The Gallatin National Forest, part of the Greater Yellowstone Area, encompasses 1.8 million acres and contains some of the highest mountains in Montana. Six mountain ranges run through the national forest land—the Absaroka, Beartooth, Bridger, Crazy, Gallatin, and Madison Ranges. Many peaks rise above 10,000 feet. The sheer grandeur of this national forest includes the protected 259,000-acre Lee Metcalf Wilderness and the 945,000-acre Absaroka-Beartooth Wilderness. The forest also contains the headwaters to the Boulder, Gallatin, and Madison Rivers plus hundreds of miles of creeks and tributaries. (Many of the rivers have a blue-ribbon rating for fishing.) The Gallatin National Forest has an abundance of wildlife, including black and grizzly bear, moose, elk, mountain lions, big horn sheep, mountain goats, and deer. Whether fishing, boating, mountain climbing, horseback riding, camping, biking, backpacking or hiking, this area has endless opportunities for outdoor recreation.

These 110 hikes lie within a 90-mile drive of Bozeman and are organized by groups in the drainages and mountain ranges that surround the city. A wide range of scenery and ecosystems accommodates all levels of hikes, from relaxing creekside strolls to all-day, high-elevation outings. The trails have been chosen for their scenery, variety, and ability to be hiked within the day.

Most of the hikes are accessed by three main routes—Highway 191 through the Gallatin Canyon, Highway 86 to the Bridgers, and Highway 89 through Paradise Valley. Within the city itself are 21 hikes.

To the north of Bozeman lies the Bridger Range, home to the Bridger Foothills National Recreation Trail and Bridger Bowl Ski Area. Many hiking and biking trails are found in this scenic mountain range because of its close proximity to Bozeman, yet this area retains a feeling of remoteness. Hikes 1—17 are located within the Bridgers.

Hikes 18–43 are in Bozeman or within a few minutes drive. The city lies in the East Gallatin Valley between the Bridgers and the Gallatin Range. Bozeman itself has a great variety of trails developed by the Gallatin Valley Land Trust. (See page 61 for more information.) Several trails access the nearby canyons and mountains from this community trail system.

South of Bozeman is the 34,000-acre Hyalite Drainage, a stunning mountain valley between the Gallatin Canyon and Paradise Valley. This drainage is a popular recreational area with a large reservoir built in the 1940s as its centerpiece. The Hyalite Reservoir has a holding capacity of 8,000 acre-feet of water and is used for drinking water for the city of Bozeman and to irrigate the Gallatin Valley. Its coves, creeks, and piers offer great trout fishing and boating opportunities. The Hyalite Drainage Recreational Area is surrounded by 10,000-foot mountain peaks and includes a large variety of biking and hiking trails, creeks, streams, lakes and numerous waterfalls. Hikes 44–55 lie in this beautiful mountain valley.

Hike 56 is located in Bear Trap Canyon in the Madison River drainage west of Bozeman. The canyon is a well known fishing and hiking area in a remote, roadless region within the Madison Range.

Hikes 57–75 are accessed from Highway 191 through the Gallatin Valley. Highway 191 snakes south through the Gallatin Canyon along the Gallatin River. The highway connects Bozeman with Big Sky and West Yellowstone, the west entrance to Yellowstone National Park. The Gallatin River and Highway 191 lie between two mountain ranges. To the east is the Gallatin Range, which includes the Hyalite Drainage. To the west is the Madison Range, which includes the Lee Metcalf Wilderness and the Spanish Peaks.

Several of the hikes are located in the rugged 78,000-acre Spanish Peaks Wilderness Area (part of the Lee Metcalf Wilderness), north of Big Sky and west of Highway 191. The steep Spanish Peaks contain some of the oldest rocks in North America. The three-billion year old metamorphic rocks were sculpted by glaciers, wind, and water. Within the area are 25 peaks rising above 10,000 feet, including Gallatin Peak at 11,015 feet. Below the peaks are wide subalpine meadows, forested valleys, and more than 175 lakes.

Continuing south on Highway 191 leads toward the headwaters of the Gallatin River and the far northwest corner of Yellowstone National Park. Hikes 76—84 are located along several tributaries of the Gallatin, traveling up through valleys to sweeping views of the landscape.

Highway 89 begins about 20 miles east of Bozeman at Livingston. The 53-mile southerly stretch connects Livingston with Gardiner at the north entrance of Yellowstone Park. The highway parallels the Yellowstone River through Paradise Valley, a wide, scenic valley flanked by majestic mountain peaks. The west side of the valley is bordered by the Gallatin Range—Hikes 85—96. The east side of the valley is bordered by the Absaroka and Beartooth Ranges—Hikes 97—110.

A quick glance at the hikes' summaries will allow you to choose a hike that is appropriate to your ability and desire. An overall map on the next page identifies the locations of most of the hikes. Several other regional maps, as well as maps for each hike, provide the essential details. Many commercial maps are available for further hiking. Suggestions are listed with each hike and on page 10.

Even though these trails are described as day hikes, many of the trails involve serious backcountry hiking. Reference the hiking statistics listed at the top of each page for an approximation of difficulty, and match the hikes to your ability. Hiking times are calculated for continuous hiking. Allow extra time for exploration. Feel free to hike farther than these day hike suggestions, but be sure to carry additional trail and topographic maps. Use good judgement about your capabilities, and be prepared with adequate clothing and supplies.

Because many of the hikes are located in high altitude terrain, be aware that the increased elevation will affect your stamina. Weather conditions undoubtedly change throughout the day and seasons. It is imperative to wear warm, layered clothing. Snacks, water, and a basic first aid kit are a must. Both black and grizzly bears inhabit the region, so wear a bear bell and hike in a group whenever possible. Some preparation and forethought will help ensure a safe, enjoyable, and memorable hike.

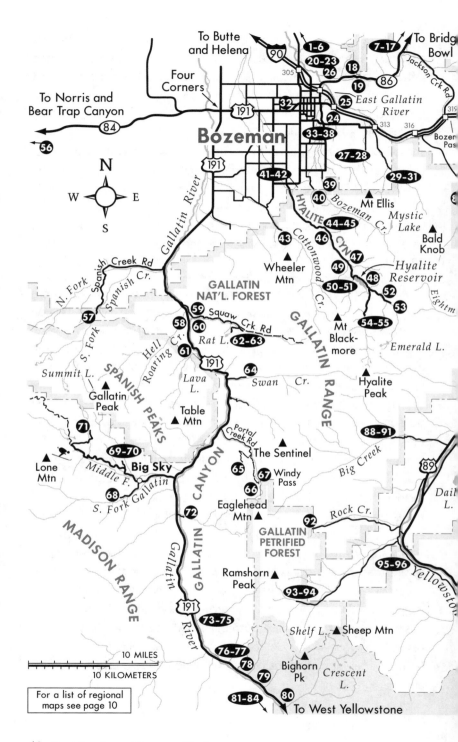

To Butte and Helena

To Bridge Bowl

1-6   7-17

20-23   18
26

19   86

Four Corners

To Norris and Bear Trap Canyon

84

56

305

32

25   East Gallatin River

313   316

Bozen Pas

24

Bozeman

191

33-38

27-28

29-31

41-42

39

Mt Ellis

Mystic Lake

40   Bozeman Cr.

Bald Knob

44-45

43   Cottonwood Cr.

46

Wheeler Mtn

49

47

Hyalite Reservoir

50-51

48

GALLATIN NAT'L. FOREST

52

Squaw Crk Rd

59

53

Spanish Creek Rd

N. Fork

Spanish Cr.

57

58   60

Rat L.   62-63

Mt Black-more

54-55

Emerald L.

S. Fork

Hell Roaring Cr.

61

191

Lava L.

64   Swan   Cr.

Hyalite Peak

Summit L.

SPANISH PEAKS

GALLATIN RANGE

Eightm

Gallatin Peak

Table Mtn

Portal Creek Rd

The Sentinel

88-91

71

Lone Mtn

69-70

Big Sky

65   67   Windy Pass

Big Creek

89

Dail L.

68   Middle F.

66

S. Fork Gallatin

Eaglehead Mtn

GALLATIN CANYON

72   92

Rock Cr.

MADISON RANGE

GALLATIN PETRIFIED FOREST

95-96

Yellowstor

Ramshorn Peak

93-94

Shelf L.   Sheep Mtn

73-75

76-77

Bighorn Pk

78

Crescent L.

10 MILES

79   80

10 KILOMETERS

81-84

To West Yellowstone

For a list of regional maps see page 10

N   W   E   S

Gallatin River

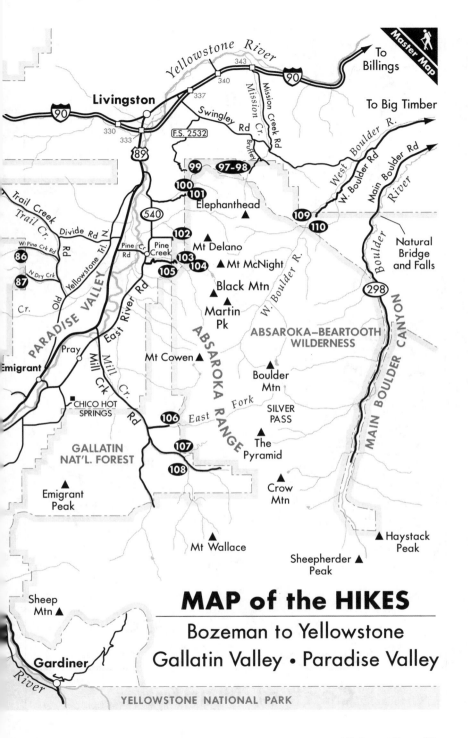

MAP of the HIKES
Bozeman to Yellowstone
Gallatin Valley • Paradise Valley

YELLOWSTONE NATIONAL PARK

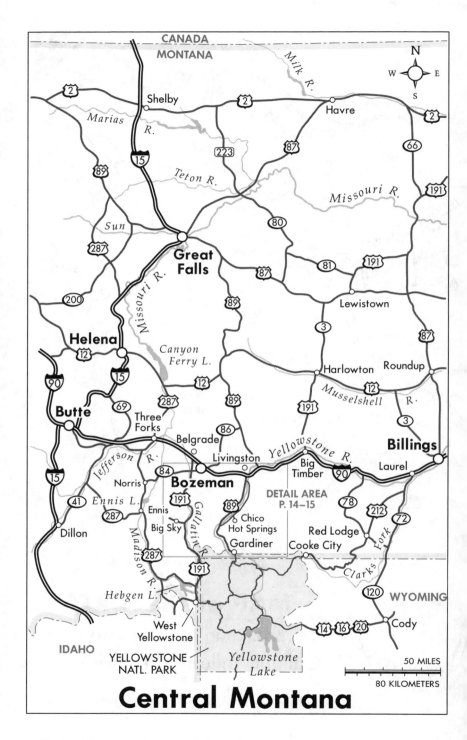

Central Montana

Bridger Mountains
and Bangtail Mountains

HIKES 1—17

map
page 18

The Bridger Mountains abruptly rise from the north end of Bozeman, forming a backdrop for the city. The 25-mile-long range is a steep fold of sedimentary rock with a distinct rolling spine. The elevation ranges from 5,000 feet up to 9,665 feet at Sacagawea Peak, the highest peak in the range (Hike 11). The range borders the fertile Gallatin Valley on the west and the Bangtail Mountains to the east, divided by Bridger Canyon.

The Bridgers are surrounded by six mountain ranges. The Gallatin and Madison stretch to the south, the Crazies lie to the east, the Big Belts are to the north, the Elkhorns lie to the northwest, and the Tobacco Roots extend along the west. From atop the ridge, these mountain ranges can all be viewed.

The Bridger Foothills National Recreation Trail parallels the ridge in a steady series of ups and downs, skirting the west side of the peaks. The trail runs 24 miles, from Baldy Mountain, at the "M" picnic area on the south end of the Bridger Range (Hike 18), to Hardscrabble Peak (Hike 10).

The Bangtail Mountains to the east are a short range within the Bridger Mountains. The Bangtails lie between Bridger Canyon and Shields Valley, north of Bozeman Pass. The mountain range has a network of logging roads and hiking/biking trails.

Hikes 1—7 explore the west side of the Bridgers, accessed from the Gallatin Valley. Hikes 8—13 travel up the east side of the range from Bridger Canyon. Many of the hikes access the spine of the range and the Bridger Foothills National Recreation Trail, forming an interconnected network of trails. Hikes 14—17 begin in Bridger Canyon and head eastward into the Bangtail Mountains.

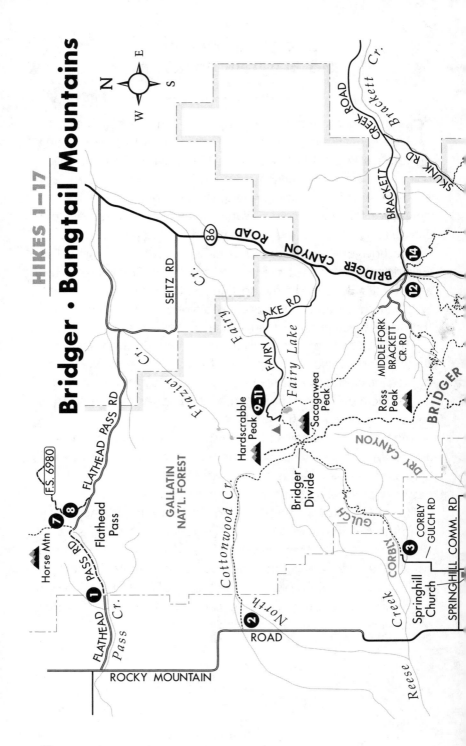

Bridger • Bangtail Mountains

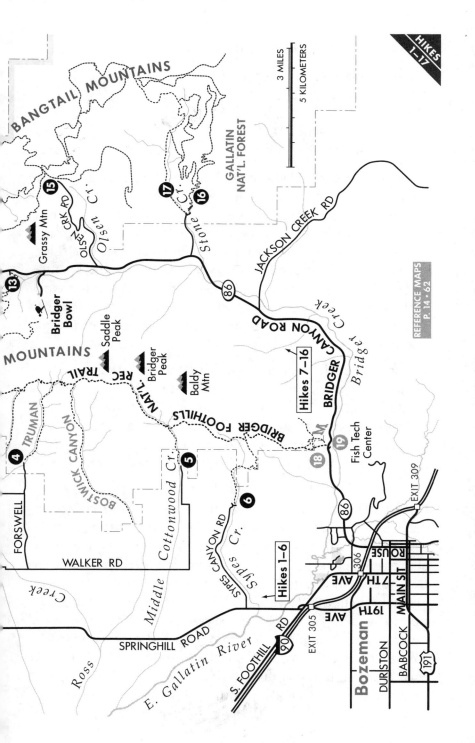

BANGTAIL MOUNTAINS

GALLATIN NAT'L. FOREST

3 MILES

5 KILOMETERS

15 Grassy Mtn

17 **16** Stone Cr.

OLSEN CRK. RD

Olsen Cr.

JACKSON CREEK RD

86

CANYON ROAD

Bridger Creek

REFERENCE MAPS P. 14 • 62

13 Bridger Bowl

Saddle Peak

MOUNTAINS

TRUMAN

NAT'L. REC. TRAIL

Bridger Peak

Baldy Mtn

BRIDGER FOOTHILLS

Hikes 7-16

BRIDGER

BOSTWICK CANYON

4 FORSWELL

5

6

Middle Cottonwood Cr.

WALKER RD

SYPES CANYON RD

Sypes Cr.

18 **19** M

Fish Tech Center

86

EXIT 309

Hikes 1-6

Ross Creek

SPRINGHILL ROAD

E. Gallatin River

S. FOOTHILL RD

90

EXIT 305

306

7TH AVE

19TH AVE

ROUSE

MAIN ST

Bozeman

DURSTON

BABCOCK

191

1. Flathead Pass

Hiking distance: 4.6 miles round trip
Hiking time: 2.5 hours
Elevation gain: 1,200 feet
Maps: U.S.G.S. Flathead Pass
        Beartooth Publishing: Bozeman, Big Sky, W. Yellowstone

Summary of hike: Flathead Pass crosses the north end of the Bridger Mountains, connecting the Gallatin Valley on the east with Bridger Canyon on the west. At the 6,922-foot pass is a beautiful alpine meadow covered in wildflowers. The stunning views from the meadow span to the surrounding peaks, Shields Valley, Gallatin Valley, and the Crazy Mountains. The trail is a forested road that hugs Pass Creek and steadily climbs past jagged rock walls and chiseled outcroppings. The narrow road can be driven, but it is rutted and rocky. It is better explored as a hiking or biking route.

Driving directions: From I-90 and the 7th Avenue overpass, drive 2 miles north on 7th Avenue (which becomes West Frontage Road) to Springhill Road. Turn right (north) and continue 19.3 miles to posted Flathead Pass Road. (En route, the pavement ends at 11.3 miles and becomes Rocky Mountain Road.) Turn right and drive 2.1 miles on the narrow dirt road to the national forest boundary. Park on the side of the road.

Hiking directions: Head east on the narrow dirt road above Johnson Canyon to the south, and enter the shaded forest. Parallel the north side of Pass Creek, steadily gaining elevation and passing unmarked side roads that veer off from the main trail. At a half mile, pass Trail 528 on the left. Walk through sloping meadows with wildflowers and tree-shaded pockets. Cross under power poles at 0.8 miles by jagged rock walls and chiseled outcroppings in a gorge. Pass through a cattle gate and climb to the open, rolling meadows to Flathead Pass by a fenceline and cattle guard. The vistas extend across Shields Valley to the Crazy Mountains in the east and the Gallatin Valley and Tobacco Root Mountains to the west. This is the turn-around spot.

To extend the hike, head north one mile up to Horse Mountain (Hike 7), or continue through the alpine meadows along the Horse Mountain Traverse (Hike 8). ■

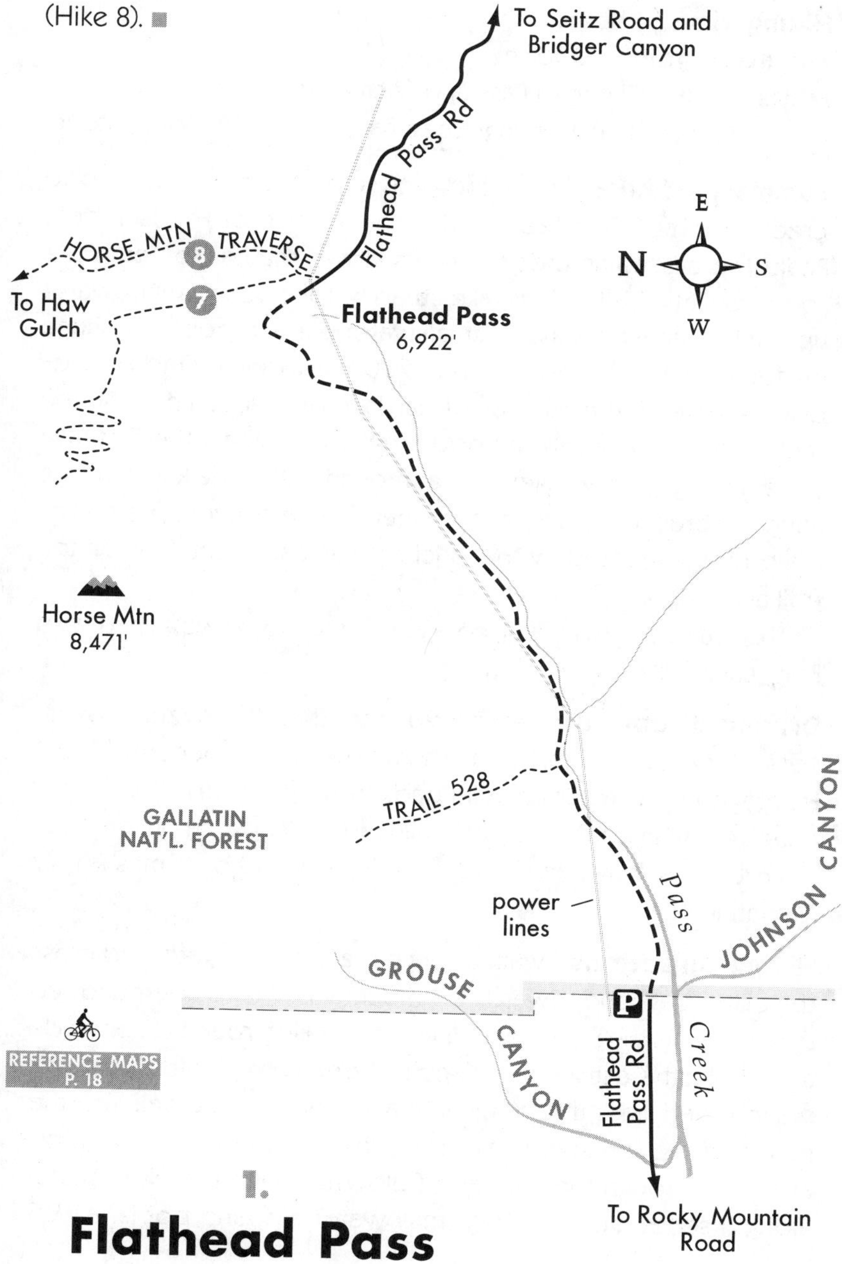

To Seitz Road and Bridger Canyon

Flathead Pass Rd

HORSE MTN TRAVERSE

8

7

To Haw Gulch

Flathead Pass
6,922'

N E S W

Horse Mtn
8,471'

TRAIL 528

GALLATIN NAT'L. FOREST

power lines

GROUSE CANYON

Pass Creek

JOHNSON CANYON

REFERENCE MAPS
P. 18

P

Flathead Pass Rd

To Rocky Mountain Road

1.
Flathead Pass

2. North Cottonwood Creek

Hiking distance: 8 miles round trip
Hiking time: 4 hours
Elevation gain: 2,000 feet
Maps: U.S.G.S. Flathead Pass and Sacagawea Peak
Beartooth Publishing: Bozeman, Big Sky, W. Yellowstone

Summary of hike: The headwaters of North Cottonwood Creek form at 8,700 feet on the north slope of Hardscrabble Peak. The cascading creek tumbles down the canyon en route to the Gallatin Valley. This hike steadily follows the whitewater up the lush canyon, passing small waterfalls and pools to a huge meadow with wildflowers. The 7,700-foot tree-rimmed meadow sits beneath the shadow of Hardscrabble Peak. En route, the trail crosses North Cottonwood Creek three times. The first mile traverses the grassy valley slope through Half Circle Ranch to the national forest boundary at the mouth of the canyon. The access is a privilege granted by the ranch, not an easement. Stay on the trail and help keep the access open.

This trail can also be hiked as an 8-mile, one-way shuttle to Fairy Lake (Hike 9).

Driving directions: From I-90 and the 7th Avenue overpass, drive 2 miles north on 7th Avenue (which becomes West Frontage Road) to Springhill Road. Turn right (north) and continue 14.5 miles to the posted trailhead parking area on the right. (En route, the pavement ends at 11.3 miles and becomes Rocky Mountain Road.)

Hiking directions: Walk through the trailhead gate, and cross the open grassland towards the mountains. The rock-embedded path parallels the ranch fenceline. At 0.7 miles, rock-hop or wade across North Cottonwood Creek. Merge with an old two-track wagon road. Pass through a gate and follow the creek into the mouth of the forested canyon and the gated U.S. forest boundary. Pass through the gate and follow the tumbling whitewater along a series of cascades, small waterfalls, and pools. At 2.3

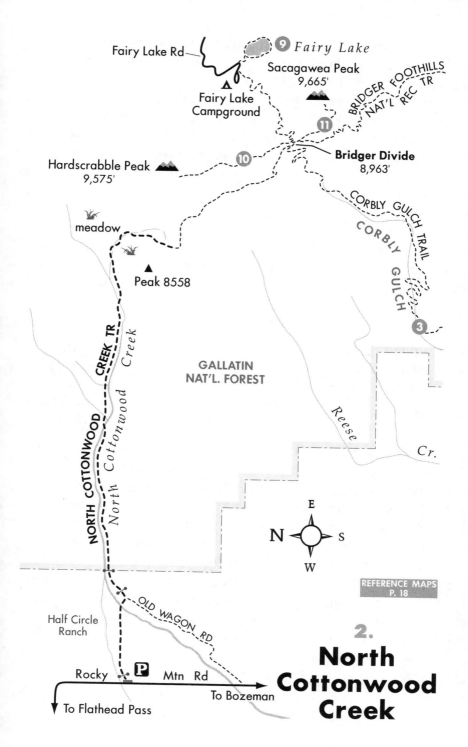

Fairy Lake Rd

9 *Fairy Lake*

Sacagawea Peak
9,665'

Fairy Lake
Campground

BRIDGER FOOTHILLS NAT'L REC TR

11

10

Bridger Divide
8,963'

Hardscrabble Peak
9,575'

CORBLY GULCH TRAIL

CORBLY GULCH

meadow

Peak 8558

3

CREEK TR

NORTH COTTONWOOD

North Cottonwood Creek

GALLATIN
NAT'L. FOREST

Reese

Cr.

E
N ✦ S
W

REFERENCE MAPS
P. 18

OLD WAGON RD

Half Circle
Ranch

Rocky   **P**   Mtn   Rd

To Bozeman

To Flathead Pass

2.
**North
Cottonwood
Creek**

miles, wade across the creek and follow the north bank. Cross two tributary streams from the north canyon slope, and cross back to the south side of the creek at 3.5 miles. Climb high above the creek on the north-facing wall to a large forested flat with a trickling stream. Cross the stream a couple of times, and follow the stream's north edge through a sloping meadow beneath Hardscrabble Peak. Curve right around Peak 8558, and follow cairns through the trail-less meadow. This is the turn-around spot.

To extend the hike, the trail steadily climbs 2 more miles, gaining 1,000 feet to the Bridger Foothills National Recreation Trail at Bridger Divide. The divide is located at the saddle between Hardscrabble Peak and Sacagawea Peak. ■

3. Corbly Gulch

Hiking distance: 4 miles round trip
Hiking time: 2.5 hours
Elevation gain: 1,500 feet

map
page 26

Maps: U.S.G.S. Miser Creek, Flathead Pass and Sacagawea Peak
        Beartooth Publishing: Bozeman, Big Sky, W. Yellowstone

Summary of hike: Corbly Creek flows from the west slope of Sacagawea Peak, joining Limestone Creek and Reese Creek on its journey to the East Gallatin River. The trail up Corbly Gulch follows the creek past its headwaters to the Bridger Foothills National Recreation Trail on the saddle between Hardscrabble Peak and Sacagawea Peak. This hike follows the lower two miles of the trail, beginning from the mouth of the canyon in the Gallatin Valley. The trail leads through forests and meadows beneath the craggy canyon walls and crosses the creek many times to overlooks of the valley and the Tobacco Root Mountains.

This trail can also be hiked as an 8-mile, one-way shuttle to Fairy Lake (Hike 9).

Driving directions: From I-90 and the 7th Avenue overpass, drive 2 miles north on 7th Avenue (which becomes West Frontage Road) to Springhill Road. Turn right (north) and continue 8.5 miles to Springhill Community Road on the right. Turn right and drive 1.5 miles to Corbly Gulch Road, just before reaching the Springhill Church. Turn left on the gravel road and zigzag 2 miles to the posted trailhead access on the left. Turn left and park in the spaces on the right.

Hiking directions: Walk up the rutted two-track road through the open grasslands toward distinct Corbly Gulch. Parallel and cross Corbly Creek, steadily gaining elevation to the mouth of the canyon and the national forest boundary. Follow the north wall of the canyon and pass through a wire gate. Climb through flowered meadows with views of the Bridger Divide. Rock-hop or balance on logs across the creek, and weave uphill to vistas across the Gallatin Valley to the Tobacco Root Mountains. Enter the shade of a pine forest, passing small meadows. Curve left, following a trail sign to the creek. Cross the creek and follow the north edge of the cascading water. At 2 miles, the trail begins zigzagging across the creek six times. This is a good turn-around spot.

To continue hiking, the trail steadily climbs 4 more miles along the gulch, gaining 2,500 feet to the Bridger Foothills National Recreation Trail at Bridger Divide. The divide is located at the saddle between Hardscrabble Peak and Sacagawea Peak. ■

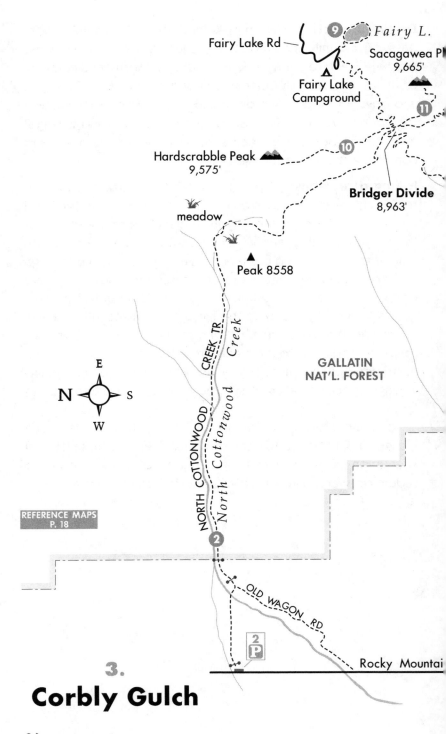

Fairy Lake Rd

9

Fairy L.

Sacagawea P
9,665'

11

Fairy Lake
Campground

Hardscrabble Peak
9,575'

10

Bridger Divide
8,963'

meadow

Peak 8558

CREEK TR.

Creek

NORTH COTTONWOOD

North Cottonwood

**GALLATIN
NAT'L. FOREST**

E

N

S

W

REFERENCE MAPS
P. 18

2

OLD WAGON RD

2
P

Rocky Mountai

3.
Corbly Gulch

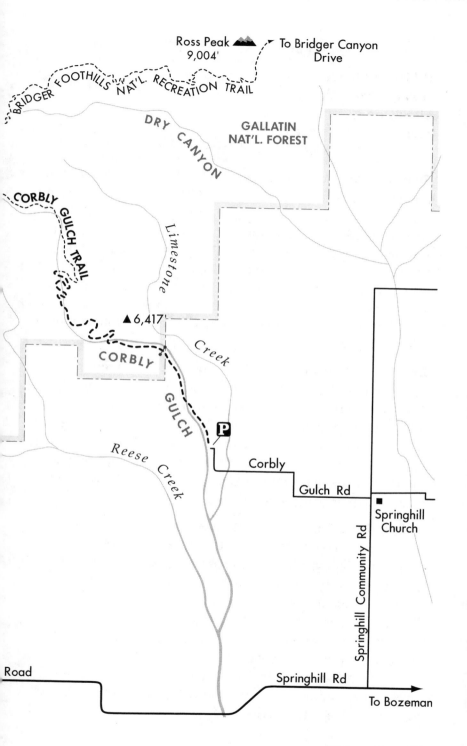

Ross Peak 9,004'

To Bridger Canyon Drive

BRIDGER FOOTHILLS NAT'L. RECREATION TRAIL

DRY CANYON

GALLATIN NAT'L. FOREST

CORBLY GULCH TRAIL

Limestone

▲6,417'

CORBLY

Creek

GULCH

Reese Creek

P

Corbly

Gulch Rd

Springhill Church

Springhill Community Rd

Road

Springhill Rd

To Bozeman

4. Truman Gulch Trail

Hiking distance: 5 miles round trip
Hiking time: 2.5 hours
Elevation gain: 1,000 feet
Maps: U.S.G.S. Saddle Peak
U.S.F.S. Gallatin National Forest: West Half or East Half

Summary of hike: Truman Gulch sits on the west slope of the Bridger Mountains eight miles north of Bozeman. The stream-fed drainage is tucked between 9,004-foot Ross Peak and 9,159-foot Saddle Peak, directly west of Bridger Bowl Ski Area on the Gallatin Valley side of the range. The Truman Gulch Trail begins at the mouth of the canyon and climbs to the Bridger Foothills National Recreation Trail below the divide. The trail is surrounded by forested, rolling mountains and follows the course of the creek to overlooks with sweeping vistas. En route are three creek crossings.

Driving directions: From I-90 and the 7th Avenue overpass, drive 2 miles north on 7th Avenue (which becomes West Frontage Road) to Springhill Road. Turn right (north) and continue 8.5 miles to Springhill Community Road on the right. There is a sign for Truman Gulch. Turn right and continue 1.6 miles to Walker Road. The Springhill Church is on this corner. Turn right and drive 1.1 mile to Forswell Road and turn left. Continue 3 miles to the trailhead parking area at road's end.

Hiking directions: Head east into the canyon on the wide trail and pass a horse gate. Cross the creek at 0.2 miles and gradually climb through the forest. Cross the stream two more times at 1.8 miles. A short distance ahead, views open up of the surrounding mountains and several drainages converge. Cross the stream and climb steeply out of the valley for a half mile to the junction with the Bridger Foothills National Recreation Trail at 2.5 miles. This is the turn-around spot.

To hike farther, the right fork (south) connects with Bostwick Canyon and Middle Cottonwood Creek Trail (Hike 5). The left fork (north) leads to Ross Pass (Hike 12). ∎

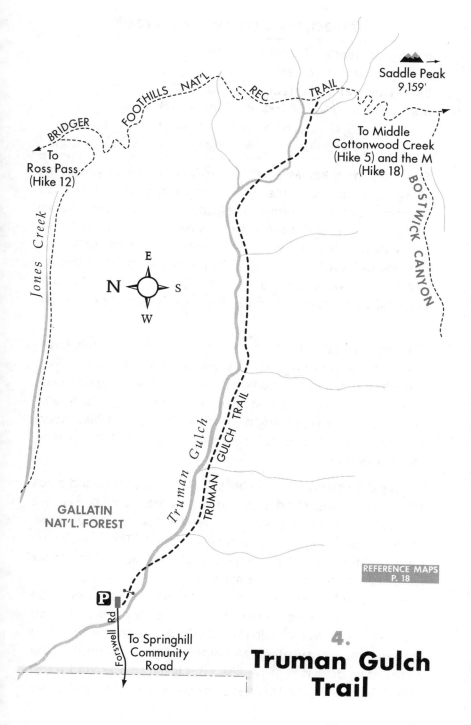

Saddle Peak
9,159'

To Middle
Cottonwood Creek
(Hike 5) and the M
(Hike 18)

BRIDGER FOOTHILLS NAT'L REC TRAIL

To
Ross Pass
(Hike 12)

Jones Creek

BOSTWICK CANYON

N
E
S
W

Truman Gulch

TRUMAN GULCH TRAIL

GALLATIN
NAT'L. FOREST

REFERENCE MAPS
P. 18

P

Forswell Rd

To Springhill
Community
Road

4.
Truman Gulch Trail

5. Middle Cottonwood Creek

Hiking distance: 2.8 miles round trip
Hiking time: 1.5 hours
Elevation gain: 450 feet
Maps: U.S.G.S. Miser Creek and Saddle Peak
U.S.F.S. Gallatin National Forest: West Half or East Half
Beartooth Publishing: Bozeman, Big Sky, W. Yellowstone

Summary of hike: Middle Cottonwood Creek begins in the Bridger Mountains on the upper west slope of Saddle Peak. The creek cascades through the canyon to the Gallatin Valley and joins the East Gallatin River. This hike begins at the mouth of the canyon and follows the cascading whitewater of Middle Cottonwood Creek. The trail climbs toward Saddle Peak through lush riparian vegetation, passing colorful rock formations, small waterfalls, and pools. En route, the trail crosses the creek five times.

Driving directions: From I-90 and the 7th Avenue overpass, drive 2 miles north on 7th Avenue (which becomes West Frontage Road) to Springhill Road. Turn right (north) and continue 3.4 miles to Toohey Road on the right. There is a sign for Middle Cottonwood Creek. Turn right and drive 1.7 miles to Walker Road. Turn right again and continue 3.2 miles to the trailhead parking area at road's end.

Hiking directions: Head east past large boulders, and cross a footbridge over Middle Cottonwood Creek. Continue up the canyon, and cross a log over the creek at 0.4 miles. Follow the course of the creek past cascades and pools. The canyon narrows at 0.8 miles. Boulder hop to the north side of the creek amid moss-covered rock formations.

At one mile, the trail joins the Bridger Foothills National Recreation Trail. To the right, the trail crosses the creek and heads 6 miles south to the M Trail (Hike 18). Continue straight ahead up the canyon. Zigzag up Baldy Mountain to a ridge overlooking the surrounding drainages at 1.4 miles. This is the turn-around spot.

To hike farther, the trail traverses the west slope of Bridger

Peak and Saddle Peak on the Bridger Foothills National Recreation Trail, connecting to the north with Bostwick Canyon and Truman Gulch (Hike 4). ■

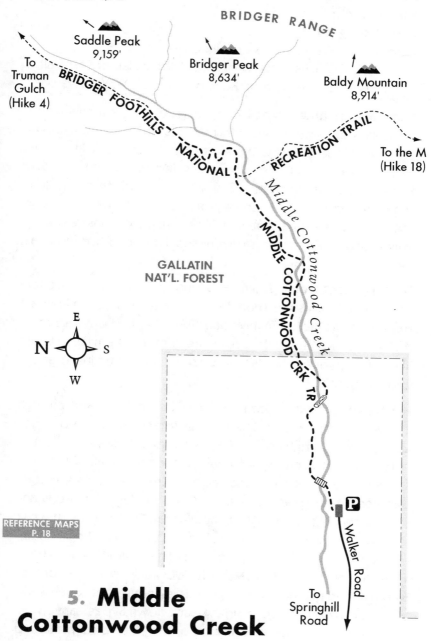

BRIDGER RANGE

Saddle Peak
9,159'

Bridger Peak
8,634'

Baldy Mountain
8,914'

To
Truman
Gulch
(Hike 4)

BRIDGER FOOTHILLS NATIONAL

RECREATION TRAIL

To the M
(Hike 18)

Middle Cottonwood Creek

MIDDLE COTTONWOOD CRK TR

GALLATIN
NAT'L. FOREST

E
N → S
W

REFERENCE MAPS
P. 18

P

Walker Road

To
Springhill
Road

5. Middle Cottonwood Creek

6. Sypes Canyon Trail

Hiking distance: 4 miles round trip
Hiking time: 2 hours
Elevation gain: 1,000 feet
Maps: U.S.G.S. Bozeman and Kelly Creek
U.S.F.S. Gallatin National Forest: West Half or East Half
Beartooth Publishing: Bozeman, Big Sky, W. Yellowstone

Summary of hike: Sypes Canyon is located on the southwest flank of Baldy Mountain at the southern end of the Bridger Mountains. The Sypes Canyon Trail begins at the edge of the Gallatin Valley and climbs up the creek-fed canyon to the Bridger Foothills National Recreation Trail. The hike leads through a lush, shady forest up the south canyon wall to an overlook. From the overlook are great vistas of Bozeman; the expansive Gallatin Valley; and the Madison, Gallatin, and Tobacco Root mountain ranges.

Driving directions: From I-90 and the 7th Avenue overpass, drive 2 miles north on 7th Avenue (which becomes West Frontage Road) to Springhill Road. Turn right and drive 1.5 miles to Sypes Canyon Road. Turn right and continue 3.2 miles to Churn Road. Turn right and go 50 yards to the signed trailhead at the end of the road.

Hiking directions: Head east past the trail sign and through a grassy fenced access. Enter a lush forest canopy into Sypes Canyon on the right side of Sypes Creek. Cross over to the north side of the creek, and head up the north wall of the canyon above Sypes Creek. At a half mile, the trail reaches a ridge. Descend alongside a rock wall cliff into the lush, forested canyon. Curve right at one mile, heading south up the canyon while skirting the edge of the national forest boundary. Begin an ascent through a lodgepole pine forest to a saddle by a trail sign with a view of the valley. Bear left 200 yards to an overlook of Bozeman and the Madison Range. This is a great spot to relax and enjoy the views before returning back down Sypes Canyon.

To hike farther, the trail climbs one mile to a cairn-marked junction with the Bridger Foothills National Recreation Trail. The right fork descends to the M Trail at the south end of the Bridger Mountains (Hike 18). The left fork climbs to the head of Middle Cottonwood Creek (Hike 5). ■

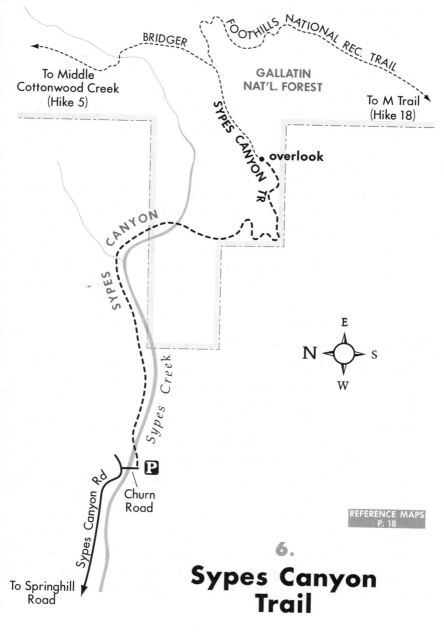

6.

Sypes Canyon Trail

7. Horse Mountain

Hiking distance: 2.2 miles round trip
Hiking time: 1 hour
Elevation gain: 700 feet
Maps: U.S.G.S. Flathead Pass
Beartooth Publishing: Bozeman, Big Sky, W. Yellowstone

Summary of hike: Horse Mountain towers 1,550 feet above Flathead Pass at the north end of the Bridger Mountains. This hike begins atop the 6,922-foot pass and climbs to a knoll overlooking Shields Valley and the Crazy Mountains. A side path continues up the east slope of Horse Mountain to amazing vistas of Hardscrabble Peak and Sacagawea Peak.

Driving directions: From Main Street in downtown Bozeman, head north on North Rouse Avenue. Drive 25.2 miles up Bridger Canyon to Seitz Road on the left. It is located 3.8 miles past Fairy Lake Road. (After crossing Griffin Drive, Rouse Avenue becomes Bridger Canyon Drive/Highway 86.) Drive 4.3 miles on the unpaved road to a signed junction. Turn left towards Flathead Pass, and continue 5.9 miles to the pass. Along the way, stay left at a fork with F.S. Road 6980. At the pass, cross a cattle guard to the power poles. Park on the right.

Hiking directions: From the meadow, veer north on the dirt road underneath the power poles. Head up the flower-covered meadow 100 yards to a Y-fork. The right fork traverses the mountain at a near-level grade to a saddle (Hike 8). Stay to the left, overlooking Shields Valley, the Crazy Mountains, and the limestone fins framing the view of the Gallatin Valley. Climb the ridge to the 7,258-foot knoll at a half mile. After savoring the views, go left and cross the meadow on the double-track trail. At the west end of the meadow, enter a pine forest and begin climbing Horse Mountain. Steadily climb, zigzagging north then west through pockets of trees and meadows. Views of Hardscrabble Peak and Sacagawea Peak lie across Flathead Pass. At 1.1 mile, the trail fades away. Return along the same route. ∎

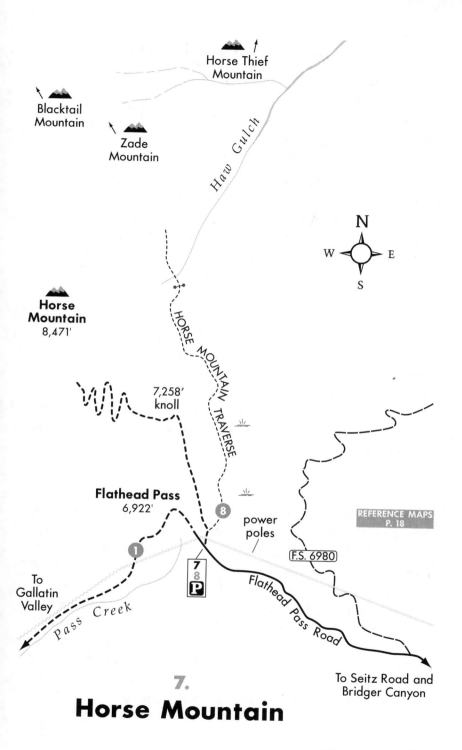

Horse Thief
Mountain

Blacktail
Mountain

Zade
Mountain

Haw Gulch

N

W ✦ E

S

**Horse
Mountain**
8,471'

HORSE MOUNTAIN TRAVERSE

7,258'
knoll

Flathead Pass
6,922'

⑧

power
poles

REFERENCE MAPS
P. 18

F.S. 6980

①

7
8
P

To
Gallatin
Valley

Pass Creek

Flathead Pass Road

To Seitz Road and
Bridger Canyon

7.

Horse Mountain

8. Horse Mountain Traverse

Hiking distance: 2.8 miles round trip
Hiking time: 1.5 hours
Elevation gain: 100 feet
Maps: U.S.G.S. Flathead Pass and Blacktail Mountain
Beartooth Publishing: Bozeman, Big Sky, W. Yellowstone

Summary of hike: The Horse Mountain Traverse is an easy hike through meadows atop Flathead Pass at 6,922 feet. The near-level path traverses the east flank of Horse Mountain, towering 1,550 feet above Flathead Pass at the north end of the Bridgers. The trail, an old logging road reclaimed by vegetation, leads to a grassy saddle at the headwaters of Haw Gulch. From the open saddle are vistas of Horsethief Mountain, Shields Valley, and the Crazy Mountains.

Driving directions: From Main Street in downtown Bozeman, head north on North Rouse Avenue. Drive 25.2 miles up Bridger Canyon to Seitz Road on the left. It is located 3.8 miles past Fairy Lake Road. (After crossing Griffin Drive, Rouse Avenue becomes Bridger Canyon Drive/Highway 86.) Drive 4.3 miles on the un-paved road to a signed junction. Turn left towards Flathead Pass, and continue 5.9 miles to the pass. Along the way, stay left at a fork with F.S. Road 6980. At the pass, cross a cattle guard to the power poles. Park on the right.

Hiking directions: From the gorgeous meadow, veer north on the dirt road under the power poles. Head up the flower-covered meadow 100 yards to a Y-fork. The left fork leads to a knoll and steeply climbs Horse Mountain (Hike 7). Veer right and traverse the east slope of Horse Mountain. The old road meanders through meadows dotted with firs and pines at a near-level grade. At just over one mile, pass through a gated fence to a 7,000-foot saddle with north views of Horsethief Mountain. Easily descend, passing the Haw Gulch stream flowing under the trail. The trail abruptly ends in a dense pocket of pine trees at 1.4 miles. Return along the same route. ∎

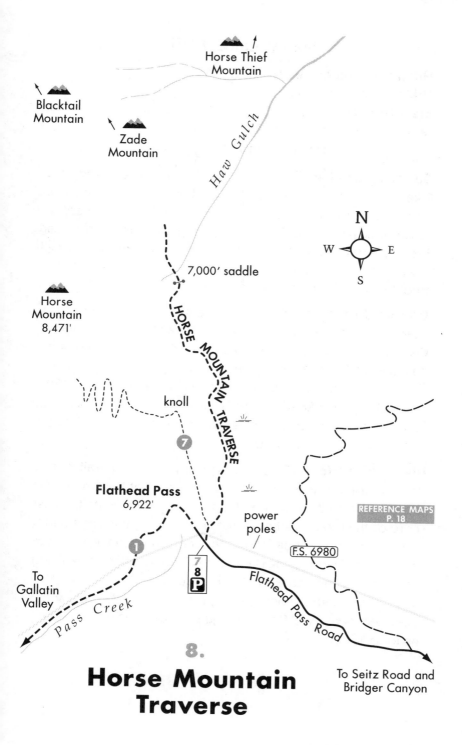

Horse Thief
Mountain

Blacktail
Mountain

Zade
Mountain

Haw Gulch

N
W E
S

7,000' saddle

Horse
Mountain
8,471'

HORSE MOUNTAIN TRAVERSE

knoll

7

Flathead Pass
6,922'

power
poles

REFERENCE MAPS
P. 18

1

To
Gallatin
Valley

Pass Creek

7
8
P

F.S. 6980

Flathead Pass Road

To Seitz Road and
Bridger Canyon

8.

Horse Mountain
Traverse

9. Fairy Lake Trail

Hiking distance: 1.2-mile loop
Hiking time: 40 minutes
Elevation gain: 100 feet
Maps: U.S.G.S. Sacagawea Peak
U.S.F.S. Gallatin National Forest: East Half

Summary of hike: Fairy Lake is a picture-perfect, tree-lined lake sitting in a forested bowl at the base of Sacagawea Peak. The 20-acre lake receives heavy use due to its easy access and close proximity to the Fairy Lake Campground, located a quarter mile away. The trail loops around the perimeter of the high mountain lake. It is a great place to have a picnic, fish for cutthroat trout, and spend the day.

Driving directions: From Main Street in downtown Bozeman, head north on North Rouse Avenue. Drive 21.4 miles up Bridger Canyon to the signed Fairy Lake turnoff on the left, 0.9 miles past the Battle Ridge Campground. (After crossing Griffin Drive, Rouse Avenue becomes Bridger Canyon Drive/Highway 86.) Turn left on Fairy Lake Road/Forest Service Road 74. Drive 6.1 miles on the unpaved road to the Fairy Lake Campground. Park at the signed trailhead on the left.

Hiking directions: Take the signed Fairy Lake Trail gently downhill for a quarter mile to the north shore of the lake. At the shoreline bear left, following the forested route along the east shore of the lake. Rock hop across Fairy Creek, the lake's outlet stream. A fisherman trail follows the shoreline, hugging the edge of the water. Various side paths meander through the forest and reconnect at the shoreline. Loop around to the west end of the lake. The path continues along the water's edge below the rocky sedimentary cliffs of Sacagawea Peak. After completing the loop, return to the left. ■

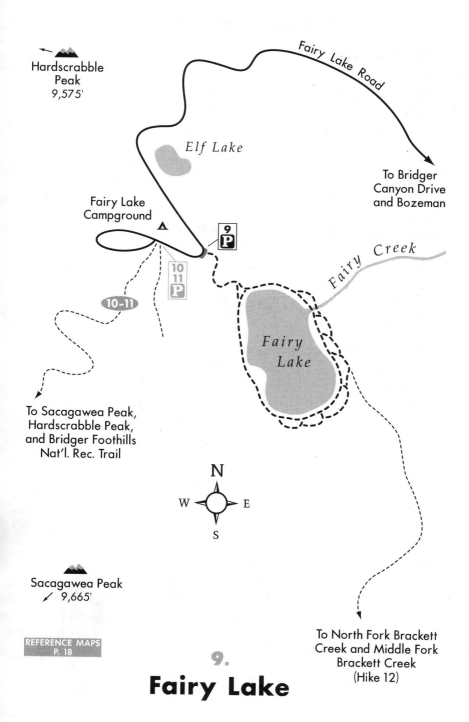

Hardscrabble
Peak
9,575'

Fairy Lake Road

Elf Lake

To Bridger
Canyon Drive
and Bozeman

Fairy Lake
Campground

Fairy Creek

9 P

10 11 P

10-11

Fairy
Lake

To Sacagawea Peak,
Hardscrabble Peak,
and Bridger Foothills
Nat'l. Rec. Trail

N
W ← → E
S

Sacagawea Peak
9,665'

REFERENCE MAPS
P. 18

To North Fork Brackett
Creek and Middle Fork
Brackett Creek
(Hike 12)

9.
Fairy Lake

10. Hardscrabble Peak

Hiking distance: 4 miles round trip
Hiking time: 3 hours
Elevation gain: 1,900 feet
Maps: U.S.G.S. Sacagawea Peak
U.S.F.S. Gallatin National Forest: East Half

Summary of hike: Hardscrabble Peak stands directly north of Sacagawea Peak in the northern Bridger Mountain Range. Frazier Lake and Ainger Lake sit on the east slope of the triple-peak mountain 1,400 feet below. This hike leads to the summit of Hardscrabble Peak at 9,575 feet, gaining 1,900 feet en route. The trail follows the drainage between Sacagawea Peak and Hardscrabble Peak to the 8,963-foot saddle at Bridger Divide. From Hardscrabble Peak are views of six surrounding mountain ranges—the Gallatin, Madison, Crazies, Tobacco Roots, Elkhorns, and Big Belts.

Driving directions: From Main Street in downtown Bozeman, head north on North Rouse Avenue. Drive 21.4 miles up Bridger Canyon to the signed Fairy Lake turnoff on the left, 0.9 miles past the Battle Ridge Campground. (After crossing Griffin Drive, Rouse Avenue becomes Bridger Canyon Drive/Highway 86.) Turn left on Fairy Lake Road/Forest Service Road 74. Drive 6.1 miles on the unpaved road to the Fairy Lake Campground. Turn right and park 0.1 mile ahead at the signed trail on the left.

Hiking directions: Head south on the signed right fork through the shady conifer forest. Traverse the hillside up several switchbacks while great views open up to the east. Cross the northern edge of a meadow abundant with wildflowers. Switchbacks lead up the exposed rocky bowl at the head of the drainage. More switchbacks climb up to the ridge on the Bridger Divide at 8,963 feet. At the divide are cairns and a signed junction. The left fork—Hike 11—leads to Sacagawea Peak, the highest peak in the Bridger Mountains. Take the right fork and follow the ridge north, gaining another 675 feet from the saddle to the

9,299' ▲

peak. After marveling at the vistas from
the rocky peak, return along
the same path. ■

*Frazier
Lake*

9,474' ▲

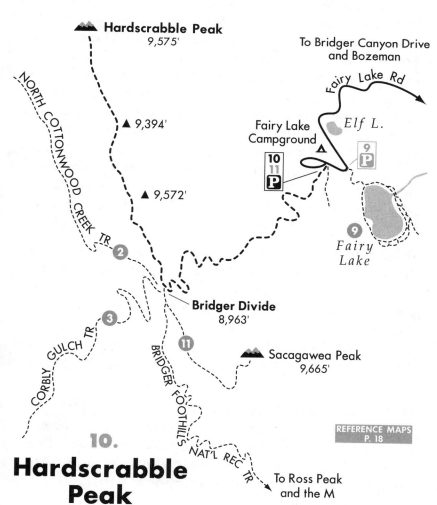

N
W ✦ E
S

Hardscrabble Peak
9,575'

To Bridger Canyon Drive
and Bozeman

Fairy Lake Rd

▲ 9,394'

**Fairy Lake
Campground**

Elf L.

10
11
P

9
P

▲ 9,572'

NORTH COTTONWOOD CREEK TR

②

9
*Fairy
Lake*

Bridger Divide
8,963'

CORBLY GULCH TR
③

BRIDGER FOOTHILLS

⑪

Sacagawea Peak
9,665'

REFERENCE MAPS
P. 18

NAT'L REC TR

10.
Hardscrabble
Peak

To Ross Peak
and the M

11. Sacagawea Peak

Hiking distance: 4 miles round trip
Hiking time: 3 hours
Elevation gain: 2,000 feet
Maps: U.S.G.S. Sacagawea Peak
U.S.F.S. Gallatin National Forest: East Half
Beartooth Publishing: Bozeman, Big Sky, W. Yellowstone

Summary of hike: Sacagawea Peak, named after Lewis and Clark's Indian guide, is the highest peak in the Bridger Range. The 9,665-foot peak sits on the northern end of the range. From the west, the peak can be accessed from the North Cottonwood Creek Trail and the Corbly Gulch Trail (Hikes 2 and 3). The shortest and most popular route, however, is this trail from the east, starting at the Fairy Lake Campground. The trail climbs the mountain, passing through a glacial cirque to Bridger Divide between Sacagawea Peak and Hardscrabble Peak. From the divide the trail winds up to the rocky summit for fantastic views of Shields Valley, Gallatin Valley, and the mountain ranges in every direction. To the south are the Gallatin and Madison Ranges; the Big Belts lie to the north; the Elkhorns and Tobacco Roots lie to the west; and the Crazies are to the east.

Driving directions: From Main Street in downtown Bozeman, head north on North Rouse Avenue. Drive 21.4 miles up Bridger Canyon to the signed Fairy Lake turnoff on the left, 0.9 miles past the Battle Ridge Campground. (After crossing Griffin Drive, Rouse Avenue becomes Bridger Canyon Drive/Highway 86.) Turn left on Fairy Lake Road/Forest Service Road 74. Drive 6.1 miles on the unpaved road to the Fairy Lake Campground. Turn right and park 0.1 mile ahead at the signed trail on the left.

Hiking directions: Head south on the signed right fork through the shady conifer forest. Traverse the hillside up several switchbacks while great views open up to the east. Cross the northern edge of a meadow abundant with wildflowers. Switchbacks lead up the exposed rocky bowl at the head of the drainage. More switchbacks climb up to the ridge on the Bridger

Divide at 8,963 feet. At the divide are cairns and a signed junction. The right fork leads up to Hardscrabble Peak (Hike 10).

Take the left fork and follow the ridge south. Pass a signed junction on the right, which heads down the mountain to Corbly Creek and North Cottonwood Creek. Continue gaining elevation southeast along the ridge. Bear left at a junction with the Bridger Foothills National Recreation Trail, and head north for the final ascent to the peak. After enjoying the incredible views at the summit, return along the same path. ■

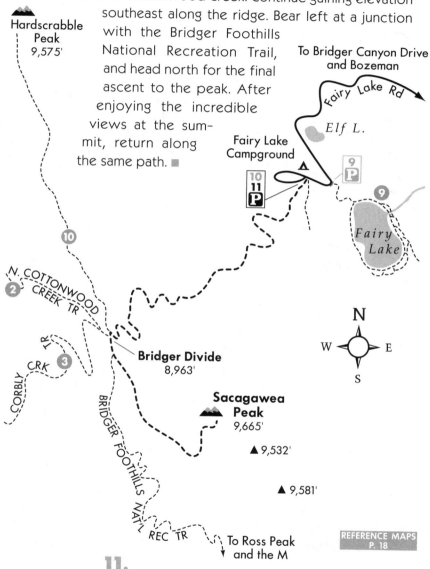

Hardscrabble Peak
9,575'

To Bridger Canyon Drive and Bozeman

Fairy Lake Rd

Elf L.

Fairy Lake Campground

10
11
P

9
P

10

9

Fairy Lake

N. COTTONWOOD CREEK TR

2

Bridger Divide
8,963'

CORBLY CRK TR

3

BRIDGER FOOTHILLS NAT'L REC TR

Sacagawea Peak
9,665'

▲ 9,532'

▲ 9,581'

N
W — E
S

REFERENCE MAPS
P. 18

To Ross Peak and the M

11.
Sacagawea Peak

12. Middle Fork Brackett Creek to Ross Pass

Hiking distance: 6 to 12.5 miles round trip
Hiking time: 3 to 6 hours
Elevation gain: 1,400 to 1,800 feet
Maps: U.S.G.S. Saddle Peak
Beartooth Publishing: Bozeman, Big Sky, W. Yellowstone

Summary of hike: Ross Peak is a jagged 9,004-foot peak between Sacagawea Peak and Bridger Bowl Ski Area. Grass-covered Ross Pass sits on the south flank of Ross Peak in a long, sweeping crescent at 7,620 feet. Dramatic limestone formations lie just west of the ridge. The vistas are breathtaking. Running along the ridge and through Ross Pass is the Bridger Foothills National Recreation Trail. This hike follows Middle Fork Brackett Creek Road—an old logging road—up to the ridgeline trail. The hike begins in Bridger Canyon but can be shortened by driving up the primitive road. The road/trail roughly follows the creek, crossing feeder streams and passing its headwaters en route to Ross Pass.

Driving directions: From Main Street in downtown Bozeman, head north on North Rouse Avenue. Drive 18.8 miles up Bridger Canyon to posted Brackett Creek Road. It is located between mile markers 18 and 19. (After crossing Griffin Drive, Rouse Avenue becomes Bridger Canyon Drive/Highway 86.) Curve right on Brackett Creek Road 100 yards to the large Bangtail Divide Trailhead parking lot on the right.

Middle Fork Brackett Creek Road—this hike—is a primitive dirt road on the west side of Bridger Canyon. It can be comfortably driven for almost 3 miles. Thereafter, the old logging road gets steeper, narrower, and rutted and is not recommended for driving. These hiking directions start from the Bangtail Divide parking area, but can be shortened if you choose to drive up the road.

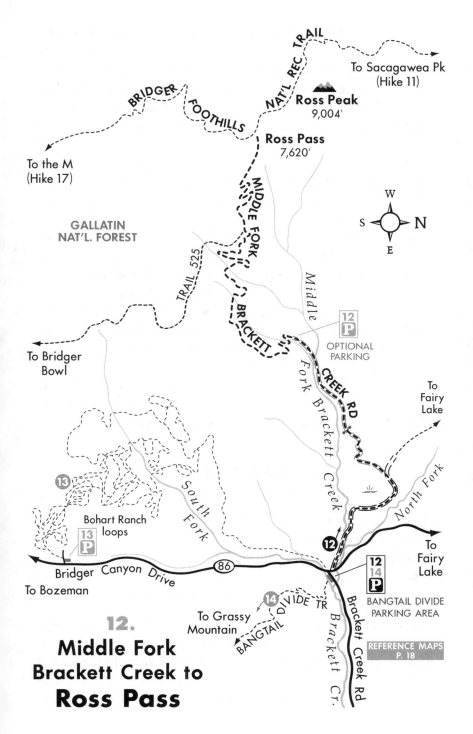

To Sacagawea Pk
(Hike 11)

BRIDGER FOOTHILLS NAT'L REC TRAIL

Ross Peak
9,004'

Ross Pass
7,620'

To the M
(Hike 17)

MIDDLE FORK

GALLATIN
NAT'L. FOREST

TRAIL 525

BRACKETT

W
S — N
E

Middle Fork Brackett Creek

12
P
OPTIONAL
PARKING

CREEK RD

To Bridger
Bowl

To
Fairy
Lake

South Fork

North Fork

13

Bohart Ranch
loops

13
P

12

Bridger Canyon Drive
86

To Bozeman

12
14
P

To
Fairy
Lake

BANGTAIL DIVIDE
PARKING AREA

14

To Grassy
Mountain

BANGTAIL DIVIDE TR

Brackett Creek Rd

Brackett Cr.

REFERENCE MAPS
P. 18

12.
Middle Fork
Brackett Creek to
Ross Pass

Hiking directions: Walk 100 yards down Brackett Creek Road and cross Highway 86. Pick up the posted Middle Fork Brackett Creek Road and head west, passing a narrow side road on the left. Skirt the east edge of an expansive sloping meadow with views of Ross Peak and Ross Pass. Loop around the north end of the meadow to a Y-fork at one mile. The right fork leads to Fairy Lake (Hike 9) on an old road bed. Stay left and continue to a metal gate at 1.8 miles. Follow the north edge of Middle Fork Brackett Creek. At 2.5 miles, wind steeply uphill to an overlook of Grassy Mountain in the Bangtail Mountains (Hike 13). Zigzag up the mountain while enjoying the continuous vistas of Ross Pass and Ross Peak. Cross a feeder stream and weave up to views of the Crazy Mountains. On a right bend, Trail 525 veers left, leading to South Fork Brackett Creek and Bridger Bowl. Climb 4 long switchbacks toward the pass. Traverse the slope to a large flower-filled meadow below the saddle. Make the final steep ascent to posted Ross Pass and a T-junction with the Bridger Foothills National Recreation Trail at 7,640 feet. Just west of the pass are the gorgeous limestone fins.

To the right (north), the national recreation trail leads to Sacagawea Peak. To the south, it leads past Bridger Bowl and to the M Trail at the south end of the Bridgers (Hike 18). ▪

13. Bohart Ranch

16621 Bridger Canyon Road

Hiking distance: 5-mile loop
Hiking time: 2.5 hours
Elevation gain: 350 feet
Maps: U.S.G.S. Saddle Peak
     Bohart Ranch Cross Country Ski Center map

*map
page 48*

Summary of hike: Bohart Ranch is a well-planned, maintained cross-country ski center with groomed and tracked trails. It is located on the lower east slopes of the Bridger Mountains in Bridger Canyon, just north of Bridger Bowl Ski Area. The ranch is also an excellent area for hiking in the snow-free months.

Eighteen miles of scenic trails loop through the natural terrain and are open to hiking, mountain biking, horseback riding, and frisbie golf. The trail system connects with forest service trails at the north and west end of Bohart Ranch. This hike utiizes several loops which wind through the rolling terrain, including a mix of spruce, fir, lodgepole pines, expansive meadows, and crossings the South Fork of Brackett Creek. Dogs are not allowed.

Driving directions: From Main Street in downtown Bozeman, head north on North Rouse Avenue. Drive 16.6 miles up Bridger Canyon to the signed Bohart Ranch on the left. It is located 0.8 miles past the Bridger Bowl Ski Area entrance between mile markers 16 and 17. (After crossing Griffin Drive, Rouse Avenue becomes Bridger Canyon Drive/Highway 86.) Turn left and park in the large parking area on the right, across from the base lodge.

Hiking directions: There are innumerable looping routes through Bohart Ranch. Throughout the hike, many trail options will present themselves. This hike is only a guideline. All the paths loop back to the lodge and many junctions are marked, making it very difficult to get lost.

Cross the entrance road and take the posted path between the base lodge and the pond. Follow the unpaved road uphill through the open forest between the north and south loops. At 0.7 miles, all the trails funnel up to Jane's Gate/Junction 20. Enter the Meadow Loops in a large flat meadow with great views of Ross Peak and Sacagawea Peak.

For a counter-clockwise loop through the center of the ranch, the Inner Meadow Trail cuts straight ahead through the meadow. The Outer Meadow Loop to the right snakes through the rolling hills in a sweeping S-pattern. The two paths rejoin at a restroom and picnic area by Junction 21. Curve right towards the posted lookout. Stay to the right in the Ridge Loops section of Bohart Ranch. Head up the forested slope to the lookout by a picnic bench. The southern view overlooks Bridger Canyon and the Bangtail Mountains to the Gallatin Range. Make a horseshoe left bend on the Bloody Gulch Trail to Junction 34.

Continue north and enter the Brackett Creek Loops. Head

downhill and steadily descend on the north-facing slope above the South Fork of Brackett Creek. Cross over the creek and walk up the hillside to Junction 43 at the east end of the ranch. The right fork enters the forest service land on the Logger's Loops for an additional 2.7-mile loop.

For this hike, go left on the Tommy's Turns Trail, and weave up the hillside onto the Little Dipper Trail. Recross the South Fork of Brackett Creek, and continue to Junction 46. Bear right, following the sign to the lodge. Veer right and descend on Meggin's Turn Trail, following the ranch boundary. Pass Junction 23 and curve left onto the Whiskey Gulch Trail. Walk through the meadow, completing the loop at Jane's Gate/Junction 20. Head back to the lodge and trailhead through the north and south loops. ■

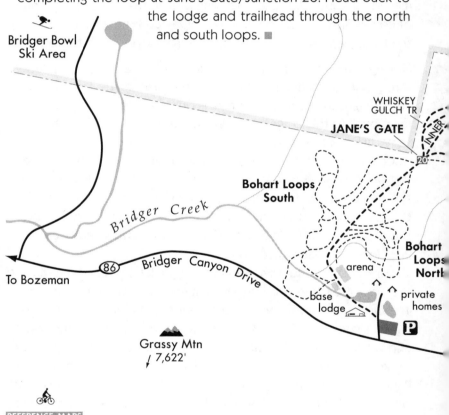

REFERENCE MAPS
P. 18

13.

Bohart Ranch

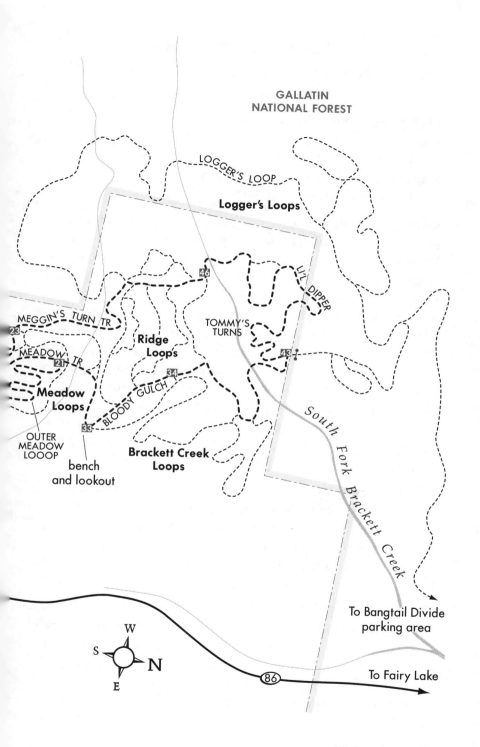

GALLATIN
NATIONAL FOREST

LOGGER'S LOOP

Logger's Loops

46

LI'L DIPPER

MEGGIN'S TURN TR

23

**Ridge
Loops**

TOMMY'S
TURNS

43

MEADOW TR

21

34

**Meadow
Loops**

BLOODY GULCH

33

S o u t h   F o r k   B r a c k e t t   C r e e k

OUTER
MEADOW
LOOOP

bench
and lookout

**Brackett Creek
Loops**

To Bangtail Divide
parking area

W

S   N

E

86   To Fairy Lake

14. Bangtail Divide Trail
North Trailhead: Brackett Creek
(GRASSY MOUNTAIN TRAIL)

Hiking distance: 7.5 miles round trip
Hiking time: 4 hours
Elevation gain: 1,400 feet
Maps: U.S.G.S. Saddle Peak and Grassy Mountain
          Beartooth Publishing: Bozeman, Big Sky, W. Yellowstone

Summary of hike: The Bangtail Divide Trail straddles the ridge of the Bangtail Range between Bridger Canyon and Shields Valley. The 23-mile trail, directly east of Bridger Bowl Ski Area, connects Brackett Creek at its north trailhead to Stone Creek at its south trailhead. This hike begins at the Brackett Creek Trailhead and follows the northern 3.5 miles of the trail to Grassy Mountain. (This section of the trail is also called the Grassy Mountain Trail.) The trail traverses through lodgepole pines and flower-filled meadows while skirting the ridgeline of the Bangtails. From the trail are sweeping vistas into the valleys on either side of the ridge, including Bridger Bowl, Sacagawea Peak, and the Crazy Mountains.

Hike 16 begins at the southern Bangtail Divide trailhead. Hike 15 begins from Olson Creek Road along the ridge between the northern and southern trailheads.

Driving directions: From Main Street in downtown Bozeman, head north on North Rouse Avenue. Drive 18.8 miles up Bridger Canyon to posted Brackett Creek Road. It is located 2 miles past the Bridger Bowl entrance between mile markers 18 and 19. (After crossing Griffin Drive, Rouse Avenue becomes Bridger Canyon Drive/Highway 86.) Curve right on Brackett Creek Road 100 yards to the Bangtail Divide Trailhead parking lot on the right.

Hiking directions: Cross the footbridge over Brackett Creek, and curve left on the northern base of Grassy Mountain. Ten switchbacks zigzag up the slope, gaining a quick 400 feet. On the eighth switchback is an overlook of Ross Pass, Ross Peak, Sacagawea Peak, Hardscrabble Peak, and Horse Mountain. Head

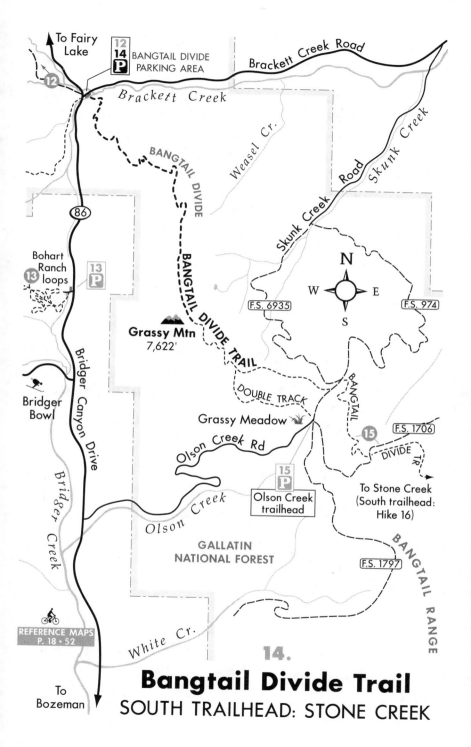

14.
Bangtail Divide Trail
SOUTH TRAILHEAD: STONE CREEK

south, traversing the drainage on the cliffside path. Weave through the lodgepole pines, with frequent views of the Bridger Range and its jagged, sculpted peaks. Four more switchbacks lead to Bangtail Divide, with eastward views down Weasel Creek Canyon to Shields Valley and the Crazy Mountains. The trail levels out and weaves through meadows dotted with pines. The views include Battle Ridge in the north and Grassy Mountain to the south. Climb through the forest, returning to the divide. Follow the ridge south, and cross a saddle through a sloping meadow, where there is a view across Bridger Canyon to Bridger Bowl and the ski runs. Descend on the east side of Grassy Mountain below the summit in a meadow at 3.7 miles, overlooking the logged area and network of roads far below. This is the turn-around spot. No routes lead directly up to the 7,622-foot peak.

To continue hiking, the trail descends to Skunk Creek Road at 7 miles, connecting with Olson Creek Road (Hike 15). ∎

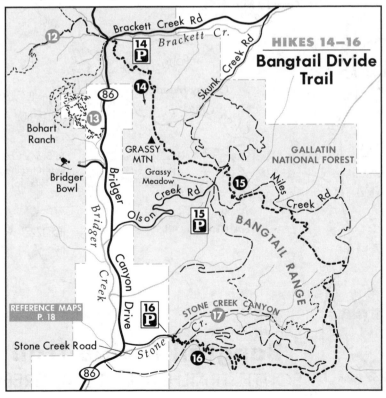

15. Bangtail Divide Trail
from Olson Creek Road

Hiking distance: 5-mile loop
Hiking time: 2.5 hours
Elevation gain: 400 feet
Maps: U.S.G.S. Grassy Mountain

map
page 54

    Beartooth Publishing: Bozeman, Big Sky, W. Yellowstone
    U.S.D.A. Gallatin National Forest West Half map

Summary of hike: The Bangtail Divide Trail is a 23-mile trail that connects Stone Creek, Olson Creek, and Brackett Creek. The trail climbs to the crest of the Bangtail Range, weaving through pine, spruce, and fir forests and across rolling meadows. Hike 14—the northern trailhead—is also known as the Grassy Mountain Trail and begins at Brackett Creek. Hike 17—the southern trailhead—begins on the banks of Stone Creek. This hike lies between the northern and southern trailheads, starting from atop Olson Creek Road. The trail begins near the crest of the Bangtails above 7,000 feet, avoiding most of the elevation gain. Throughout the hike are great views of the Bridger Mountains, the Crazy Mountains, Shields Valley, the Olson Creek drainage, and the Miles Creek canyon.

Driving directions: From Main Street in downtown Bozeman, head north on North Rouse Avenue. Drive 14.5 miles up Bridger Canyon to Olson Creek Road on the right, located between mile markers 14 and 15. (After crossing Griffin Drive, Rouse Avenue becomes Bridger Canyon Drive/Highway 86.) Turn right and continue 4.6 miles to the signed trailhead on both sides of the road. The trailhead is located 0.1 mile beyond the sign which reads "Entering National Forest Land." Park alongside the road.

Hiking directions: From the east (right) side of the road, take the signed trail into the open pine forest. Head up the slope, enjoying the spectacular views of the Bridger Mountains, Shields Valley, and the Crazy Mountains. Top the slope and curve right, leaving the Olson Creek drainage. Traverse the east-facing hillside high above Miles Creek. Walk through meadows at a near-level grade with far-reaching vistas. Cross over Miles Creek to Miles Creek Road at 1.25 miles. Cross the road and pick up the trail, beginning the loop. Roughly follow the top of the rolling mountains. Slowly descend on a long, sweeping left bend. At 2.5 miles is a small clearing on the left, where the trail comes within 100 yards of Miles Creek Road. At this point, the Bangtail Divide Trail veers away from the road, continuing 4 miles to Bishop Park Road and 14 miles to the Stone Creek Trailhead (Hikes 16 and 17).

For this hike, leave the trail and scramble down the slope to the dirt road. Bear left on Miles Creek Road and cross over Canyon Creek. Follow the contours of the hills, and bend left on a couple of curves, returning to the Miles Creek drainage. After walking 1.4 miles on the road, complete the loop at the posted Bangtail Divide Trail at the beginning of the loop. Bear right on the trail, and return 1.25 miles to the trailhead. ■

15.
Bangtail Divide Trail
from OLSON CREEK ROAD

16. Bangtail Divide Trail
South Trailhead: Stone Creek

Hiking distance: 6 miles round trip
Hiking time: 3 hours
Elevation gain: 2,000 feet

map
page 56

Maps: U.S.G.S. Grassy Mountain and Bozeman Pass
Beartooth Publishing: Bozeman, Big Sky, W. Yellowstone
U.S.D.A. Gallatin National Forest West Half map

Summary of hike: The Bangtail Divide Trail straddles the ridge of the Bangtail Range between Bridger Canyon and Shields Valley. The 23-mile trail, directly east of Bridger Bowl Ski Area, connects Brackett Creek at its north trailhead to Stone Creek at its south trailhead. (Olsen Creek Road can be accessed midway through the trail—Hike 15.) This hike begins from the southern access at Stone Creek. The trail climbs to the crest of the Bangtail Range and weaves through evergreen forests and open, rolling meadows. Throughout the hike are great views of the Bridger Mountains and the surrounding terrain, including Stone Creek Canyon and Spring Creek Canyon.

Hike 14 begins at the northern Brackett Creek trailhead.

Driving directions: From Main Street in downtown Bozeman, head north on North Rouse Avenue. Drive 12 miles up Bridger Canyon to Stone Creek Road on the right. (After crossing Griffin Drive, Rouse Avenue becomes Bridger Canyon Drive/Highway 86.) Turn right and continue 1.2 miles to the posted trailhead parking area on the left.

Hiking directions: Walk 50 yards up Stone Creek Road to the posted trailhead on the right. Head up the south canyon wall, weaving through an open pine forest. Zipper up the hillside at an easy uphill grade with the aid of 22 switchbacks. Along the way, views open up across Bridger Canyon to the east slope of the Bridger Mountains and up Stone Creek Canyon.

After the switchbacks, the trail reaches a signed ridge at an old logging road. Cross the road and follow School Gulch Canyon at a level grade above School Gulch Creek. At the upper end of the minor canyon, curve left to a grassy saddle straddling both Stone Creek and School Gulch Creek canyons. Curve right, leaving the ridge, and traverse the slope, with alternating views into Stone Creek Canyon and Spring Canyon. Return to the ridge atop a grassy meadow. Parallel the ridge and drop into another open meadow. Continue straight ahead, crossing the rolling terrain while enjoying the great views of the Bridger peaks. At 3.5 miles, switchback left and head north. Skirt through a pocket of lodgepole pines, crossing the head of Stone Creek Canyon. This is the turn-around point for a 6-mile round-trip hike.

To extend the hike, the trail continues another 7 miles to Bishop Park Road and 13 miles to Olson Creek Road by Grassy Meadow (Hike 15). From the meadow, the Bangtail Divide Trail continues 7 miles along the Grassy Mountain Trail section to Grassy Mountain and the trailhead at Brackett Creek (Hike 14). ■

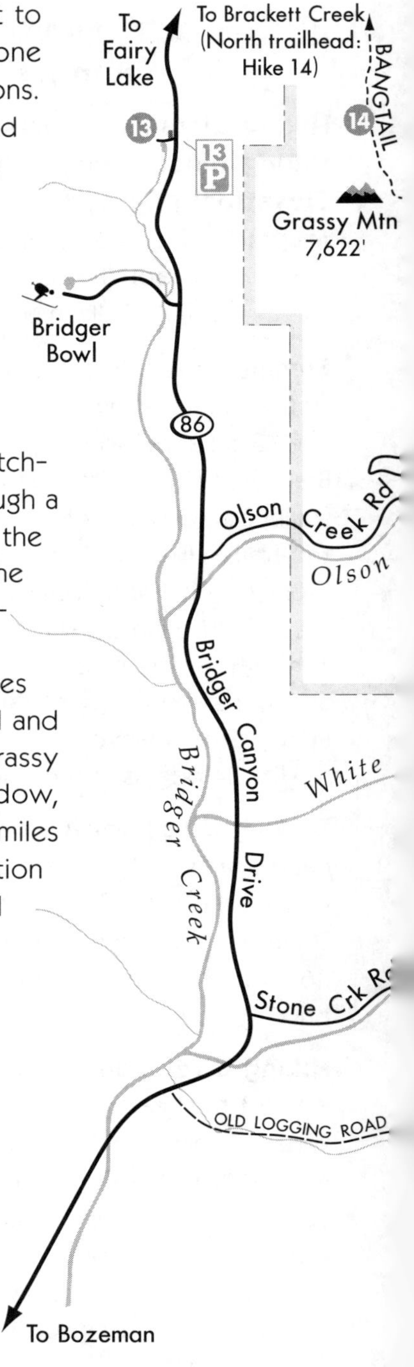

To Fairy Lake

To Brackett Creek (North trailhead: Hike 14)

BANGTAIL

13

13 P

14

Grassy Mtn 7,622'

Bridger Bowl

86

Olson Creek Rd

Olson

Bridger Canyon Drive

White

Bridger Creek

Stone Crk Rd

OLD LOGGING ROAD

16.
Bangtail Divide Trail
SOUTH TRAILHEAD: STONE CREEK

To Bozeman

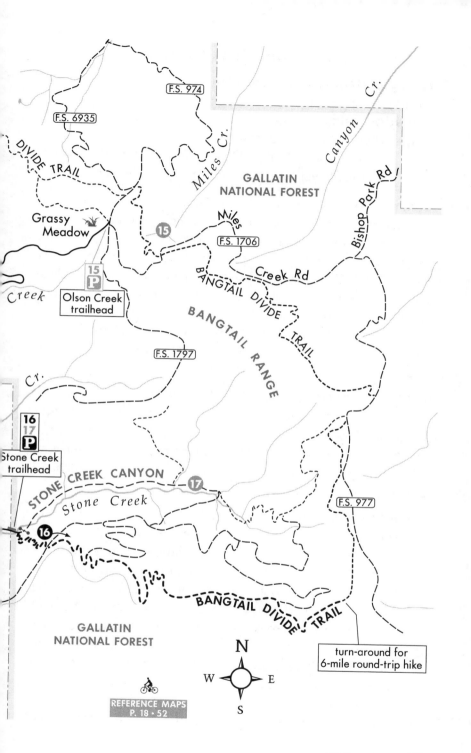

F.S. 974

F.S. 6935

DIVIDE TRAIL

Miles Cr.

GALLATIN
NATIONAL FOREST

Canyon Cr.

Bishop Park Rd

Grassy
Meadow

15

Miles

F.S. 1706

Creek Rd

BANGTAIL DIVIDE TRAIL

15
P
Olson Creek
trailhead

Creek

BANGTAIL RANGE

F.S. 1797

Cr.

16
17
P
Stone Creek
trailhead

STONE CREEK CANYON

Stone Creek

17

F.S. 977

16

BANGTAIL DIVIDE TRAIL

GALLATIN
NATIONAL FOREST

turn-around for
6-mile round-trip hike

N
W E
S

REFERENCE MAPS
P. 18 · 52

17. Stone Creek Road

Hiking distance: 4 miles round trip
Hiking time: 2 hours
Elevation gain: 400 feet
Maps: U.S.G.S. Grassy Mountain
U.S.F.S. Gallatin National Forest: East Half or West Half
Beartooth Publishing: Bozeman, Big Sky, W. Yellowstone

Summary of hike: Stone Creek Canyon drains out of the Bangtail Mountains on the east side of Bridger Canyon, directly south of Grassy Mountain. The creek begins at a 7,700-foot ridge and tumbles 2,300 feet downhill in 4.4 miles to Bridger Creek. The Stone Creek Trail winds through a beautiful rolling mountain and meadow landscape. It is more of a stroll through the mountains than a backcountry hike, as the trail begins on a vehicle-restricted logging road. The road heads up the drainage on a gradual incline along the north bank of cascading Stone Creek. This is also a popular cross-country ski trail.

Driving directions: From Main Street in downtown Bozeman, head north on North Rouse Avenue. Drive 12 miles up Bridger Canyon to Stone Creek Road on the right. (After crossing Griffin Drive, Rouse Avenue becomes Bridger Canyon Drive/Highway 86.) Turn right and continue 1.2 miles to the posted trailhead parking area on the left.

Hiking directions: Walk east up forested Stone Creek Road, crossing over Stone Creek. Pass the Bangtail Divide Trail on the right at 50 yards, reaching the vehicle restricted gate a short distance ahead. Go around the gate and head gently uphill, parallel to Stone Creek. Pass a home tucked into a side canyon on the left. At 0.5 miles, an old abandoned log house sits to the right of the trail by Stone Creek. While traversing the north canyon hillside above the creek, pass a small cluster of homes on the left. At 1.2 miles, the Moody Creek Trail heads north up Moody Gulch. Stay on the Stone Creek Road to the end of the draw at 2 miles. The road curves sharply to the right and crosses Stone Creek, continuing to the right. A posted foot trail leaves the road at this curve and crosses the creek to the left. This is the turn-around spot.

From here, the trail ascends steeply out of the canyon. The trail gains 1,400 feet to the Bangtail Divide Trail, overlooking the Bangtail Creek drainage, Shields Valley, and the Crazy Mountains. ■

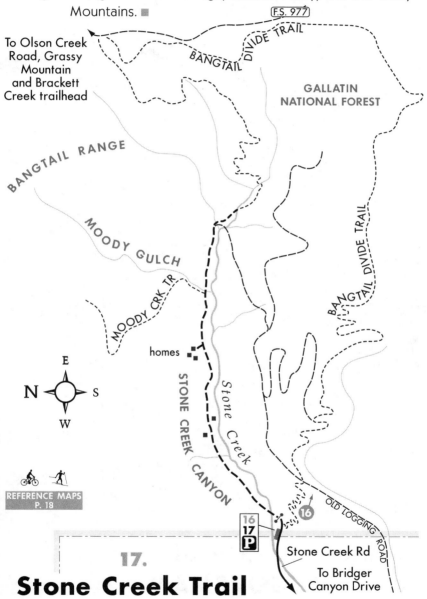

17.
Stone Creek Trail

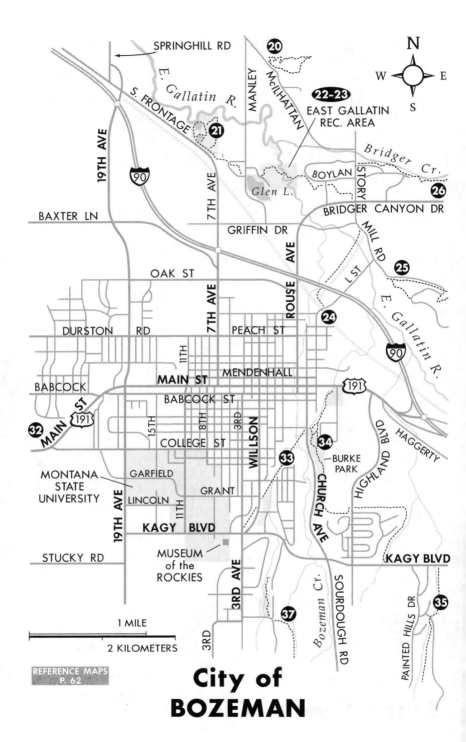

N

W   E

S

SPRINGHILL RD

20

MANLEY

McILHATTAN

E. *Gallatin R.*

S. FRONTAGE

22-23

EAST GALLATIN
REC. AREA

BOYLAN

STORY

Bridger   *Cr.*

26

19TH AVE

I-90

7TH AVE

21

Glen L.

BRIDGER CANYON DR

BAXTER LN

GRIFFIN DR

ROUSE AVE

MILL RD

L ST

25

OAK ST

7TH AVE

24

E. *Gallatin R.*

DURSTON   RD

PEACH ST

11TH

I-90

BABCOCK

MAIN ST

MENDENHALL

191

MAIN ST

32

191

BABCOCK ST

15TH

8TH

3RD

WILLSON

33

34

BURKE
PARK

COLLEGE ST

HIGHLAND BLVD

HAGGERTY

MONTANA
STATE
UNIVERSITY

GARFIELD

GRANT

LINCOLN

11TH

CHURCH AVE

19TH AVE

KAGY BLVD

STUCKY RD

3RD AVE

MUSEUM
of the
ROCKIES

KAGY BLVD

SOURDOUGH RD

Bozeman Cr.

35

37

PAINTED HILLS DR

1 MILE

2 KILOMETERS

3RD

REFERENCE MAPS
P. 62

City of
BOZEMAN

In and Around Bozeman

HIKES 18–43

These 26 hikes lie within a 10-mile radius of Bozeman. They include several miles of hiking and biking routes within the open space of the city, which sits between mountain ranges in the East Gallatin Valley. The northern end of the Gallatin Range slopes down to the southeast end of Bozeman, offering many beautiful canyon hikes only a few minutes drive from downtown. The southern reaches of the Bridger Range curves toward Bozeman from the northeast. Hikes 18 and 19 are located at the end of this range at the large Montana State University "M."

The hikes within Bozeman itself are part of the Main Street to the Mountains trail system, developed and expanded by the hard work and dedication of the Gallatin Valley Land Trust (see below). Hikes 20–26 and 32–38 are part of this trail system, which accesses the East Gallatin Recreation Area, Burke Park, Highland Ridge, and Bozeman Creek.

Mount Ellis and Chestnut Mountain rise at Bozeman's southeast end. New World Gulch and Bear Creek drainages flow between the mountains, feeding the East Gallatin. Hikes 27–31 explore this fairly remote yet nearby area.

Bozeman Creek Trail—Hike 39—is a popular destination for hiking, biking, and horse packing. To the west of this canyon is Leverich Canyon (Hike 40), Kirk Hill (Hikes 41–42), Hyalite Canyon (Hikes 44–55), and South Cottonwood Canyon (Hike 43).

The Gallatin Valley Land Trust (GVLT) is a non-profit organization dedicated to the protection and preservation of open space, including conservation easements, wildlife habitat, and the creation of public trails in and around Gallatin County. They are primarily responsible for building *Main Street to the Mountains*, Bozeman's community trail system. The trail network weaves through Bozeman's neighborhoods, connecting historic corridors, open grasslands, riparian waterways, and scenic ridgelines with views of the Gallatin Valley and surrounding peaks. The trails will eventually link downtown Bozeman with the Bridger Mountains and the Gallatins. Their efforts and accomplishments are largely due to volunteer labor, donations, and grants. To contact GVLT, call (406) 587-8404.

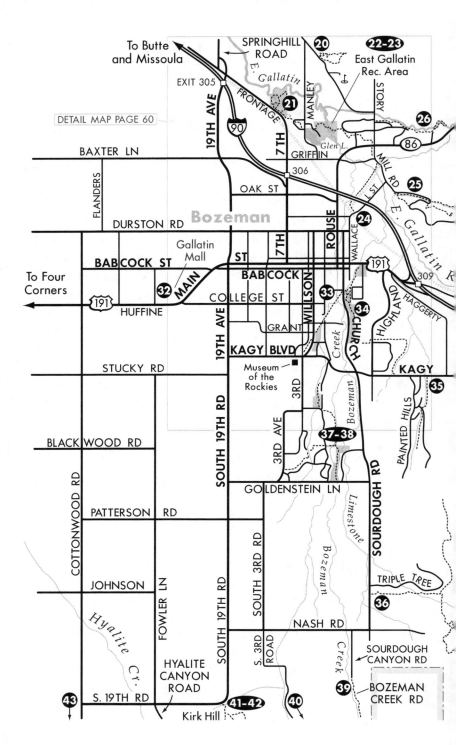

To Butte and Missoula

SPRINGHILL ROAD

E. *Gallatin*

DETAIL MAP PAGE 60

EXIT 305

FRONTAGE

19TH AVE

I-90

7TH

BAXTER LN

FLANDERS

OAK ST

GRIFFIN

306

Glen L.

Bozeman

DURSTON RD

Gallatin Mall

ST

BABCOCK ST

7TH

BABCOCK

ROUSE

WALLACE

To Four Corners

191

MAIN

COLLEGE ST

WILLSON

191

309

HUFFINE

GRANT

CHURCH

Creek

HIGHLAND

HAGGERTY

19TH AVE

KAGY BLVD

Museum of the Rockies

3RD

Bozeman

KAGY

STUCKY RD

SOUTH 19TH RD

3RD AVE

PAINTED HILLS

BLACKWOOD RD

COTTONWOOD RD

GOLDENSTEIN LN

SOURDOUGH RD

Limestone

PATTERSON RD

Bozeman

JOHNSON

FOWLER LN

TRIPLE TREE

Hyalite Cr.

SOUTH 19TH RD

SOUTH 3RD RD

NASH RD

Creek

SOURDOUGH CANYON RD

HYALITE CANYON ROAD

S. 3RD ROAD

BOZEMAN CREEK RD

S. 19TH RD

Kirk Hill

20
22-23
East Gallatin Rec. Area
21
26
86
25
24
32
33
34
35
37-38
36
39
43
41-42
40

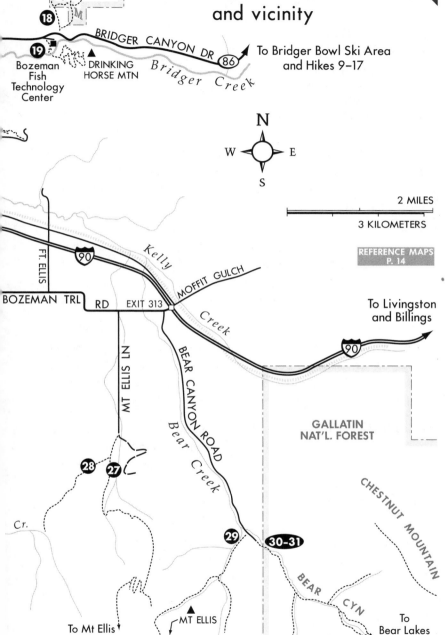

To Fairy Lake

18

BRIDGER CANYON DR **86**

19

Bozeman Fish Technology Center

DRINKING HORSE MTN

Bridger Creek

To Bridger Bowl Ski Area and Hikes 9–17

N
W ✦ E
S

2 MILES

3 KILOMETERS

REFERENCE MAPS P. 14

FT. ELLIS

90

Kelly

MOFFIT GULCH

BOZEMAN TRL RD EXIT 313

Creek

To Livingston and Billings

90

MT ELLIS LN

BEAR CANYON ROAD

Bear Creek

GALLATIN NAT'L. FOREST

28 **27**

Cr.

29 **30–31**

BEAR CYN

CHESTNUT MOUNTAIN

To Mt Ellis

MT ELLIS

To Bear Lakes

18. M Trail

Hiking distance: 1.6-mile loop
Hiking time: 1 hour
Elevation gain: 850 feet
Maps: U.S.G.S. Kelly Creek
U.S.F.S. Gallatin National Forest: East Half
Beartooth Publishing: Bozeman, Big Sky, W. Yellowstone

Summary of hike: The landmark Montana State University "M" is located at the mouth of Bridger Canyon on the south flanks of Baldy Mountain. The M was created by MSU students back in 1915. The 250-foot whitewashed rock letter has two access routes. The right fork follows the ridge for a steep but direct route. The left fork switchbacks through a fir and juniper forest, making a more gradual ascent. The left fork is the beginning of the Bridger Foothills National Recreation Trail, a 24-mile ridge route following the contours of the Bridger Range. This popular hike to the M climbs up the steeper ridge route and descends through the forest via the switchbacks.

Driving directions: From Main Street in downtown Bozeman, head north on North Rouse Avenue 4.2 miles to the signed trailhead on the left, across from the fish hatchery. (After crossing Griffin Drive, Rouse Avenue becomes Bridger Canyon Drive/Highway 86.) Turn left into the trailhead parking lot.

Hiking directions: Head north past the trailhead gate and picnic area to a junction with wide, clearly defined trails. Begin the loop by taking the right fork in a counter-clockwise direction. Head steeply up the ridge, hiking mercilessly up to the base of the M. Beyond the M is a junction. The right fork loops back to the top of the M and the ridge. The left fork levels out and begins the return loop. Bear left at a second junction, and begin the descent on the switchbacks to a junction with the Bridger Foothills National Recreation Trail (Trail #534). Go left (south), returning to the base of the mountain and completing the loop. Return to the trailhead on the right. ▪

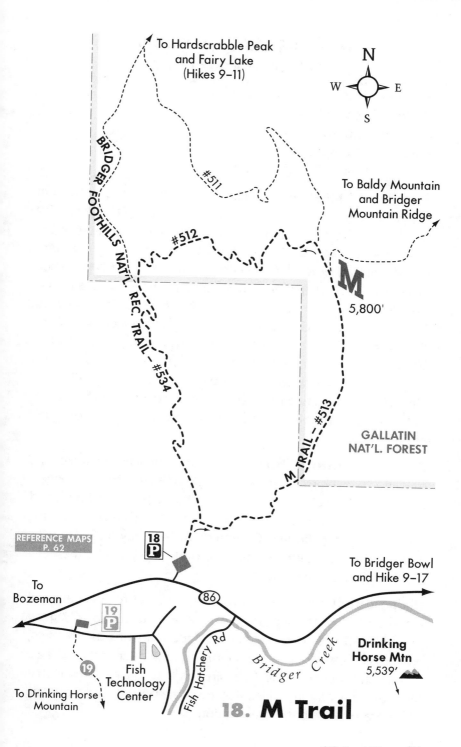

To Hardscrabble Peak
and Fairy Lake
(Hikes 9–11)

N
W E
S

#511

To Baldy Mountain
and Bridger
Mountain Ridge

BRIDGER FOOTHILLS NAT'L. REC. TRAIL – #534

#512

M
5,800'

M TRAIL – #513

GALLATIN
NAT'L. FOREST

REFERENCE MAPS
P. 62

18
P

To
Bozeman

86

To Bridger Bowl
and Hike 9–17

19
P

19

To Drinking Horse
Mountain

Fish
Technology
Center

Fish Hatchery Rd

Bridger Creek

Drinking
Horse Mtn
5,539'

18. **M Trail**

110 Great Hikes - **65**

19. Drinking Horse Mountain
FISH TECHNOLOGY CENTER

Hiking distance: 2.4-mile loop
Hiking time: 1.5 hours
Elevation gain: 700 feet
Maps: U.S.G.S. Kelly Creek
       Gallatin Valley Land Trust map

Summary of hike: Drinking Horse Mountain is the prominent mountain rising above the Bozeman Fish Technology Center. The 40-acre property around the mountain is located across the road from the M Trail parking lot. The scenic trail to the summit of Drinking Horse Mountain offers 360-degree panoramas, including views of the Gallatin Mountains, the Absaroka Range, the Spanish Peaks, Bridger Canyon, and across the Gallatin Valley. The trail is configured like a figure-eight, switchbacking through the evergreen forest, meadows, wildflower-dotted hillsides, and rock outcroppings. From the trailhead, the path descends through riparian vegetation to Bridger Creek. The Kevin Mundy Memorial Bridge, a beautiful 50-foot-long covered bridge, spans the creek near the fish hatchery. Dogs are allowed but bicycles are prohibited.

Driving directions: From Main Street in downtown Bozeman, head north on North Rouse Avenue. Drive 4.1 miles to the signed Bozeman Fish Technology Center on the right, across the road from the M Trail—Hike 18. (After crossing Griffin Drive, Rouse Avenue becomes Bridger Canyon Drive/Highway 86.) Turn right into the fish technology center, and drive 100 yards to the trailhead parking lot on the left.

Hiking directions: Cross the entrance road to the trailhead kiosk, and walk through the lush, vegetated corridor. Zigzag downhill to a trail split. Continue straight, following the trail sign, and cross the Kevin Mundy Memorial Bridge over Bridger Creek. Cross Fish Hatchery Road (the dirt road) to the Drinking Horse Mountain trail entrance. Head up from the base of the mountain on the serpentine path to a junction.

Begin the loop to the right, ascending Drinking Horse Mountain. Weave up the forested mountainside to overlooks that span across the Gallatin Valley to the Tobacco Root Mountains. Leave the forest to the sloping, tree-dotted meadows and rock out-croppings. Continue uphill to views of the Gallatin Range. Weave around the hillside, high above Bridger Canyon, to a saddle and a trail split. Veer right to reach the 5,539-foot summit that over-looks Bridger Canyon.

After enjoying the views, drop down and steadily descend, completing the double loop around its perimeter. Bear to the right and retrace your steps back to the covered bridge, return-ing to the trailhead. ■

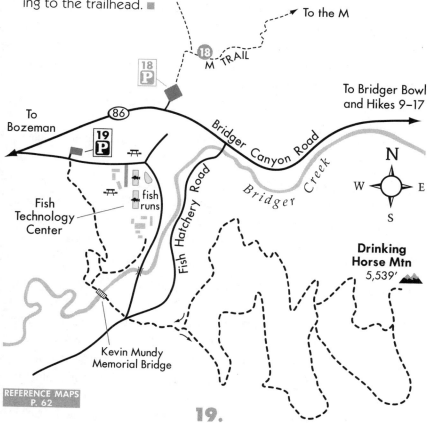

Drinking Horse Mountain
FISH TECHNOLOGY CENTER

20. Snowfill Dog Recreation Area

Hiking distance: 1.25-mile loop
Hiking time: 30 minutes
Elevation gain: 160 feet
Maps: U.S.G.S. Bozeman
Gallatin Valley Land Trust map

Summary of hike: The Snowfill Dog Recreation Area is a 37-acre dogs-off-leash parkland. The park was named *Snowfill* as it is located just north of the city landfill and offers easy access for Nordic skiing and sledding. The recreation area is open year-round. The Hedvig Flowers Memorial Trail, a 1.25-mile loop, roughly circles the perimeter of the park. The trail is named in memory of Hedvig Rappe-Flowers, a local Nordic skier who gave tirelessly to the art community and died of cancer in 2007. The path weaves through rolling fields with spectacular vistas of the Bridger Mountains, the north end of the Gallatin Range, and the Gallatin Valley. The area is owned by the city of Bozeman and maintained by Bozeman Parks Division and the Gallatin Valley Land Trust.

Driving directions: From Main Street in downtown Bozeman, head north on North Rouse Avenue 1.4 miles to Griffin Drive. Turn left and drive 0.3 miles to Manley Road. Turn right and continue 1.8 miles to McIlhattan Road. Make a sharp right turn and go a quarter mile to the trailhead parking lot on the left.

Hiking directions: Pass through the trailhead gate to a trail split. The Hedvig Flowers Memorial Trail is a loop that roughly follows the parkland's perimeter and can be hiked in either direction. The right fork heads up the slope and follows a minor ridge above McIlhattan Road. The left fork weaves up the northern side of the park. Both routes lead to the highest point in the northeast corner of the recreation area. Throughout the hike are sweeping vistas across the Gallatin Valley to the Bridger Mountains, Gallatin Range, and the Tobacco Root Mountains. ■

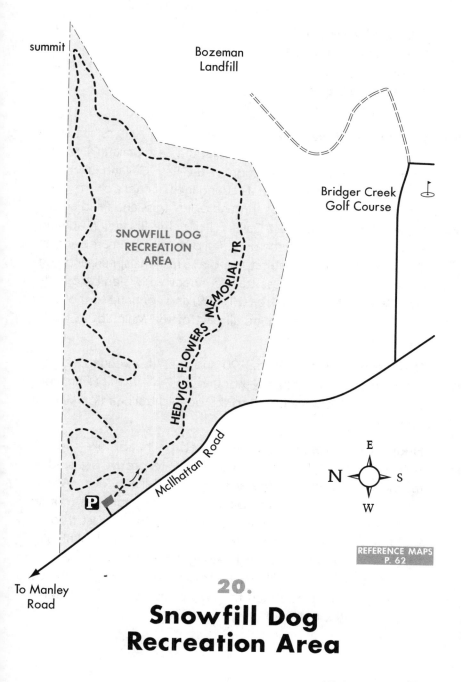

summit

Bozeman
Landfill

Bridger Creek
Golf Course

SNOWFILL DOG
RECREATION
AREA

HEDVIG FLOWERS MEMORIAL TR.

McIlhattan Road

P

E

N — S

W

To Manley
Road

REFERENCE MAPS
P. 62

20.
Snowfill Dog
Recreation Area

21. Cherry River Loop
CHERRY RIVER FISHING ACCESS

Hiking distance: 0.8-mile loop
Hiking time: 30 minutes
Elevation gain: Level
Maps: U.S.G.S. Bozeman
       Gallatin Valley Land Trust map

Summary of hike: The Cherry River Fishing Access sits at the northwest corner of Bozeman along the East Gallatin River. The Cherry River (actually a section of the East Gallatin River) was named in the early 1800s for its abundance of choke cherry trees. An interpretive trail loops through open grasslands and around the wetlands to the East Gallatin River. The Bridger Mountains serve as a backdrop to the beautiful preserve. Interpretive signs describe the riparian habitat, the birds, mammals, fish, and vegetation. The fishing access trails connect with Glen Lake in the East Gallatin Recreation Area (Hike 22) and continue to the Story Mill Trail (Hike 24), which are all part of the Main Street to the Mountains trail system.

Driving directions: From I-90 and the 7th Avenue overpass in Bozeman, drive 1 mile northbound on 7th Avenue (which becomes West Frontage Road) to the posted trailhead parking lot on the right.

Hiking directions: From the posted trailhead, take the left fork—the Cherry River Loop Trail. Pass interpretive signs while meandering clockwise toward the East Gallatin River. At the north end, a side path leads to the river. On the northeast corner of the main trail is a trail split. The left fork heads east through the grasslands and connects with the East Gallatin Trail at Glen Lake (Hike 22). Stay to the right along the east side of the wetland, passing cattails, willows, and dogwood. On the south side of the loop, skirt between the two ponds on a raised berm, returning to the trailhead.

To extend the walk, head east from the southeast corner of the parking lot for 300 yards. This path connects with the trail from the northeast corner of the loop by a footbridge. Continue one mile to the East Gallatin Recreation Area (Hikes 22–23). ■

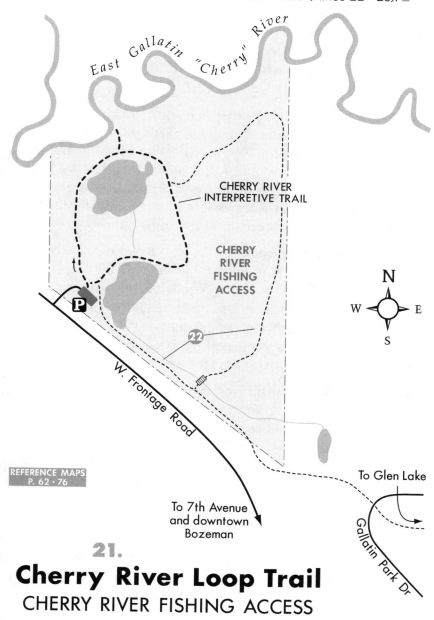

East Gallatin "Cherry" River

CHERRY RIVER
INTERPRETIVE TRAIL

CHERRY
RIVER
FISHING
ACCESS

P

W. Frontage Road

N
W ← → E
S

REFERENCE MAPS
P. 62 · 76

To Glen Lake

To 7th Avenue
and downtown
Bozeman

Gallatin Park Dr

21.
Cherry River Loop Trail
CHERRY RIVER FISHING ACCESS

22. Glen Lake to Cherry River

EAST GALLATIN RECREATION AREA to
CHERRY RIVER FISHING ACCESS

Hiking distance: 2.2 miles round trip
Hiking time: 1 hour
Elevation gain: 40 feet
Maps: U.S.G.S. Bozeman
Gallatin Valley Land Trust map

Summary of hike: The East Gallatin River stretches about 25 miles northeast of Bozeman before joining the Gallatin River by the Horseshoe Hills out of Belgrade. This hike begins in the East Gallatin Recreation Area, an 83-acre park adjacent to the East Gallatin River at the northeast corner of Bozeman. The trail begins from Glen Lake and heads west to a loop through the Cherry River Fishing Access, a preserve which borders the river.

Driving directions: From Main Street in downtown Bozeman, head north on North Rouse Avenue 1.4 miles to Griffin Drive. Turn left and drive 0.3 miles to Manley Road. Turn right and continue 0.6 miles to the signed East Gallatin Recreation Area. Turn right and drive 0.15 miles to the parking spaces on the left (just inside the fence) or 0.3 miles to the parking spaces on the right at the end of the road. All parking is on the east side of Glen Lake.

Hiking directions: Head west on the wide gravel path along the north side of Glen Lake to Manley Road. Cross the road and walk 100 yards down Gallatin Park Drive to the trail on the right, or walk 100 yards up Manley Road to the trail on the left. Both routes merge in a short distance and head west. Pass a pond on the right and skirt the base of the hill 50 feet below 7th Avenue. At a half mile, about 300 yards shy of the Cherry River Fishing Access parking lot, is a posted junction by a footbridge. Bear right and cross the bridge over the stream. Walk north through the grasslands towards the Bridger Range. Before reaching the tree-lined East Gallatin River, curve left to a T-junction with the Cherry River Loop Trail (Hike 21). Both directions lead back to

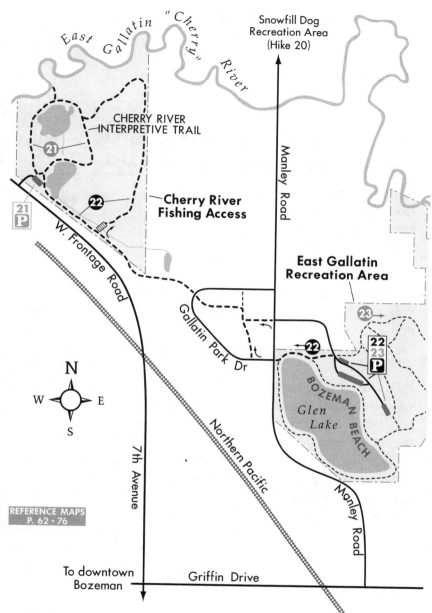

Map labels:

East Gallatin "Cherry" River

Snowfill Dog
Recreation Area
(Hike 20)

CHERRY RIVER
INTERPRETIVE TRAIL

21

Cherry River
Fishing Access

22

21
P

W. Frontage Road

Manley Road

East Gallatin
Recreation Area

23

Gallatin Park Dr

22

22
23
P

N
W ⟡ E
S

BOZEMAN BEACH

Glen
Lake

7th Avenue

Northern Pacific

REFERENCE MAPS
P. 62 · 76

To downtown
Bozeman

Manley Road

Griffin Drive

22. Glen Lake to Cherry River
EAST GALLATIN RECREATION AREA
CHERRY RIVER FISHING ACCESS

the Cherry River parking area. Pick up the trail on the southeast corner of the parking lot and head east, completing the loop by the footbridge. After the footbridge, retrace you route back to Glen Lake. ■

23. East Gallatin River Trail to Story Mill
EAST GALLATIN RECREATION AREA

Hiking distance: 2.2 miles round trip
Hiking time: 1 hour
Elevation gain: Level
Maps: U.S.G.S. Bozeman
      Gallatin Valley Land Trust map

map
page 76

Summary of hike: The East Gallatin Recreation Area is an 83-acre park adjacent to the East Gallatin River at the northeast corner of Bozeman. The centerpiece of the park is Glen Lake (also called East Gallatin Lake), developed over an old gravel pit. Bozeman Beach lies on the east side of the lake, a 300-foot sandy beach strand. The popular lake is used for swimming, canoeing, kayaking, windsurfing, fishing, and sunbathing.

Trails lead in both directions from the lake. To the west, the recreation area connects with the Cherry River Fishing Access (Hike 21—22). This hike leads east along the serpentine East Gallatin River, a popular bird-watching area. The trail crosses the river on a 70-foot pedestrian bridge. Two loops wind through the riparian corridor between the river and the Bridger Creek Golf Course. The trail continues east to the Story Mill Trail (Hike 24).

The trails in the East Gallatin Recreation Area are part of the Main Street to the Mountains trail system.

Driving directions: From Main Street in downtown Bozeman, head north on North Rouse Avenue 1.4 miles to Griffin Drive. Turn left and drive 0.3 miles to Manley Road. Turn right and continue

0.6 miles to the signed East Gallatin Recreation Area. Turn right and drive 0.15 miles to the parking spaces on the left (just inside the fence) or 0.3 miles to the parking spaces on the right at the end of the road. All parking is on the east side of Glen Lake.

Hiking directions: From Glen Lake, take either of the posted trails east. Both routes meet a short distance ahead in an open, grassy meadow. Skirt the east edge of the meadow, bordering the lush vegetation that engulfs the river, to a signed junction at 0.3 miles by the pedestrian bridge. Straight ahead, the path follows the west edge of the river to the Rouse Avenue trailhead 0.3 miles ahead. Along the way, side paths lead to the riverbank.

Bear left on the East Gallatin Connector Trail, and cross the East Gallatin Pedestrian Bridge, an arched metal bridge over the creek. At the T-junction, begin the loop on the right fork, following the river in a lush forest. Pass elbow bends in the river to a Y-fork. The main route goes left. For now go 12 yards to the right and another fork. This is a short loop through the forest and along the river. Return to the Y-fork and continue to another trail split. The left fork is our return route. Bear right and leave the forest, following the south edge of Bridger Creek Golf Course to Boylan Road. Curve right, staying on the footpath, with a view of the west flank of the Bridger Mountains. Head south, then east, passing homes and open grasslands. Cross Birdie Drive and weave along the gravel path to the Story Mill Connector Trail. This is the turn-around spot.

Return to the forested junction. This time bear right on the loop, and weave through the forest, crossing five bridges over the wetlands before completing the loop at the pedestrian bridge. Cross the bridge over the East Gallatin River, and retrace your steps back to the parking area.

Trails continue northwest to the Cherry River Fishing Access, Hikes 21–22. ■

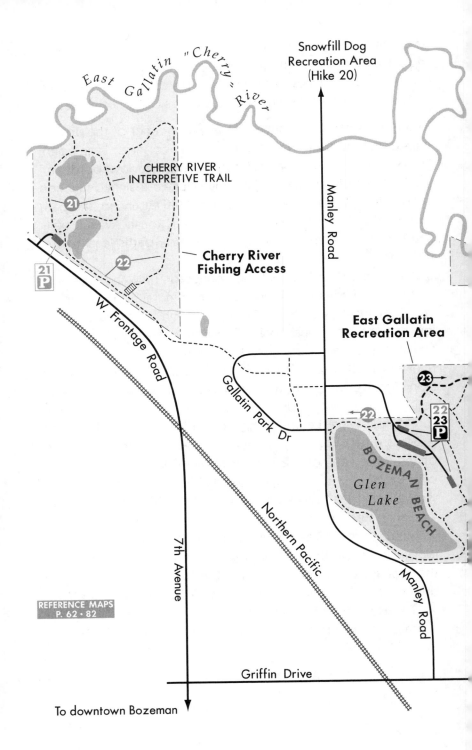

East Gallatin "Cherry" River

CHERRY RIVER
INTERPRETIVE TRAIL

21

22

**Cherry River
Fishing Access**

**21
P**

W. Frontage Road

Snowfill Dog
Recreation Area
(Hike 20)

Manley Road

**East Gallatin
Recreation Area**

23

22

**22
23
P**

BOZEMAN BEACH

*Glen
Lake*

Gallatin Park Dr

7th Avenue

Northern Pacific

REFERENCE MAPS
P. 62·82

Manley Road

Griffin Drive

To downtown Bozeman

23.
East Gallatin River Trail to Story Mill
EAST GALLATIN RECREATION AREA

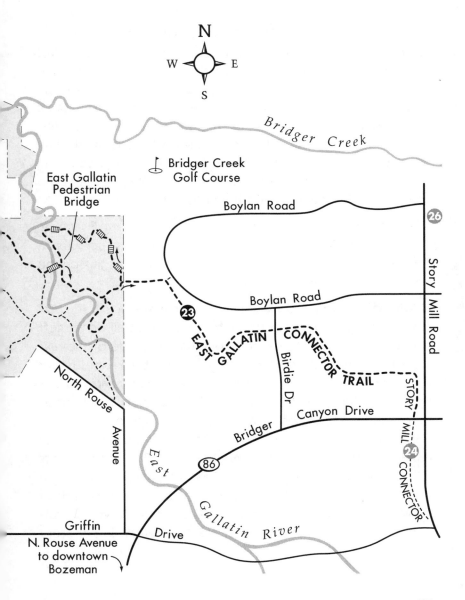

24. Story Mill Spur Trail

Hiking distance: 2.2 miles round trip
Hiking time: 1 hour
Elevation gain: Level
Maps: U.S.G.S. Bozeman

map page 80

Summary of hike: Back in 1883, Story Mill was the largest flour mill in Montana. It was also the first business in Bozeman serviced by the railroad. Railroad tracks, known as the Story Mill Spur, lead 4,400 feet to the historic mill. The Story Mill Spur Trail is an interpretive trail along the railroad right-of-way. The trail crosses the East Gallatin River, where benches have been placed in the shade of the cottonwood trees. The hike continues past the remains of the Bozeman livestock yards and the historic Story Mill to Bridger Canyon Drive, where it now connects to the East Gallatin River Trail (Hike 23). The Gallatin Valley Land Trust worked 9 years to make this historic trail into a reality.

Driving directions: From Main Street in downtown Bozeman, take North Wallace Avenue 0.6 miles to East Tamarack Street. Turn right and park alongside the road. The trail begins on the north side of the railroad tracks.

Hiking directions: Walk north on North Wallace Street 0.1 mile, crossing the railroad tracks to the signed trail on the left side of the road. Take the trail along the right side of the railroad tracks heading north. Cross over the tracks and under I-90. The trail narrows and the shrub-lined path heads directly towards the Bridger Mountains. Continue past farmhouses, barns, and horses. Cross a wooden footbridge over the East Gallatin River, and pass the cottonwood grove by the historic remains of the Gallatin Valley Auction Yard. The trail connects with the unpaved Story Mill Road. Bear left past the mills to the signed footpath on the left side of the road. The trail ends at Bridger Drive. To extend the hike, cross Bridger Drive and follow the Story Mill Connector Trail along the west side of Story

Mill Road. A short distance ahead is a posted junction with the East Gallatin Connector Trail that leads to Glen Lake and the East Gallatin Recreation Area (Hike 23). ∎

25. Story Hills Trails

Hiking distance: 3-mile loop
Hiking time: 1.5 hours
Elevation gain: 300 feet
Maps: U.S.G.S. Bozeman and Kelly Creek
  Gallatin Valley Land Trust map

**map
page 80**

Summary of hike: The Story Hills sit on the northeast corner of Bozeman, off of Story Mill Road. The privately owned property is a great in-town destination that is open for hiking, biking, and equestrian use during daylight hours. Dogs are also allowed. The trail forms a loop around Big Gulch and meanders through pockets of aspen, pine, and open pastureland with livestock at large. The trail offers views of the Gallatin Range, the city of Bozeman, and the Gallatin Valley.

The landowner has provided recreational access to his land and has generously worked with the Gallatin Valley Land Trust, who improved the trails. As a working cattle ranch, the owner occasionally closes access while moving cattle, spraying weeds, or for periodic upkeep. The trails may also be closed if they are too muddy or when fire danger is high. Future access to this trail system depends on users respecting the land. To help keep this section of the ranch open to the public, please treat the land well, stay on the trails, and respect the temporary closures.

Driving directions: From Main Street in downtown Bozeman, head north on Wallace Avenue. Drive 1.3 miles to Story Mill Road. (After crossing over the railroad tracks, Wallace Avenue becomes L Street.) Turn right on Story Mill Road and continue 0.2 miles to the posted trailhead on the right. Park off the road on the right.

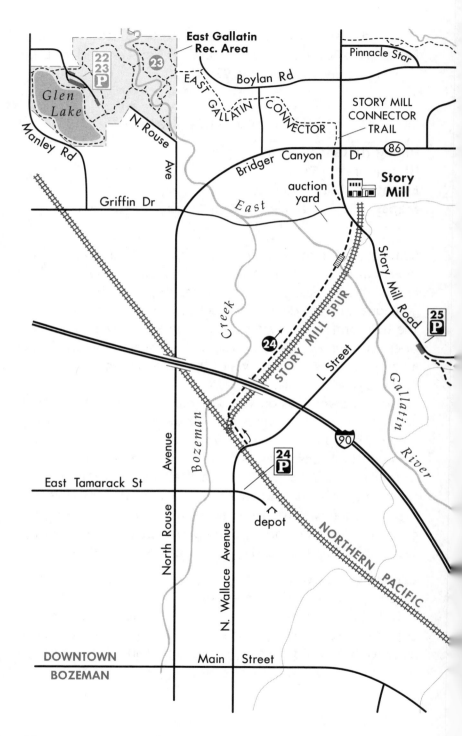

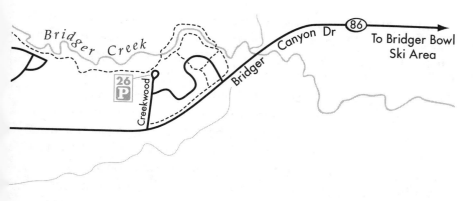

Bridger Creek

26
P

Creekwood

Bridger Canyon Dr

86

To Bridger Bowl
Ski Area

STORY HILLS

N
W • E
S

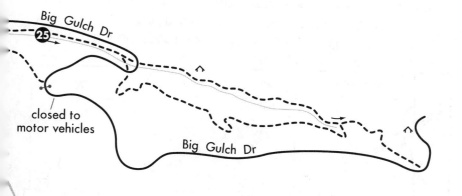

Big Gulch Dr

25

closed to
motor vehicles

Big Gulch Dr

REFERENCE MAPS
P. 62 • 82

HIKE 24
Story Mill Spur Trail

HIKE 25
Story Hills Trails

Hiking directions: Pass through the trailhead gate and head east. Follow the base of the hill, parallel to Big Gulch Drive. At a half mile, Big Gulch Road curves right and heads up the hill. Cross the road and begin the loop, continuing straight along the north-facing slope of Big Gulch. Pass a home on the hillside across the road, and slowly gain elevation to views across north Bozeman. As the walls of the gulch narrow, the trail reaches a junction at 1.3 miles. The return route goes across the gully to the right. For now, detour straight ahead. Continue gaining elevation and cross over the gulch to the open pastureland. The trail ends at the east end of vehicle-restricted Big Gulch Drive. From the end of the trail are vistas of Mount Ellis, Chestnut Mountain, and into the mouth of Bear Canyon.

Return a quarter mile to the junction and bear left, crossing the gulch. Follow the single track trail down canyon on the south gulch slope. Pass through a grove of pines to views across the city. Wind down a forested side drainage, and return to the exposed grassland. Follow the ridge and zigzag down to Big Gulch Drive, completing the loop. Cross the road and bear left, returning a half mile to the trailhead. ∎

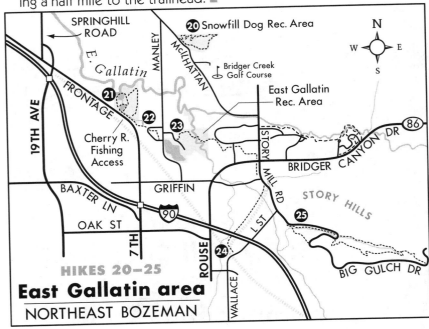

26. Legends—Creekwood— Bridger Creek Trail

Hiking distance: 2.5 miles round trip
Hiking time: 1 hour
Elevation gain: level
Maps: U.S.G.S. Kelly Creek and Bozeman
     Gallatin Valley Land Trust map

map
page 84

Summary of hike: This hike, which follows a scenic stretch of Bridger Creek, is named after the adjacent Legends and Creekwood Subdivisions. The trail is located at the northeast end of Bozeman off of Bridger Canyon Drive, just before entering the Bridger Canyon. The easy, level trail follows the banks of Bridger Creek, framed by huge alders, cottonwoods, and lush undergrowth.

Driving directions: CREEKWOOD LANE—EAST TRAILHEAD: From Main Street in downtown Bozeman, head north on North Rouse Avenue. Drive 2.7 miles to Creekwood Lane on the left. (After crossing Griffin Drive, Rouse Avenue becomes Bridger Canyon Drive/Highway 86.) Turn left (north) on Creekwood Lane, and continue 0.15 miles to the cul-de-sac and trailhead parking area.

STORY MILL ROAD—WEST TRAILHEAD: From Main Street in downtown Bozeman, head north on North Rouse Avenue 1.9 miles to Story Mill Road, located 0.8 miles before Creekwood Lane. Turn left (north) on Story Mill Road and drive 0.3 miles to the trailhead on the right, located just after passing Pinnacle Star Street. Turn left on Boylan Road and park.

Hiking directions: From the Creekwood Lane trailhead, begin on the trail to the left. Head west on the gravel path, and meander through open grassland, paralleling the riparian brush along Bridger Creek. As the trail nears Boylan Road and Medicine Wheel Lane, the brush thins, allowing easy creek access. Continue downstream, following the watercourse of the wooded creek. Skirt the Legends Subdivision, and stroll through the wide greenbelt

with continued creek access. The trail ends at one mile at Story
Mill Road, across from Boylan Road. Return to the trailhead.

Additional trails lie to the east of Creekwood Lane. For a
short loop, head east (right) from the trailhead, staying on the
paved path. Pass the picnic shelter to a trail split, where the

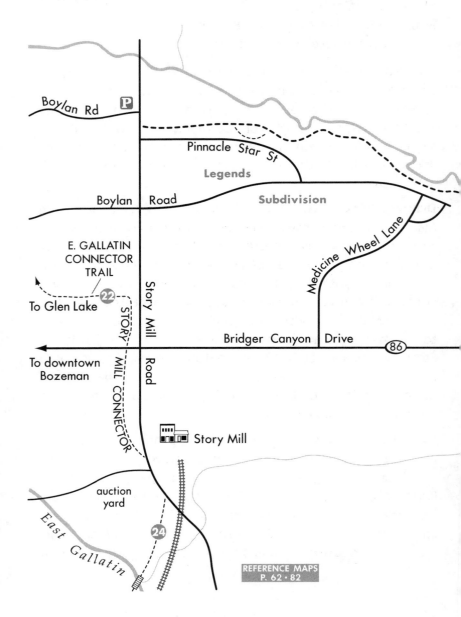

pavement ends. Begin the loop to the left, and cross the metal bridge over Bridger Creek. Curve right and follow the creek upstream. Continue along the northern boundary of the open space, tucked between the wood fence and the creek, to a second bridge. Recross the creek and bend right, following the south banks of Bridger Creek back to the trailhead. ∎

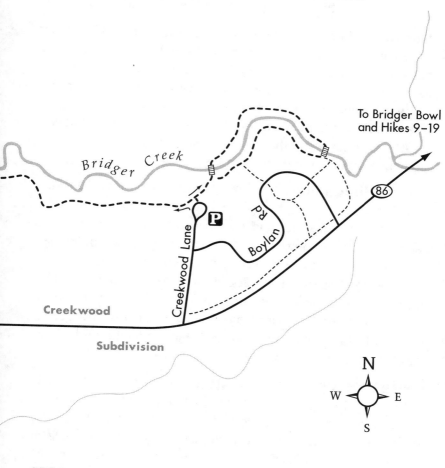

26.
Legends–Creekwood– Bridger Creek Trail

27. Lower Mount Ellis

Hiking distance: 6 miles round trip
Hiking time: 3.5 hours
Elevation gain: 2,400 feet
Maps: U.S.G.S. Kelly Creek and Mount Ellis
 Beartooth Publishing: Bozeman, Big Sky, W. Yellowstone

map
page 89

Summary of hike: Mount Ellis lies on the southeast edge of Bozeman at the north end of the Gallatin Range. The mountain has two peaks, with the higher 8,331-foot peak to the south. A long, sweeping saddle connects the two summits, which rise between New World Gulch and Bozeman Creek Canyon. This hike climbs up the northeast slope of Mount Ellis to the lower 7,690-foot peak. Atop the lower peak is a clearing with Madison limestone outcroppings and gorgeous vistas.

Driving directions: From Bozeman, drive east on I-90 to the Bear Canyon Road exit, the first exit east of Bozeman. Turn right on Bozeman Trail Road, and continue 0.7 miles to Mount Ellis Lane. Turn left and drive 1.75 miles to the end of the public road by private property gates. Park on the side of the road.

From Kagy Boulevard and Sourdough Road in Bozeman, drive 3.5 miles east on Kagy Boulevard to Mount Ellis Lane, across from a large, old barn. (En route, Kagy Boulevard becomes Bozeman Trail Road.) Turn right and continue 1.75 miles to the end of the public road by private property gates.

Hiking directions: Pass through the wooden state land gate. Follow the old jeep road on an upward slope through the open pastureland. Head toward the treeline at the base of prominent Mount Ellis. Along the way are sweeping vistas across the Gallatin Valley to the Bangtail, Bridger, and Tobacco Root Mountains. At 0.35 miles, enter the shade of an aspen and pine forest. Pass a wide, grassy path on the right that leads to Limestone Creek (Hike 28). Continue 70 yards to a cattle gate. Climb the west wall of the canyon and curve left, looping out of the draw. Traverse the north face of Mount Ellis through lodgepole pines, curving around a second drainage. At 2 miles, the old road tops out on an open flat with a trail split. To the left, the grassy path descends toward New World Gulch (Hike 29). One hundred yards along this route is an overlook into the canyon. (Continuing into the gulch, this path becomes vague and is hard to follow.)

Back on the main trail, continue up the right (west) fork, and make a horseshoe bend through the old logging area. Make a sweeping left bend and head south, with views of Upper Mount Ellis and Bozeman Creek Canyon. Make another U-shaped bend to views of Bozeman and the Gallatin Valley. A footpath veers to the right and leads to the old-growth forest. Steeply climb to the summit of Lower Mount Ellis.

To extend the hike, a path follows the ridge across the sweeping saddle for 1.4 miles, climbing nearly 1,000 feet to the upper peak. ■

28. Limestone Creek

Hiking distance: 4 miles round trip
Hiking time: 2 hours
Elevation gain: 500 feet
Maps: U.S.G.S. Kelly Creek and Mount Ellis

map
page 89

Summary of hike: Limestone Creek forms on the northern slope of Mount Ellis at the north end of the Gallatin Mountains. The seasonal stream drains into Bozeman Creek en route to the Gallatin River. The trail traverses the base of Mount Ellis into a minor but scenic drainage that offers great views across Gallatin Valley. There is no distinct destination for this hike, but the journey itself is pastoral, scenic, and offers easy, close-to-town access.

Driving directions: From Bozeman, drive east on I-90 to the Bear Canyon exit, the first exit east of Bozeman. Turn right on Bozeman Trail Road, and continue 0.7 miles to Mount Ellis Lane. Turn left and drive 1.75 miles to the end of the public road by private property gates. Park on the side of the road.

From Kagy Boulevard and Sourdough Road in Bozeman, drive 3.5 miles east on Kagy Boulevard to Mount Ellis Lane, across from a large, old barn. (En route, Kagy Boulevard becomes Bozeman Trail Road.) Turn right and continue 1.75 miles to the end of the public road by private property gates.

Hiking directions: Pass through the wooden state land gate. Follow the old jeep road on a gradual upward slope through the open, flower-filled pastureland. Head toward the treeline at the base of prominent Mount Ellis. Along the way are sweeping vistas across the Gallatin Valley to the Bangtail, Bridger, and Tobacco Root Mountains. At 0.35 miles, enter the shade of an aspen and pine forest to an unsigned Y-fork. The main trail, straight ahead, leads to Lower Mount Ellis (Hike 27). Veer right on the wide, grassy path and pass through a trail gate. Traverse the northern foot of Mount Ellis while gaining elevation to a small meadow on a flat. Continue straight ahead through the lodgepole pine forest, curving along the contours of the mountainside. Gently descend to the end of the grassy road at the east edge of the Limestone Creek drainage at 2 miles. A footpath veers left and heads up the drainage. Choose your own turn-around spot. ■

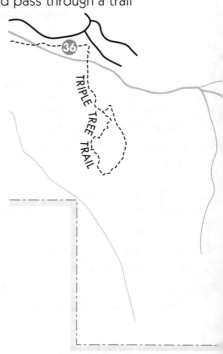

REFERENCE MAPS
P. 62·92

HIKE 27
Lower Mount Ellis

HIKE 28
Limestone Creek

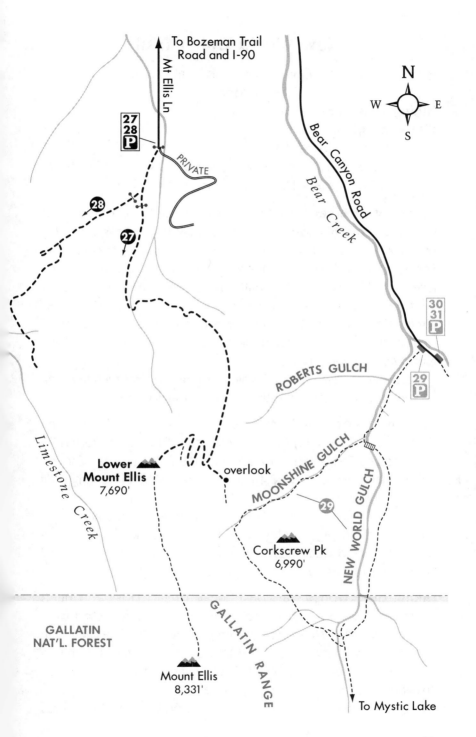

To Bozeman Trail
Road and I-90

Mt Ellis Ln

27
28
P

PRIVATE

28

27

N
W   E
S

Bear Canyon Road

Bear Creek

30
31
P

ROBERTS GULCH

29
P

Limestone Creek

Lower
Mount Ellis
7,690'

overlook

MOONSHINE GULCH

29

NEW WORLD GULCH

Corkscrew Pk
6,990'

GALLATIN
NAT'L. FOREST

GALLATIN RANGE

Mount Ellis
8,331'

To Mystic Lake

29. New World Gulch Trail

Hiking distance: 4 miles round trip to meadow
or 5.5-mile loop
Hiking time: 2.5—3 hours
Elevation gain: 1,350 feet
Maps: U.S.G.S. Mount Ellis
Beartooth Publishing: Bozeman, Big Sky, W. Yellowstone
U.S.F.S. Gallatin National Forest: West Half or East Half

Summary of hike: New World Gulch is located southeast of Bozeman, branching off of Bear Canyon along the east slope of Mount Ellis. The stream-fed gulch is due north of Mystic Lake. The New World Gulch Trail climbs up the drainage 4.7 miles to the lake. This hike takes the trail halfway up the narrow drainage for 2.2 miles to a meadow and canyon. From the meadow, the trail circles Corkscrew Peak, forming a return loop on the slopes of Mount Ellis. (The area around the meadow retains water, creating muddy spots early in the season.)

Past the meadow, the trail gains another 500 feet in elevation en route to Mystic Lake at the head of Sourdough Canyon.

Driving directions: From Bozeman, drive east on I-90 to the Bear Canyon Road exit, the first exit east of Bozeman. Turn right on Bozeman Trail Road, and continue 0.2 miles to Bear Canyon Road. Turn left and drive 3.4 miles to the trailhead parking area on the right.

From Kagy Boulevard and Sourdough Road in Bozeman, drive 4 miles east on Kagy Boulevard to Bear Canyon Road. (En route, Kagy Boulevard becomes Bozeman Trail Road.) Turn right and continue 3.4 miles to the parking area on the right.

Hiking directions: Walk past the trailhead kiosk and head south up the slope of the foothill. Follow the forested path above cascading New World Creek. Traverse the east canyon wall, then meet and cross New World Creek. A short distance ahead, cross Moonshine Gulch. Twenty yards after crossing is an unsigned footpath on the right, the return loop.

Begin the loop straight ahead, staying on the main trail. Cross

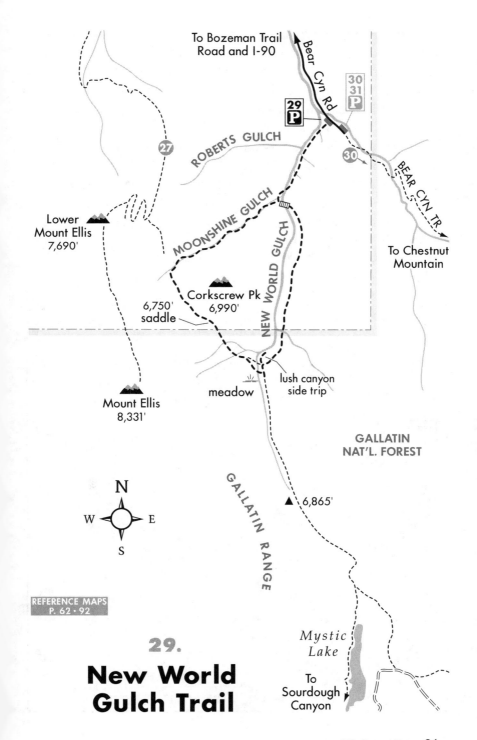

To Bozeman Trail
Road and I-90

Bear Cyn Rd

30
31
P

29
P

ROBERTS GULCH

27

30

BEAR CYN TR

Lower
Mount Ellis
7,690'

MOONSHINE GULCH

NEW WORLD GULCH

To Chestnut
Mountain

Corkscrew Pk
6,990'

6,750'
saddle

Mount Ellis
8,331'

meadow

lush canyon
side trip

GALLATIN
NAT'L. FOREST

N
W · E
S

▲ 6,865'

GALLATIN RANGE

REFERENCE MAPS
P. 62 · 92

29.
New World
Gulch Trail

*Mystic
Lake*

To
Sourdough
Canyon

a bridge over New World Creek and continue uphill. At 1.9 miles, descend once again to the gulch and a drainage stream. From the stream, detour on the faint trail downstream 400 yards to a beautiful, lush canyon with small waterfalls and ferns.

Return to the main trail, and continue upstream 0.2 miles to a large meadow and an unsigned trail fork. The main route continues beyond the meadow and leads to Mystic Lake, 2.5 miles farther. To hike the loop, take the faint path west and cross the stream. Head up the slope to a 6,750-foot saddle between Mount Ellis and Corkscrew Peak. Descend to the headwaters of a feeder stream through Moonshine Gulch. Veer right and descend along the drainage, crossing the stream several times. Complete the loop on the floor of New World Gulch. Retrace your steps back to the left. ■

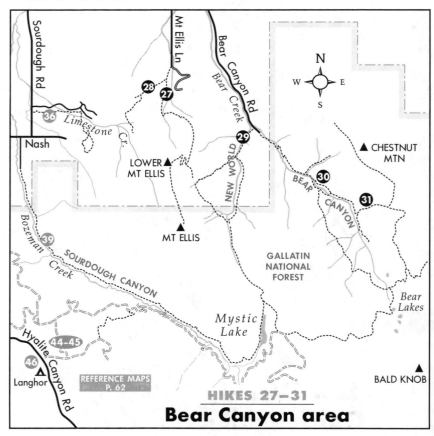

30. Bear Canyon Trail

Hiking distance: 4.4 miles round trip

Hiking time: 2.5 hours

map
page 95

Elevation gain: 400 feet

Maps: U.S.G.S. Mount Ellis

Beartooth Publishing: Bozeman, Big Sky, W. Yellowstone

U.S.F.S. Gallatin National Forest: West Half or East Half

Summary of hike: Bear Canyon is a stream-fed canyon that drains between Mount Ellis and Chestnut Mountain southeast of Bozeman. The headwaters of Bear Creek form on the upper north slope of Bald Knob and flow through the canyon en route to the East Gallatin River. The Bear Canyon Trail follows Bear Creek five miles up the lush, shady canyon to the Bear Lakes. This hike takes in the first 2.2 miles of the trail, which includes several creek crossings and a one-mile loop. The trail stays close to the cascading waters of the creek, gaining relatively little elevation. Beyond the turn-around for this hike, the Bear Canyon Trail climbs 1,400 feet to the Bear Lakes, which sit on a moist flat at 6,900 feet. En route to the lakes, the Chestnut Mountain Trail—Hike 31—veers off to the east to overlooks of the canyon and surrounding peaks.

Driving directions: From Bozeman, drive east on I-90 to the Bear Canyon Road exit, the first exit east of Bozeman. Turn right on Bozeman Trail Road, and continue 0.2 miles to Bear Canyon Road. Turn left and drive 3.6 miles to the trailhead parking area on the left at the end of the road.

From Kagy Boulevard and Sourdough Road in Bozeman, drive 4 miles east on Kagy Boulevard to Bear Canyon Road. (En route, Kagy Boulevard becomes Bozeman Trail Road.) Turn right and continue 3.6 miles to the trailhead parking area on the left at the end of the road.

Hiking directions: Walk past the trailhead gate, and head southeast on the old jeep road. Parallel the southwest side of Bear Creek through the lush forest. Continue beneath the weathered sandstone formations along Francham Mountain, and cross a wooden bridge over Bear Creek as the canyon narrows. Zigzag up two switchbacks, and traverse the north canyon wall above the creek. Head gently uphill, with frequent dips and rises. Climb up two more switchbacks, with a view up Shoefelt Gulch across the canyon. Slowly descend to a trail gate by Bear Creek. Pass through the gate and cross a bridge over Dean Gulch, where a side path curves left into the draw. Stay on the main trail, and cross another bridge by a footpath on the left.

Begin the loop straight ahead. Follow the southwest side of the drainage, slowly descending to the creek. Cross the creek on a wooden bridge to a grassy meadow beneath Chestnut Mountain. One hundred feet ahead is a faint footpath on the left—our return route. The main trail continues up Chestnut Mountain (Hike 30); the trail also continues around a loop for 3 miles to the 6,900-foot Bear Lakes.

For this hike, take the footpath to the left and walk downstream. Meander through the rolling, tree-filled meadows and cross a few feeder streams. The path fades in and out, but is easy to locate again. Cross the old creekbed and complete the loop at the bridge. Retrace your steps down canyon back to the trailhead. ∎

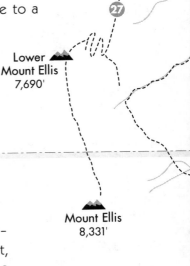

Lower
Mount Ellis
7,690'

Mount Ellis
8,331'

GALLATIN
NAT'L. FOREST

REFERENCE MAPS
P. 62 • 92

30.
Bear Canyon Trail Loop

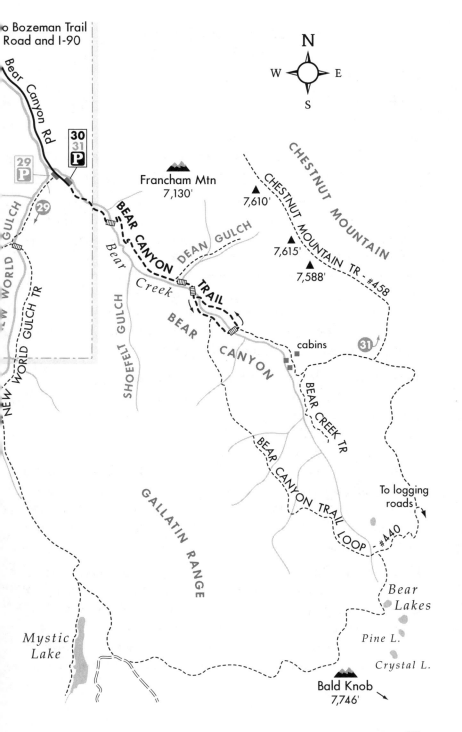

To Bozeman Trail Road and I-90

Bear Canyon Rd

N
W   E
S

30
31
P

29
P

29

NEW WORLD GULCH

NEW WORLD GULCH TR

Francham Mtn
7,130'

CHESTNUT MOUNTAIN

7,610'

CHESTNUT MOUNTAIN TR - #458

7,615'

7,588'

BEAR CANYON

DEAN GULCH

Bear

Creek

TRAIL

SHOEFELT GULCH

BEAR

CANYON

cabins

31

BEAR CREEK TR

GALLATIN RANGE

BEAR CANYON TRAIL LOOP - #440

To logging roads

Bear Lakes

Pine L.

Crystal L.

Mystic Lake

Bald Knob
7,746'

31. Bear Canyon Trail to Chestnut Mountain

Hiking distance: 10 miles round trip

Hiking time: 5 hours

Elevation gain: 2,100 feet

map
page 98

Maps: U.S.G.S. Mount Ellis and Bald Knob

Beartooth Publishing: Bozeman, Big Sky, W. Yellowstone

U.S.F.S. Gallatin National Forest: West Half or East Half

Summary of hike: Chestnut Mountain sits on the northeast tip of the Gallatin Range a few miles east of Bozeman. The 7,615-foot mountain rises between Mount Ellis and Bozeman Pass. At the west foot of Chestnut Mountain lies Bear Canyon, which provides the easiest access to the ridge. This hike follows Bear Creek through the canyon, then weaves through grassy meadows with old log cabins. The trail ascends Chestnut Mountain from its southern end and follows the ridge to far-reaching vistas of the surrounding peaks and mountain ranges.

Driving directions: From Bozeman, drive east on I-90 to the Bear Canyon Road exit, the first exit east of Bozeman. Turn right on Bozeman Trail Road, and continue 0.2 miles to Bear Canyon Road. Turn left and drive 3.6 miles to the trailhead parking area on the left at the end of the road.

From Kagy Boulevard and Sourdough Road in Bozeman, drive 4 miles east on Kagy Boulevard to Bear Canyon Road. (En route, Kagy Boulevard becomes Bozeman Trail Road.) Turn right and continue 3.6 miles to the trailhead parking area on the left at the end of the road.

Hiking directions: Walk past the trailhead gate, and traverse the southwest canyon wall through a lush forest. Parallel Bear Creek beneath the weathered sandstone formations along Francham Mountain. Cross a wooden bridge over Bear Creek as the canyon narrows. Zigzag up two switchbacks and traverse the north canyon wall above the creek. Head gently uphill with frequent dips and rises. Climb up two more switchbacks, with a view up Shoefelt Gulch across the canyon. Slowly descend to a trail gate by Bear Creek. Pass through the gate and cross a bridge over Dean Gulch, where a side path curves left into the draw. Stay on the main trail, and cross another bridge by a footpath on the left.

Begin the loop straight ahead. Follow the southwest side of the drainage, slowly descending to the creek. Cross the creek on a wooden bridge to a grassy meadow beneath Chestnut Mountain at 2.2 miles. To the left is the return loop. Go right (southeast), and stroll through the meadows. Climb through pine groves, with intermittent views of Bald Knob, where the headwaters of Bear Creek are formed. Walk through another huge meadow with an old log cabin and two sheds on the right. Another cabin sits at the far north end of the meadow. Steeply climb out of the meadow (passing the faint continuation of the Bear Creek Trail on the right) to a flat ridge and a Y-fork. The right fork leads one mile to logging roads. Bear left and climb to the south end of Chestnut Mountain. Climb the grassy ridge northwest to 360-degree views that include Bear Canyon; Bald Knob; Mount Ellis; and the Absaroka, Crazy, Bangtail, and Bridger Mountains. Continue up the spine to the tree-dotted summit. Follow the ridge over minor ups and downs, choosing your own turn-around spot. ■

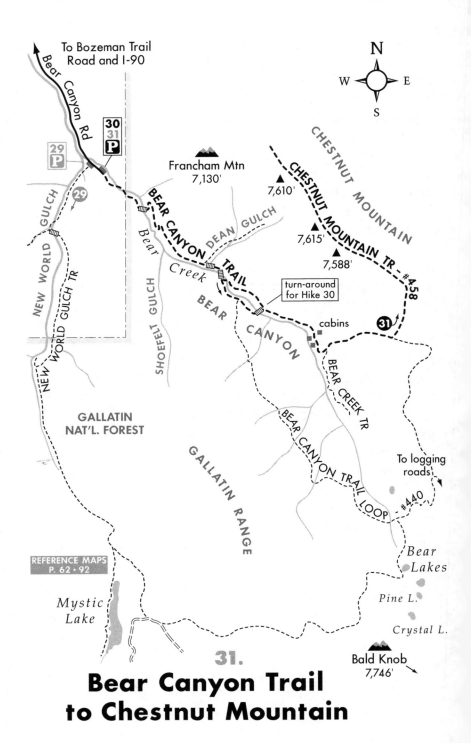

N
W   E
S

To Bozeman Trail
Road and I-90

Bear Canyon Rd

30
31
P

29
P

29

NEW WORLD GULCH

NEW WORLD GULCH TR

Francham Mtn
7,130'

DEAN GULCH

BEAR CANYON

Bear

Creek

SHOEFELT GULCH

BEAR

CANYON

turn-around
for Hike 30

cabins

7,610'

7,615'

7,588'

CHESTNUT MOUNTAIN

CHESTNUT MOUNTAIN TR - #458

31

BEAR CREEK TR

BEAR CANYON TRAIL LOOP - #440

GALLATIN
NAT'L. FOREST

GALLATIN RANGE

To logging
roads

Bear
Lakes

Pine L.

Crystal L.

REFERENCE MAPS
P. 62 • 92

Mystic
Lake

Bald Knob
7,746'

31.

Bear Canyon Trail
to Chestnut Mountain

32. Bozeman Pond Loop

Hiking distance: 0.5-mile loop
Hiking time: 30 minutes
Elevation gain: Level
Maps: U.S.G.S. Bozeman

map
page 100

Summary of hike: Bozeman Pond is a little 17-acre gem tucked away on the west side of Bozeman, adjacent to the Gallatin Valley Mall. The park, a former gravel pit, once had three ponds. It has since been developed into one lake with two sandy beaches, including an off-leash dog beach on the west end, a fishing pier, a grassy park with picnic tables, an open-air pavilion, and a walking path that circles the pond. It is a popular area for fishing, kayaking, canoeing, swimming, and walking. The pond is stocked with rainbow, brook, and brown trout.

Driving directions: From downtown Bozeman, drive 2.4 miles west on Main Street to Fowler Avenue, the first street past the Gallatin Valley Mall. (Fowler Avenue is located 1.2 miles west of 19th Avenue.) Turn right and drive one block to the park entrance on the right.

Hiking directions: From the picnic pavilion just north of the parking lot, take the main path to the left, hiking clockwise. Pass a sandy beach and side paths leading to the edge of the pond. One path leads to a fishing pier that extends over the water. The trail curves right and parallels Fowler Avenue between a stream on the left and Bozeman Pond on the right. Pass a fenced dog beach and a bridge crossing over the stream. Along the lush, forested north side of the pond are vistas of the Bridger Mountains. Cross a bridge over the pond's outlet stream, and return between the pond and the Gallatin Valley Mall. Just before completing the loop, a path leads out to a small peninsula. ■

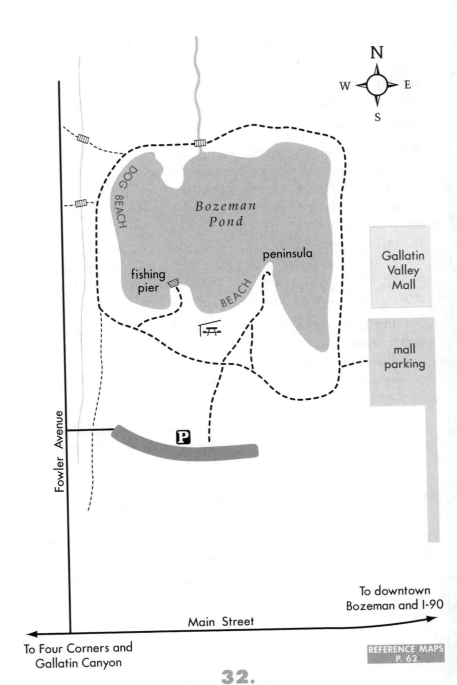

N
W   E
S

Bozeman Pond

DOG BEACH

peninsula

Gallatin Valley Mall

fishing pier

BEACH

mall parking

P

Fowler Avenue

To downtown Bozeman and I-90

Main Street

To Four Corners and Gallatin Canyon

REFERENCE MAPS
P. 62

32.
Bozeman Pond Loop

33. Gallagator Trail to Museum of the Rockies

Hiking distance: 2.2 miles round trip
Hiking time: 1 hour
Elevation gain: Level
Maps: U.S.G.S. Bozeman
Gallatin Valley Land Trust map

map
page 103

Summary of hike: The Gallagator Trail follows the route of the old Milwaukee Road railroad track, which took passengers between Bozeman and the Gallatin Gateway. The route was abandoned in the late 1930s. The right-of-way is now a hiking and biking trail in the Main Street to the Mountains trail system. The trail begins at the base of Peets Hill by Burke Park. The path crosses several bridges over Bozeman (Sourdough) Creek and Mathew Bird Creek, ending at a picnic area by the Museum of the Rockies. En route, a spur trail leads through Langohr Park. There are several street crossings along the route.

Driving directions: From Main Street at the east end of downtown Bozeman, drive south on South Church Avenue 0.4 miles to the parking area on the left, across from Story Street at the base of Peets Hill.

Hiking directions: Cross South Church Avenue to the corner of Story Street. Take the signed trail southwest along Gallagator Linear Park. Follow the wide, tree-lined path along the old railroad right-of-way. Cross a wooden bridge over Bozeman Creek. At 0.2 miles, cross a second bridge over Mathew Bird Creek to a junction. The side path on the right leads to a fork. The right fork goes through an aspen grove and exits by Anderson Street, just east of Black Avenue. The left fork loops back to the main trail. Continue along Mathew Bird Creek past scenic backyards. Pass a bridge on the right that crosses over the creek to the south end of Black Avenue. Cross another bridge over Mathew Bird Creek at a half mile, 30 yards shy of Garfield Street. After crossing the road, follow the trail along the right side of the creek to the signed Langohr Spur Trail on the left. The spur trail leads through the streamside park on the west side of the water-way to Langohr Gardens at Mason Street and Tracy Avenue. En route, the spur passes a climbing rock on the left and a trail that crosses a bridge over the creek to Tracy Avenue.

On the main trail, continue southwest, passing a pond on the left to South Willson Avenue. Cross the road and bear left 70 yards to Lincoln Street. Pick up the path again by the wooden trail posts on the southwest corner. Follow the hedge-lined path to Kagy Boulevard. Cross the road to the Museum of the Rockies. Follow the path to a picnic area by the metal horse sculpture. To return, retrace your steps. ■

34. Chris Boyd—Highland Ridge Trail

Hiking distance: 4.4 miles round trip
Hiking time: 2 hours
Elevation gain: 100 feet
Maps: U.S.G.S. Bozeman
       Gallatin Valley Land Trust map

*map
page 104*

Summary of hike: Burke Park is a 42-acre linear park that par-allels South Church Avenue. It is at the hub of the Main Street to the Mountains trail system. Highland Ridge is a low 100-foot bluff that runs above South Church Avenue the length of the park. The Highland Ridge Trail begins at Peets Hill in Burke Park and heads south along the ridge to the city water tower. From the top of the hill are views across Bozeman to the Bridger, Gallatin, and Madison Ranges. Benches are placed along the ridge for sa-voring the views, which include the Bozeman Creek corridor. The first segment of the trail has been renamed and dedicated to Chris Boyd, founder of the Gallatin Valley Land Trust. Beyond the ridge, the path skirts the edge of a subdivision and meanders through rolling grasslands, connecting with the Painted Hills Trail (Hike 35).

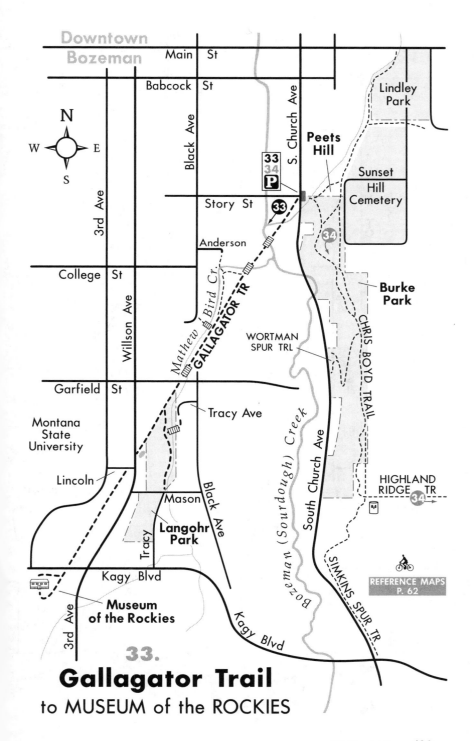

N W E S

Downtown Bozeman

Main St

Babcock St

Black Ave

S. Church Ave

Lindley Park

33 **34** P

Story St **33**

Anderson

College St

Willson Ave

3rd Ave

Mathew Bird Cr.

GALLAGATOR TR

Garfield St

Montana State University

Lincoln

Mason

Black Ave

Tracy

Langohr Park

Kagy Blvd

3rd Ave

Museum of the Rockies

Kagy Blvd

Tracy Ave

WORTMAN SPUR TRL

Bozeman (Sourdough) Creek

South Church Ave

Peets Hill

Sunset Hill Cemetery

34

Burke Park

CHRIS BOYD TRAIL

HIGHLAND RIDGE TR **34**

SIMKINS SPUR TR

REFERENCE MAPS P. 62

33.

Gallagator Trail
to MUSEUM of the ROCKIES

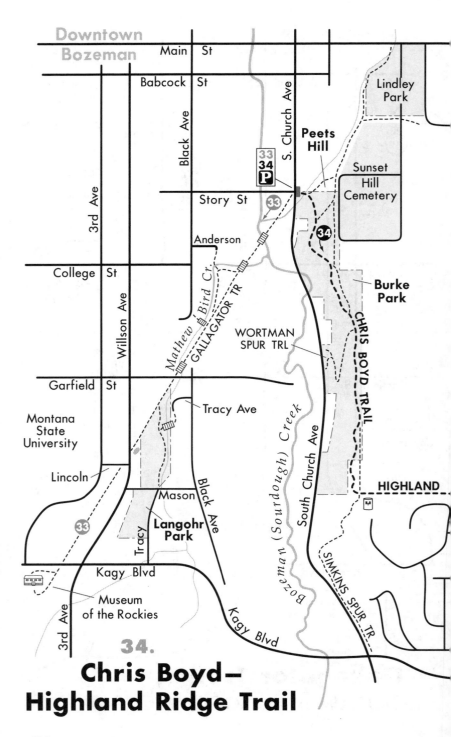

34.
Chris Boyd–
Highland Ridge Trail

Driving directions: From Main Street at the east end of downtown Bozeman, drive south on South Church Avenue 0.4 miles to the parking area on the left, across from Story Street at the base of Peets Hill.

Hiking directions: Walk 20 yards up the posted path to a trail split and map kiosk in Burke Park. The left fork climbs northeast to Lindley Park. Bear right and head up Peets Hill to the ridge. From the top are several paths. Take the Chris Boyd Trail (which begins in Lindley Park) and head south. Follow the hillside ridge through Burke Park. Pass the Wortman Spur Trail on the right that leads down the hillside to Church Avenue. Continue along the ridge 0.7 miles to a signed junction with the Simkins Spur Trail at the water tower. Bear left on the Highland Ridge Trail. Follow the wooden rail fence to the east to Highland Boulevard, between farmland to the north and a row of homes to the south. Go to the left 75 yards on the paved bike path and cross the road, picking up the signed trail again. The path curves around the perimeter of New Hyalite View subdivision and curves south through the rolling grasslands. At 2.3 miles, the trail forks. Curve left, reaching Kagy Boulevard. Follow the Kagy Connector Trail east, crossing the road to the Painted Hills Trailhead 0.4 miles ahead (Hike 35). Continue with Hike 35, or return on the same path. ■

Highland Blvd

RIDGE TRAIL

34

New Hyalite View subdivision

N

W ← → E

S

REFERENCE MAPS
P. 62

35
P

Kagy Blvd

KAGY CONNECTOR TR

35 PAINTED HILLS TRAIL

35. Painted Hills Trail

Hiking distance: 2.5 miles round trip
Hiking time: 1 hour
Elevation gain: Level
Maps: U.S.G.S. Bozeman
      Gallatin Valley Land Trust map

Summary of hike: The Painted Hills are tucked into the southeast corner of Gallatin Valley and Bozeman, just north of Mount Ellis. The Painted Hills Trail begins near the south end of the Highland Ridge Trail—Hike 34. (The Kagy Connector Trail links these two trails together.) The trail passes through dedicated parkland along a gully near the Painted Hills subdivision. The path heads south, crossing a small stream, and currently ends at a private property fenceline. The Gallatin Valley Land Trust is actively working to connect it with the Triple Tree Trail (Hike 36).

Driving directions: From Main Street at the east end of downtown Bozeman, drive south on South Church Avenue 1.6 miles to Kagy Boulevard. (South Church Avenue becomes Sourdough Road after Kagy Boulevard.) Turn left (east) on Kagy Boulevard, and drive 0.9 miles to the trailhead parking area on the right.

Hiking directions: Head south past the trail sign, following the east edge of the draw. Continue across a series of small rises and dips. Cross a wooden footbridge over a seasonal drainage. At 0.6 miles, cross McGee Drive in the Painted Hills subdivision. Pick up the trail again and cross another footbridge. Bear left on the narrow footpath and continue up the draw. The trail currently ends at 1.25 miles at a private property fence. Return by retracing your steps. ■

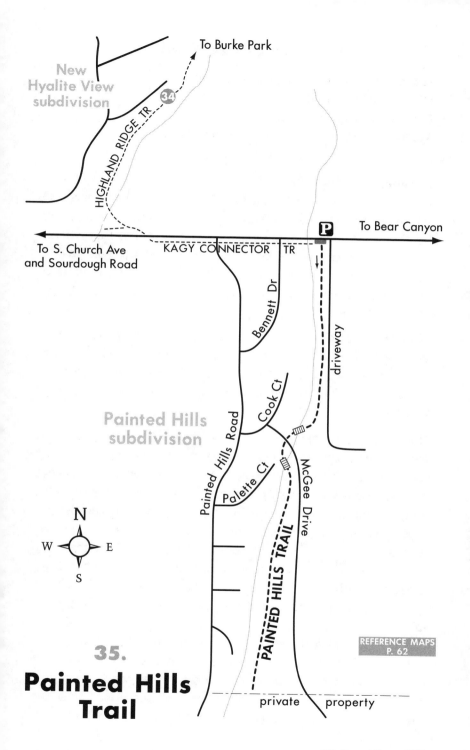

To Burke Park

New Hyalite View subdivision

HIGHLAND RIDGE TR. 34

To Bear Canyon

P

KAGY CONNECTOR TR

To S. Church Ave and Sourdough Road

Bennett Dr

driveway

Painted Hills subdivision

Cook Ct

Painted Hills Road

Palette Ct

McGee Drive

N
W   E
S

PAINTED HILLS TRAIL

REFERENCE MAPS
P. 62

35.
Painted Hills Trail

private   property

36. Triple Tree Trail

Hiking distance: 4.5 miles round trip
Hiking time: 2 hours
Elevation gain: 800 feet
Maps: U.S.G.S. Wheeler Mountain and Mount Ellis
      Gallatin Valley Land Trust map

Summary of hike: The Triple Tree Trail is on the southeast corner of Gallatin Valley just south of Bozeman. It begins on a grassy ridge, crosses Limestone Creek, and loops through the northwest slope of Mount Ellis on state land. The trail weaves through shaded woodlands to a hilltop knoll in a wildflower-covered meadow. From the summit are 360-degree views of Gallatin Valley and the Gallatin, Madison, Tobacco Root, and Bridger Ranges.

Driving directions: From Main Street in downtown Bozeman, drive south on South Church Avenue 4.6 miles to the signed parking lot on the left. The parking lot is 200 feet south of Triple Tree Road. (South Church Avenue becomes Sourdough Road after Kagy Boulevard.)

Hiking directions: Follow the wide grassy path east past the trailhead sign, and cross the rolling slopes. Enter an aspen grove and cross two footbridges over Limestone Creek. Emerge from the forest into the open meadow, and climb the slope to a signed junction at one mile. The left fork continues across the grasslands and crosses several subdivision roads. (The path will eventually connect with the Painted Hills Trail.) Take the right fork and follow the buck fence south, down into the drainage. Cross the bridge over Limestone Creek and another bridge over the wetlands. Ascend the hill into the forest to a trail split at 1.5 miles.

Take the right fork, beginning the loop, and head up the west side of the draw into state land. Bear sharply to the right, and climb up the hillside. Follow the ridge up a winding course. At the top is a meadow with fantastic vistas. After enjoying the views, cross the meadow and begin the descent into the forested drainage. Head down the draw along the right side of a trickling stream. Near the bottom, cross the stream, completing the loop. Retrace your steps to return. ■

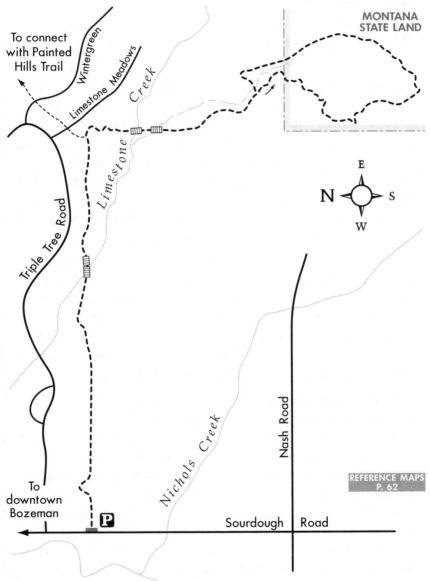

36. **Triple Tree Trail**

37. Sourdough Trail

Hiking distance: 3.2 miles round trip
Hiking time: 1.5 hours
Elevation gain: 100 feet
Maps: U.S.G.S. Bozeman
Gallatin Valley Land Trust map

Summary of hike: Bozeman (Sourdough) Creek begins from Mystic Lake on the southeast flank of Mount Ellis. The creek, Bozeman's only major stream corridor, threads its way through the city en route to the East Gallatin River. The Sourdough Trail follows a portion of Bozeman Creek under the shade of aspen and cottonwoods at the south end of Bozeman. After several creek crossings, the path breaks out into the grassy meadows, skirts the Valley View Golf Course, and meanders through Graf Park. In the winter, the Sourdough Trail is a popular cross-country ski trail.

Driving directions: From Main Street in downtown Bozeman, drive south on South Church Avenue 3.1 miles to Goldenstein Lane. It is 1.5 miles south of Kagy Boulevard. (En route, South Church Avenue becomes Sourdough Road.) Turn right on Goldenstein Lane, and drive 0.5 miles to the posted trailhead parking area on the right, 100 yards after crossing Bozeman Creek.

Hiking directions: Walk 100 yards east on the Goldenstein Trail, paralleling Goldenstein Lane to Bozeman Creek. Curve left and head north on the forested path downstream along the west edge of the creek. Short side paths lead to the creek bank. Wind through the shaded forest to a posted trail split at a half mile. Detour right, crossing a 60-foot arching metal bridge over the creek in Gardner Park. On the upstream side of the bridge is a pool in the creek.

Return to the main trail, and cross over a stream to a junction with the Sundance Trail on the left (Hike 38). Continue straight, staying on the forested Sourdough Trail. Cross a bridge over Nash-Spring Creek, and follow the creek to the fenced Valley View Golf Course. Curve left, skirting the edge of the golf course to Graf Street, just south of Spring Meadow Drive. Go to the right, picking up the signed footpath at Graf Park on the right. Walk through the parkland meadow on the east side of aspen-lined Mathew Bird Creek. The trail ends on Fairway Drive between homes. ■

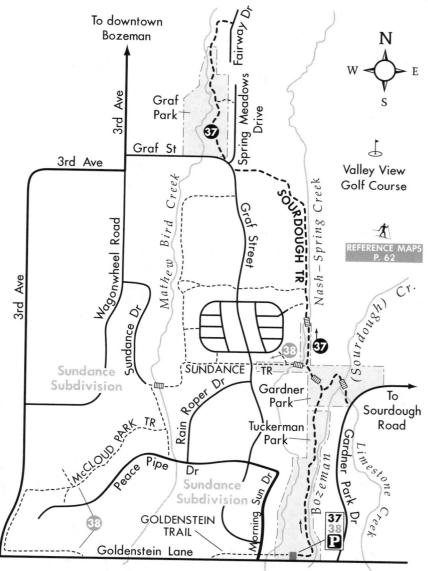

37. Sourdough Trail

38. Sundance Trail Loop

Hiking distance: 2.5-mile loop
Hiking time: 1.5 hours
Elevation gain: Level
Maps: U.S.G.S. Bozeman
Gallatin Valley Land Trust map

Summary of hike: The Sundance subdivision sits on the south side of Bozeman between 3rd Avenue and Goldenstein Lane. The first half mile of this loop hike follows the forested Sourdough Trail (Hike 37) along Bozeman Creek. It then leaves the forest and weaves through the open grasslands preserved within the subdivision, crossing bridges over Nash–Spring Creek and Mathew Bird Creek.

Driving directions: From Main Street in downtown Bozeman, drive south on South Church Avenue 3.1 miles to Goldenstein Lane. It is 1.5 miles south of Kagy Boulevard. (En route,

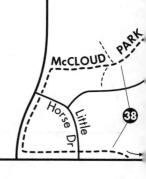

38.

Sundance Trail Loop

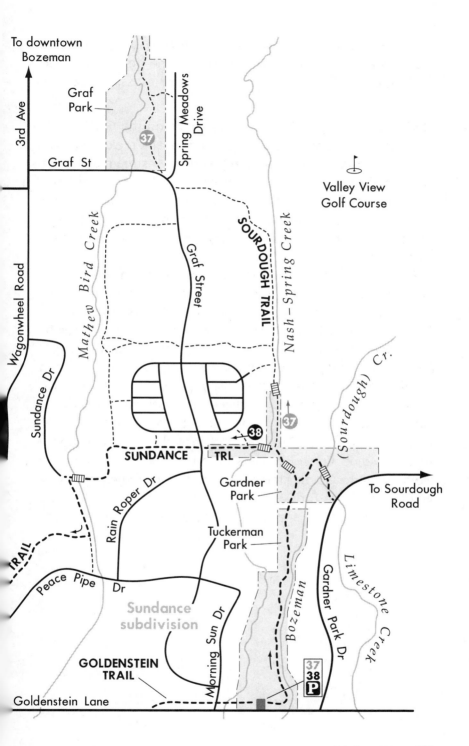

South Church Avenue becomes Sourdough Road.) Turn right on Goldenstein Lane, and drive 0.5 miles to the posted trailhead parking area on the right, 100 yards after crossing Bozeman Creek.

Hiking directions: Walk 100 yards east on the Goldenstein Trail, paralleling Goldenstein Lane to Bozeman Creek. Curve left and head north on the forested path downstream along the west edge of the creek. Short side paths lead to the creek bank. Wind through the shaded forest to a posted trail split at a half mile. Detour right, crossing a 60-foot arching metal bridge over the creek in Gardner Park. On the upstream side of the bridge is a pool in the creek.

Return to the main trail, and cross over a stream to a junction with the Sundance Trail on the left. The Sourdough Trail (Hike 37) continues straight. Bear left and cross a bridge over serpentine Nash-Spring Creek. Meander through the open grasslands in the Sundance subdivision and cross Graf Street. Weave to a junction, located just after crossing a bridge over Mathew Bird Creek. The right fork leads to a trailhead at the end of Sundance Drive. Stay to the left and parallel an irrigation ditch to another junction. The trail straight ahead ends at Peace Pipe Drive. Bear right on the McCloud Park Trail, and stroll through the meadow to 3rd Avenue. Curve left, parallel to the road, and cross Little Horse Drive to Goldenstein Lane. Head east on the path along Goldenstein Lane for 0.2 miles, where the path ends. Walk 0.3 miles along the road, and return to the trail and the trailhead. ■

39. Bozeman Creek Trail
(SOURDOUGH CANYON ROAD)

Hiking distance: 0.5 to 16 miles round trip (to Mystic Lake)
Hiking time: 30 minutes to 9 hours
Elevation gain: Approximately 200 feet/mile
Maps: U.S.G.S. Wheeler Mountain and Mount Ellis
      Beartooth Publishing: Bozeman, Big Sky, W. Yellowstone

*map
page 116*

Summary of hike: The headwaters of Bozeman (Sourdough) Creek flow from Mystic Lake and the east slope of Palisade Mountain. The creek, which provides a major source of water for the city of Bozeman, weaves through the city en route to the East Gallatin River. The Bozeman Creek Trail is an old logging road. It parallels the creek for 8 miles through a pine, fir, spruce and cottonwood forest from the mouth of Sourdough Canyon to Mystic Lake. The close proximity to town and easy grade makes this a popular hiking, biking, equestrian, and cross-country skiing route.

Driving directions: From the east end of downtown Bozeman, drive south on South Church Avenue 5.2 miles to Nash Road. (South Church Avenue becomes Sourdough Road after Kagy Boulevard.) Turn right on Nash Road, and continue 0.2 miles to Sourdough Canyon Road on the left. Turn left and drive 0.9 miles to the trailhead parking area at road's end.

Hiking directions: Pass the trailhead gate and head southeast along the wide, forested road. Parallel Bozeman Creek through Sourdough Canyon at a steady but gradual uphill grade. At 4.7 miles is a junction and a bridge crossing over the creek. The Mystic Lake Trail (known locally as the Wall of Death) stays on the northwest side of the creek and continues 3 miles to the south end of Mystic Lake. The road (to the right) crosses over the bridge to a junction. The right fork climbs to Moser Creek Road and descends to Langohr Campground (Hikes 44 and 45). The left fork also leads to Mystic Lake and to the Wild Horse Trail, which drops downhill to the Hyalite Reservoir (Hike 47). Choose your own turn-around spot. ■

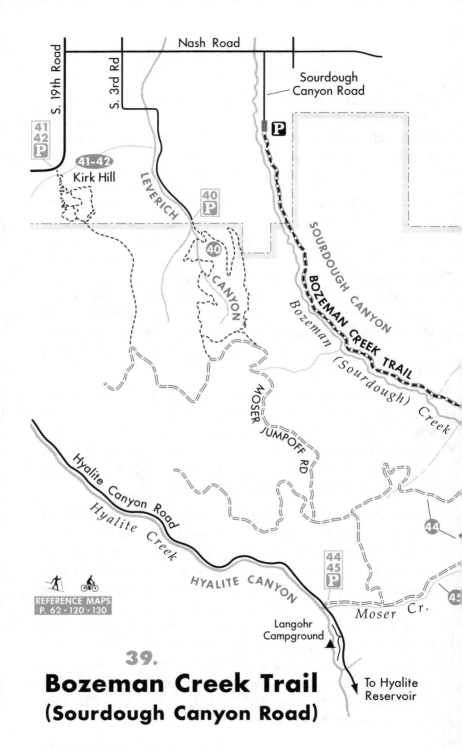

Nash Road

S. 19th Road

S. 3rd Rd

Sourdough
Canyon Road

41
42
P

41-42
Kirk Hill

LEVERICH

40
P

40

CANYON

SOURDOUGH CANYON

BOZEMAN CREEK TRAIL

Bozeman (Sourdough) Creek

MOSER JUMPOFF RD

Hyalite Canyon Road

Hyalite Creek

HYALITE CANYON

44

44
45
P

45

Moser Cr.

REFERENCE MAPS
P. 62 · 120 · 130

Langohr
Campground

To Hyalite
Reservoir

39.
Bozeman Creek Trail
(Sourdough Canyon Road)

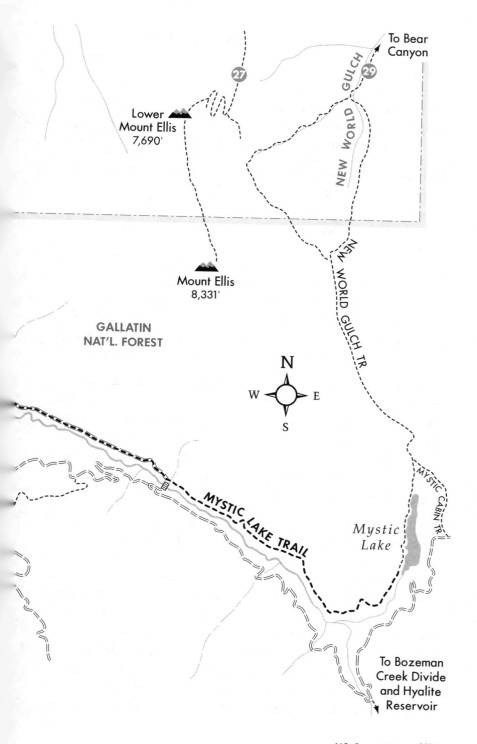

To Bear
Canyon

27

29

NEW WORLD GULCH

Lower
Mount Ellis
7,690'

Mount Ellis
8,331'

GALLATIN
NAT'L. FOREST

NEW WORLD GULCH TR.

N

W ─◆─ E

S

MYSTIC LAKE TRAIL

Mystic
Lake

MYSTIC CABIN TR.

To Bozeman
Creek Divide
and Hyalite
Reservoir

40. Leverich Canyon Trail

Hiking distance: 4.5-mile loop
Hiking time: 2.5 hours
Elevation gain: 1,200 feet
Maps: U.S.G.S. Wheeler Mountain
Beartooth Publishing: Bozeman, Big Sky, W. Yellowstone

Summary of hike: Leverich Canyon is a beautiful, narrow canyon south of Bozeman that is tucked between the two prominent drainages of Hyalite Canyon and Sourdough Canyon. The trail forms a loop on the canyon walls and follows the ridge overlooking Bozeman Creek and Sourdough Canyon. The trail crosses the head of Leverich Canyon on the Moser Creek Road. The old logging road atop the ridge provides access into both Sourdough Canyon (Hike 39) and Hyalite Canyon by Langohr Campground. The Leverich Canyon Trail passes a mineshaft and an old miner's cabin, offering great views of Bozeman, the Bridger Mountains, and the surrounding mountains and drainages.

Driving directions: From Main Street at the west end of Bozeman, drive south on 19th Avenue for 5 miles to Nash Road. Turn left and drive 0.4 miles to South Third Road. Turn right and continue one mile to the end of the pavement. Follow the narrow unpaved lane straight ahead for one mile to the trailhead parking lot. At 0.8 miles, road moguls may make driving difficult. If so, park and walk 0.2 miles up the road.

Hiking directions: Head up the slope along the east side of Leverich Creek to a switchback and trail split. Begin the loop to the left on the left switchback, hiking clockwise. (The right fork—the return route—is much steeper.) Continue uphill through the open forest on the east canyon slope at a moderate grade along three more switchbacks. After the fourth switchback, the trail levels out and follows the ridge with minor dips and rises. This section offers great panoramic views—from Leverich Canyon to the Gallatin Valley in the west and from the forested Bozeman Creek drainage to Mount Ellis in the east. After the ridge, gently descend, with views up the length of Bozeman Creek Canyon.

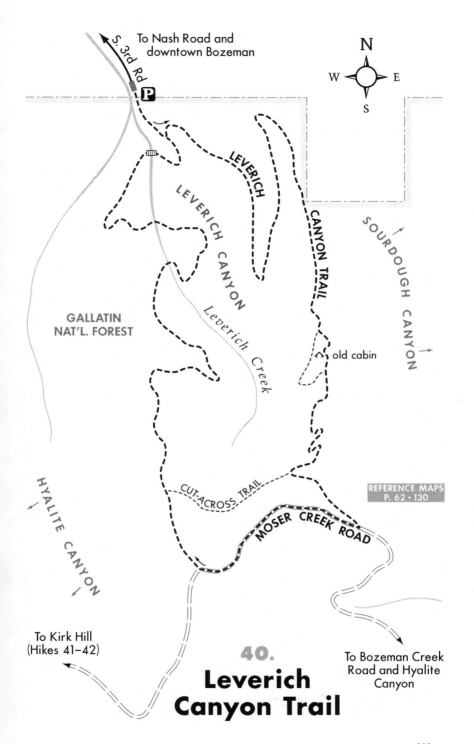

To Nash Road and
downtown Bozeman

S. 3rd Rd

P

N

W · E

S

LEVERICH

LEVERICH CANYON

CANYON TRAIL

SOURDOUGH CANYON

GALLATIN
NAT'L. FOREST

Leverich Creek

old cabin

REFERENCE MAPS
P. 62 · 130

CUT-ACROSS TRAIL

MOSER CREEK ROAD

HYALITE CANYON

To Kirk Hill
(Hikes 41–42)

40.
Leverich
Canyon Trail

To Bozeman Creek
Road and Hyalite
Canyon

Pass a mineshaft and an old log cabin on the right, then wind up the mountain at a steeper grade. Return to and follow the ridge again to a junction and switchback. The right fork, straight ahead, is a cut-across, shortening the hike by 0.6 miles.

For this hike, bear left and head east on the near-level path 0.3 miles to Moser Creek Road, an old logging road. To the left, the road leads east to Bozeman Creek Trail and west to Langohr Campground in Hyalite Canyon. Bear right on the narrow dirt road, with views of the Bridger Mountains. Follow the road 0.4 miles to a 90-degree left bend. The Moser Creek Road connects with Kirk Hill (Hikes 41 and 42). Instead, take the two-track road on the right and continue with the loop. Drop down a narrow, steep shoot, and pass the cut-across trail on the right. Steadily descend, weaving through the forest on the west wall of Leverich Canyon. At the bottom, cross a small bridge over the creek and complete the loop. Return straight ahead to the trailhead. ■

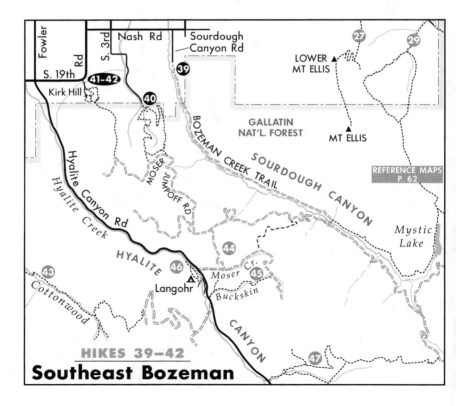

HIKES 39-42
Southeast Bozeman

41. Kirk Hill (LOOPS 1 · 3)

Hiking distance: 1.7 miles round trip
Hiking time: 45 minutes
Elevation gain: 600 feet
Maps: U.S.G.S. Wheeler Mountain
      Kirk Hill Nature Trail Map
      Beartooth Publishing: Bozeman, Big Sky, W. Yellowstone

map
page 122

Summary of hike: Kirk Hill is an open space with a triple loop trail in the northern foothills of the Gallatin Mountains. The open space sits on the south edge of the Gallatin Valley, due south of Bozeman off of South 19th Road. The trail system begins in marshy meadows and climbs through aspen groves and Douglas fir to a ridge covered with juniper and sage. This hike follows a figure-8 pattern around Loops 1 and 3. At the top of Kirk Hill is a panoramic overlook with a map that identifies the peaks and canyons of the Madison Range. Dogs are not allowed on these trails.

Driving directions: From Main Street at the west end of Bozeman, drive south on 19th Avenue for 6 miles to the signed trailhead parking area on the left at a sharp right bend in the road. (En route, 19th Avenue becomes South 19th Road.) Turn left and park.

Hiking directions: Head south past the trailhead gate and cross the grassy meadow. Head up the foothills through the shady forest, crossing the footbridge over the irrigation ditch. Switchbacks lead uphill to a signed junction at 0.5 miles. The left fork leads to Loop 2 (Hike 42). Take the right fork uphill to junction F. Bear left on the cut-across trail, and traverse the hillside on the near-level path to junction D. Head uphill to the right through the pine and fir forest, reaching junction E at the top of the hill. Go to the right, following the hilltop ridge past Rocky Mountain juniper. On the left is a short side path to the panoramic overlook of the Madison Range. Back on the main trail, begin the descent back to the cut-across trail at junction F. Bear right and traverse the hillside again to junction D. This time, bear left and descend through the forest to junction C. Bear left again, completing the figure-8 at junction B. Take the right fork downhill, returning to the trailhead. ▪

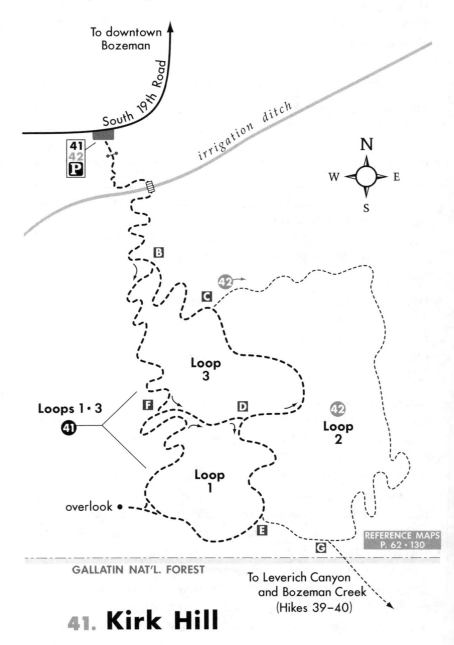

To downtown
Bozeman

South 19th Road

irrigation ditch

41
42
P

N
W ⬥ E
S

B

42→

C

Loop
3

Loops 1 · 3
41

F

D

42
Loop
2

Loop
1

overlook •

E

G

REFERENCE MAPS
P. 62 · 130

GALLATIN NAT'L. FOREST

To Leverich Canyon
and Bozeman Creek
(Hikes 39–40)

41. **Kirk Hill**

42. Kirk Hill (LOOP 2)

Hiking distance: 1.9 miles round trip
Hiking time: 1 hour
Elevation gain: 750 feet

map
page 124

Maps: U.S.G.S. Wheeler Mountain
Kirk Hill Nature Trail Map
Beartooth Publishing: Bozeman, Big Sky, W. Yellowstone

Summary of hike: Kirk Hill borders the Gallatin National Forest above Leverich Canyon and Hodgman Canyon. The open space has three interconnected self-guided loops. Interpretive signs identify the surrounding peaks, canyons, and the native and wild plants. From the ridge, a trail leaves the open space, connecting with Hyalite, Leverich, and Sourdough Canyons. This hike (Loop 2) is the largest and steepest of the three loops. The Kirk Hill trails are managed by the Museum of the Rockies and maintained by Kiwanis of the Bridgers.

Driving directions: From Main Street at the west end of Bozeman, drive south on 19th Avenue for 6 miles to the signed trailhead parking area on the left at a sharp right bend in the road. (En route, 19th Avenue becomes South 19th Road.) Turn left and park.

Hiking directions: Hike past the trailhead gate and cross the meadow, heading south. Head up the foothills through the shady forest. Cross the wooden footbridge over the irrigation ditch, and zigzag up the trail, steadily gaining elevation. At 0.5 miles is a signed junction. Take the left fork, weaving up the trail to junction C. Bear left and begin the loop. Head east across the hillside through the forest of aspen, pine and fir. The path curves south and heads steadily uphill, including some short, steep ascents. At the top, the trail levels out and crosses the hilltop. Stay to the right past junction G, which leads to Leverich Canyon, the Moser Jumpoff Road, and Bozeman Creek. Continue to junction E and Loop 1. Go to the right, returning downhill to the cut-across trail dividing Loops 1 and 3. Again stay to the right, completing the loop at junction C. Go left, back to junction B. Take the right fork downhill, returning to the trailhead. ■

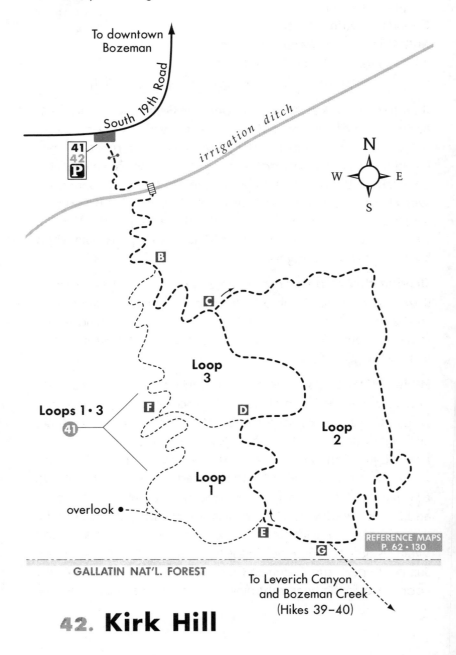

To downtown Bozeman

South 19th Road

irrigation ditch

41
42
P

N
W ◆ E
S

B

C

Loop 3

Loops 1·3
41

F

D

Loop 2

Loop 1

overlook •

E

REFERENCE MAPS
P. 62 · 130

G

GALLATIN NAT'L. FOREST

To Leverich Canyon and Bozeman Creek
(Hikes 39–40)

42. Kirk Hill

43. South Cottonwood Creek Trail

Hiking distance: 4 to 12 miles round trip
Hiking time: 2.5 to 6 hours
Elevation gain: 300 to 900 feet
Maps: U.S.G.S. Wheeler Mountain and Mount Blackmore
      Beartooth Publishing: Bozeman, Big Sky, W. Yellowstone

**map
page 126**

Summary of hike: South Cottonwood Creek flows from the upper reaches of Mount Blackmore to the Gallatin River at Gallatin Gateway. The creek gently tumbles down South Cottonwood Canyon, located on the north face of the Gallatin Range between Hyalite Canyon and Wheeler Mountain. The trail follows the creek on the northeast slope of Wheeler Mountain through a dense old-growth forest with lush riparian areas and meadows. The soft dirt path connects to Hyalite Canyon via the History Rock Trail at 6 miles (Hike 49) and the Mount Blackmore Trail at 8 miles.

Driving directions: From downtown Bozeman, drive 4 miles west on Main Street (Highway 191) toward Four Corners to Cottonwood Road at a stop light. Turn left and continue 7.6 miles to Cottonwood Canyon Road on the left. Turn left and drive 2.1 miles to the trailhead parking area at road's end.

From Big Sky, drive 27.7 miles north on Highway 191 to Cottonwood Road on the right. Turn right and continue 4.8 miles to Cottonwood Canyon Road on the right. Turn right and drive 2.1 miles to the trailhead parking area at road's end.

Hiking directions: Take the posted trail by the west corner of the parking area. Enter the lodgepole pine forest and zigzag up four switchbacks, gaining a quick 150 feet. Traverse the canyon wall along the mountain's contours. Gradually descend and pass through a trail gate to a meadow and South Cottonwood Creek. Veer left and cross a bridge over the creek. Climb the hill to a grassy meadow and follow the east slope upstream. Continue on the cliffside path high above the creek, skirting the Wheeler Mountain. The trail alternates from shaded pockets of conifers to wildflower-covered meadows with scattered rock

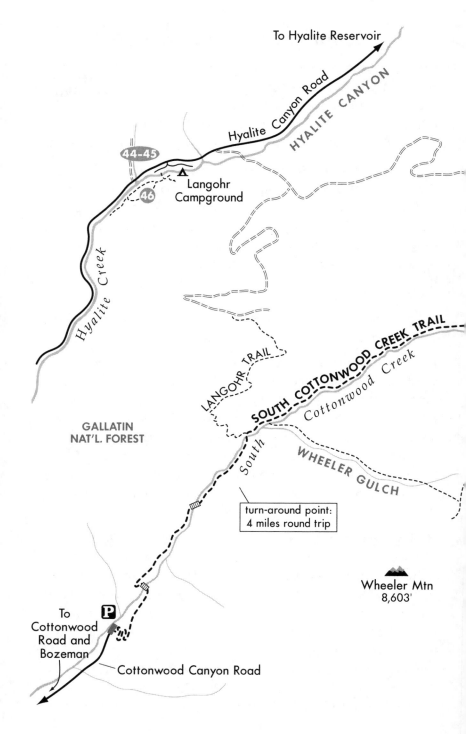

To Hyalite Reservoir

Hyalite Canyon Road

HYALITE CANYON

44-45

46

Langohr
Campground

Hyalite Creek

LANGOHR TRAIL

SOUTH COTTONWOOD CREEK TRAIL

Cottonwood Creek

GALLATIN
NAT'L. FOREST

South

WHEELER GULCH

turn-around point:
4 miles round trip

Wheeler Mtn
8,603'

To
Cottonwood
Road and
Bozeman

P

Cottonwood Canyon Road

outcroppings. Cross a log bridge to the south bank of the creek at 1.3 miles, and cross again at 2 miles. This is the turn-around for a 4-mile, round-trip hike.

To contnue, pass a trail on the left (which is diffi-cult to see) that climbs to the Langohr Campground in Hyalite Canyon. For the next 2 miles, the path rises and falls from high above the creek to the stream-side. The trail continues to a small Forest Service cabin by the History Rock Trail junction at 6 miles (Hike 49). The South Cottonwood Creek Trail continues south another 2 miles to Mount Blackmore. Choose your own turn-around spot. ∎

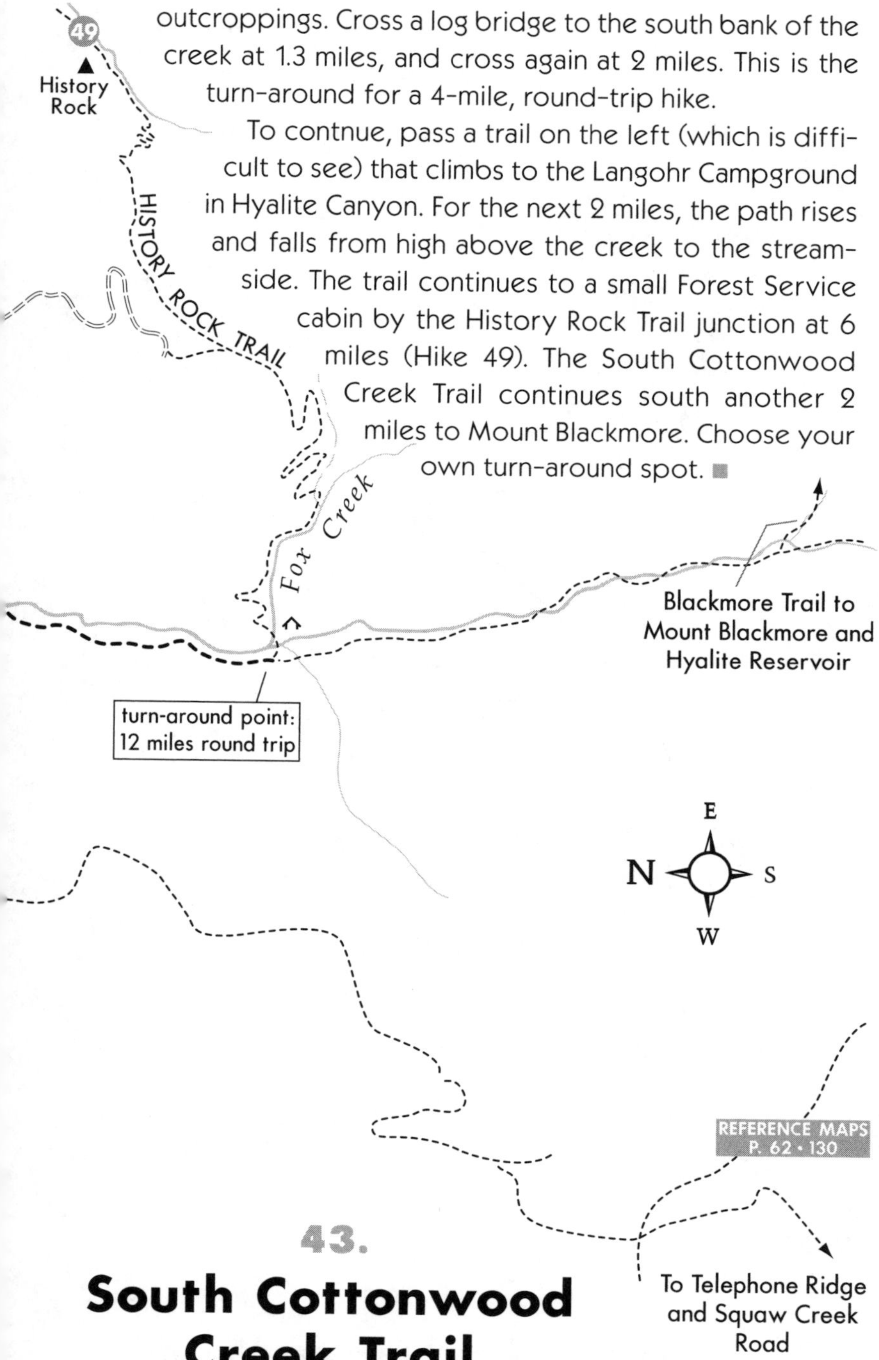

49

▲
History
Rock

HISTORY ROCK TRAIL

Fox Creek

turn-around point:
12 miles round trip

Blackmore Trail to
Mount Blackmore and
Hyalite Reservoir

E
N ◇ S
W

REFERENCE MAPS
P. 62 · 130

43.

South Cottonwood
Creek Trail

To Telephone Ridge
and Squaw Creek
Road

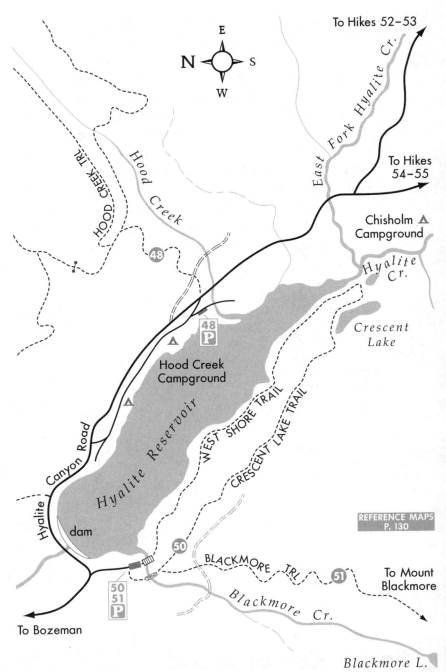

To Hikes 52–53

East Fork Hyalite Cr.

To Hikes 54–55

Chisholm ⛺ Campground

Hyalite Cr.

Crescent Lake

HOOD CREEK TRL

Hood Creek

48

48 P

Hood Creek Campground

Hyalite Reservoir

WEST SHORE TRAIL

CRESCENT LAKE TRAIL

Hyalite Canyon Road

REFERENCE MAPS
P. 130

dam

50

BLACKMORE TRL

51

To Mount Blackmore

50 51 P

Blackmore Cr.

To Bozeman

Blackmore L.

Hyalite Reservoir

Hyalite Reservoir and Canyon

HIKES 44—55

The Hyalite Canyon drainage is a 34,000-acre recreational oasis in the Gallatin Range just south of Bozeman. The centerpiece of the canyon is the Hyalite Reservoir, a 200-acre lake constructed in the late 1940s and enlarged in 1993. It serves as a water source for the city of Bozeman and the Gallatin Valley's agriculture. The picturesque reservoir sits in a broad, glacially sculpted U—shaped valley with canyons and steep-walled cirques. Framing the head of Hyalite Canyon are 10,000-foot mountain peaks. The reservoir is also a popular fishing area with cutthroat trout and arctic grayling.

A network of old logging roads, hiking trails, and multi-use trails lie within Hyalite Canyon. The trail system follows creeks, streams, and mountain slopes, leading to more than a dozen waterfalls, several alpine lakes, meadows covered in wild flowers, open ridges, and up to the surrounding peaks. Large boulders called erratics, deposited after the glacial ice melted, can be seen along the trails.

Hikes 44—46 begin near Langohr Campground, four miles downstream from the reservoir. Hike 46 explores the creekside, while Hikes 44 and 45 climb up the divide between Hyalite Canyon and Bozeman Creek (Hike 39).

Hikes 47—51 are located around Hyalite Reservoir. The hikes range from an easy lakeside stroll to more strenuous hikes that climb through the surrounding canyons to views high above the reservoir.

Two major drainages feed the lake from its headwaters—the main Hyalite Creek and the East Fork Hyalite Creek. Hike 52 is an easy hike on the East Fork to the picturesque Palisade Falls. Hike 53 continues up the beautiful drainage to the headwaters at Mount Chisholm.

The Hyalite Creek Trail—Hikes 54 and 55—is considered the most spectacular trail in the Bozeman area. Grotto Falls (Hike 54) is a short walk from the trailhead. Hike 55 continues 5.5 miles up the drainage, passing eleven waterfalls to Hyalite Lake.

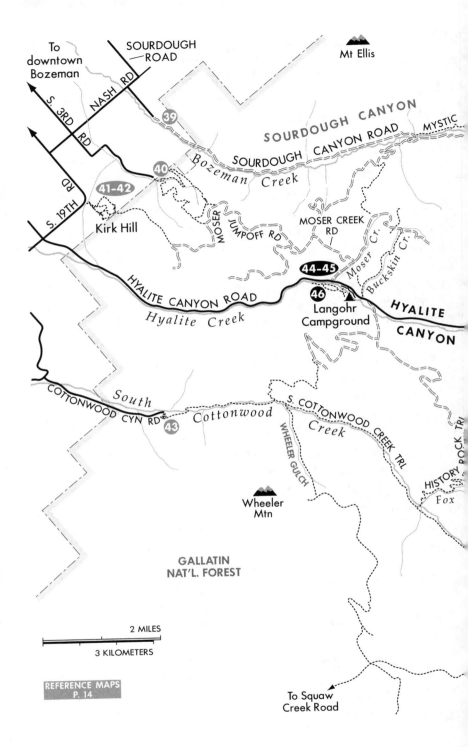

To
downtown
Bozeman

S. 3RD RD

NASH RD

SOURDOUGH
ROAD

Mt Ellis

SOURDOUGH CANYON

SOURDOUGH CANYON ROAD

MYSTIC

39

Bozeman Creek

S. 19TH RD

40

41-42

Kirk Hill

MOSER JUMPOFF RD

MOSER CREEK
RD

Moser Cr.

Buckskin Cr.

44-45

46

HYALITE

Langohr
Campground

HYALITE CANYON ROAD

Hyalite Creek

CANYON

COTTONWOOD CYN RD

South

43

Cottonwood

Creek

S. COTTONWOOD CREEK TRL

WHEELER GULCH

HISTORY ROCK TRL

Fox

Wheeler
Mtn

GALLATIN
NAT'L. FOREST

2 MILES

3 KILOMETERS

To Squaw
Creek Road

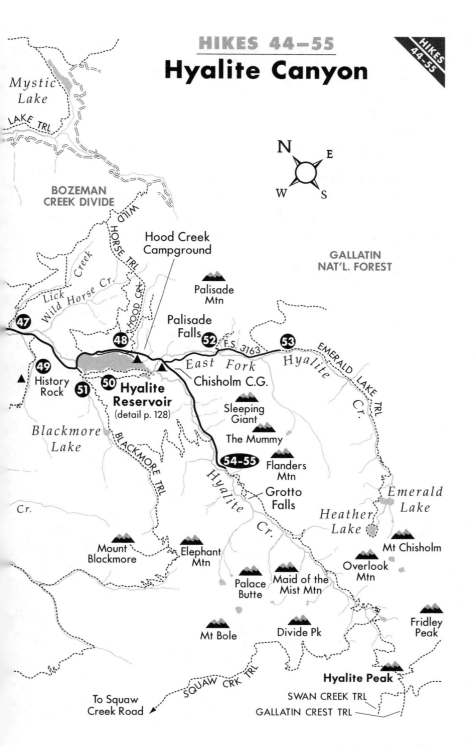

Hyalite Canyon

Mystic Lake

LAKE TRL

N
E
W
S

BOZEMAN
CREEK DIVIDE

WILD HORSE TRL

Hood Creek
Campground

GALLATIN
NAT'L. FOREST

Lick Creek

Wild Horse Cr.

HOOD CRK.

Palisade
Mtn

47

Palisade
Falls

48

52 F.S. 3163 **53**

EMERALD LAKE TRL

Hyalite Cr.

East Fork

49

History
Rock

51 **50** **Hyalite Reservoir**
(detail p. 128)

Chisholm C.G.

Sleeping
Giant

Blackmore
Lake

BLACKMORE TRL

The Mummy

54-55 Flanders
Mtn

Emerald
Lake

Cr.

Hyalite Cr.

Grotto
Falls

Heather
Lake

Mount
Blackmore

Elephant
Mtn

Mt Chisholm

Overlook
Mtn

Palace
Butte

Maid of the
Mist Mtn

Mt Bole

Divide Pk

Fridley
Peak

To Squaw
Creek Road

SQUAW CRK TRL

Hyalite Peak

SWAN CREEK TRL

GALLATIN CREST TRL

44. Moser Creek Loop

Hiking distance: 7.4 miles round trip
Hiking time: 3.5 hours
Elevation gain: 750 feet
Maps: U.S.G.S. Wheeler Mountain and Mount Ellis
　　　Beartooth Publishing: Bozeman, Big Sky, W. Yellowstone

Summary of hike: Moser Creek Road is an old logging road connecting Hyalite Canyon with Sourdough Canyon and Bozeman Creek Trail. This loop hike begins alongside Moser Creek, just north of Langohr Campground, and climbs over the divide between the canyons into the Bozeman Creek

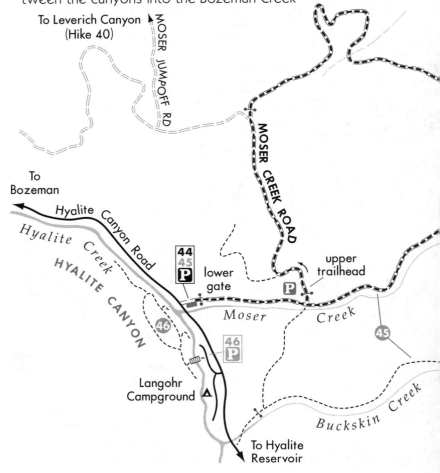

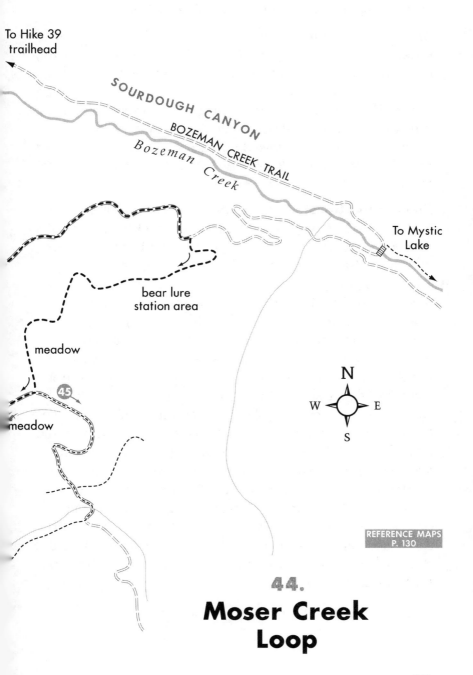

To Hike 39
trailhead

SOURDOUGH CANYON

BOZEMAN CREEK TRAIL

Bozeman Creek

To Mystic
Lake

bear lure
station area

meadow

45

meadow

N
W E
S

REFERENCE MAPS
P. 130

44.
Moser Creek
Loop

drainage. The trail weaves through shady pine forests and grassy meadows covered in flowers. Throughout the hike are great vistas of the surrounding mountains and canyons.

Driving directions: From Main Street and 19th Avenue in Bozeman, drive south on 19th Avenue 7 miles to Hyalite Canyon Road on the left. (19th Avenue becomes South 19th Road at Kagy Boulevard.) Turn left and continue 5.6 miles to the unpaved road on the left, located a quarter mile north of Langohr Campground. Turn left and park in the pullout on the right by the lower gate. When the gate is open, drive 0.5 miles up the dirt road to a road fork. Curve left and park in the wide parking area on the left at the upper trailhead.

Hiking directions: From the lower gate at Hyalite Canyon Road, walk a half mile up unpaved Moser Creek Road to a road fork and the upper trailhead. Begin the loop to the left, hiking clockwise. Gently climb through lodgepole pines, pockets of aspen, and grassy meadows with flowers. Stay to the right at a road split. At 1.4 miles is a gated road on the right. The main road veers left to Leverich Canyon (Hike 40).

Pass through the trail gate on the right, and descend on the grass-covered, two-track road. Pass an overlook of Mount Ellis to the south rim of Sourdough Canyon. Loop around a gulch and cross a feeder stream of Bozeman Creek at 2.8 miles. Follow the canyon contours to a horseshoe left bend at 4.4 miles. One hundred yards beyond the bend is an unmarked footpath on the right. The road descends to Bozeman Creek—Hike 39. Instead, take the unmarked footpath on the right, and head up the forested slope. Skirt the south wall of the forested drainage. Steadily climb to the ridge, with vistas across Hyalite Canyon and the upper peaks. Descend past a trail gate to a large sloping meadow and a junction with a dirt road. Head to the right and take the dirt road downhill 0.9 miles, completing the loop at the upper trailhead junction. ■

45. Moser—Buckskin Loop

Hiking distance: 4.7-mile loop
Hiking time: 2.5 hours
Elevation gain: 800 feet
Maps: U.S.G.S. Wheeler Mountain and Mount Ellis
      Beartooth Publishing: Bozeman, Big Sky, W. Yellowstone

map
page 136

Summary of hike: Moser Creek and Buckskin Creek are tributaries of Hyalite Creek, draining down the east canyon wall. This hike parallels Moser Creek past its headwaters and returns along Buckskin Creek. The Moser–Buckskin Loop utilizes an old logging road and a forested footpath. The trails weave through flower-filled meadows and dense riparian forests.

Driving directions: From Main Street and 19th Avenue in Bozeman, drive south on 19th Avenue 7 miles to Hyalite Canyon Road on the left. (19th Avenue becomes South 19th Road at Kagy Boulevard.) Turn left and continue 5.6 miles to the unpaved road on the left, located a quarter mile north of Langohr Campground. Turn left and park in the pullout on the right by the lower gate. When the gate is open, drive 0.5 miles up the dirt road to a road fork. Curve left and park in the wide parking area on the left at the upper trailhead.

Hiking directions: From the lower gate at Hyalite Canyon Road, walk a half mile up unpaved Moser Creek Road to a road fork and the upper trailhead. The left fork leads to Leverich Canyon. Begin the loop straight ahead on the right fork. Climb up the forested road to a huge sloping meadow at 1.4 miles. Continue on the road through the meadow, curving to the right. Steadily gain elevation and curve left on a horseshoe bend to a 4-way junction at 2.2 miles. Continue straight through and descend into the Buckskin Creek drainage. Climb a short distance to a left bend and an unsigned footpath on the right.

Leave the road and take the path into the dense conifer forest. Follow the south side of the stream-fed canyon on the old narrow roadbed with a view of Wheeler Mountain. Curve right and cross over trickling Buckskin Creek. Head down the north side of the creek, passing tree-rimmed meadows. A few paths on the left lead to the creek. At the lower end of a large meadow is a trail gate and junction. The left fork passes through the gate to Hyalite Canyon Road. Bear right and climb north through the meadow. Top the slope and enter a forest, returning to Moser Creek Road and completing the loop.

Return to the left. ■

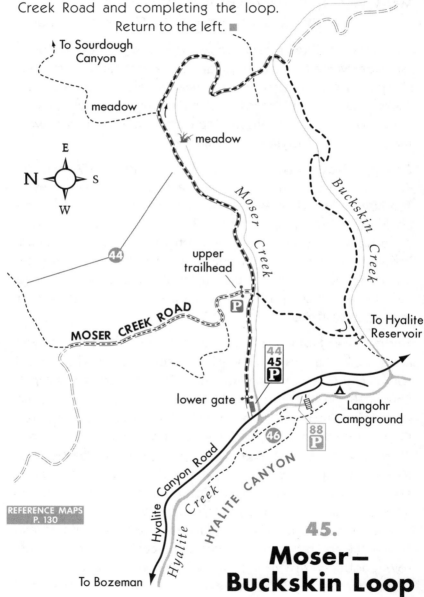

46. Langohr Loop Accessible Trail

Hiking distance: 0.3-mile loop to 2 miles round trip
Hiking time: 30 minutes to 1 hour
Elevation gain: Level
Maps: U.S.G.S. Wheeler Mountain
      U.S.F.S. Hyalite Drainage map
      Crystal Bench Maps: Bozeman, Montana

**map
page 138**

Summary of hike: The Langohr Loop Accessible Trail (also called the Hyalite Creek Interpretive Trail) is an easy, forested stroll along the banks of Hyalite Creek. The wheelchair-accessible trail is at the north end of Langohr Campground, four miles downstream of Hyalite Reservoir. Throughout the scenic hike are wildflower-covered meadows, impressive rock formations, fishing accesses, and benches.

Driving directions: From Main Street and 19th Avenue in Bozeman, drive south on 19th Avenue (which becomes South 19th Road) 7 miles to Hyalite Canyon Road on the left. Turn left and continue 5.9 miles to the signed turnoff for Langohr Campground. Turn right and make an immediate right again to the signed trailhead parking area 0.1 mile ahead.

Hiking directions: Pass the trailhead sign and cross the wooden bridge over Hyalite Creek. A well-defined side path follows Hyalite Creek upstream and ends at a massive rock formation. A fork to the right climbs up the hillside and scrambles along the cliffs above the creek. Head back toward the bridge, and take the paved path to the north, following Hyalite Creek through a conifer forest. A short distance ahead is a trail fork, the beginning of the loop. Take the right fork downstream, staying close to the creek. Along the way, two paved side paths lead to the creek on the right. At the far end of the paved loop, a footpath continues north, following the creek through the forest. On the return portion of the paved loop, the trail continues through the forest past meadows with log benches. Complete the loop and return to the bridge. ∎

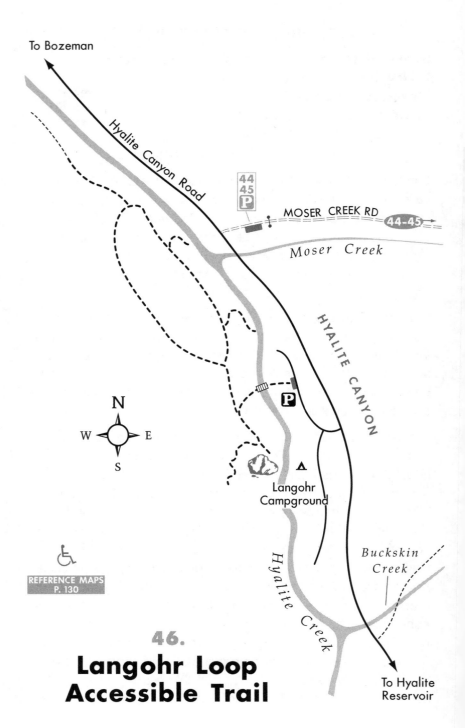

To Bozeman

Hyalite Canyon Road

44
45
P

MOSER CREEK RD 44-45

Moser Creek

HYALITE CANYON

N
W · E
S

P

Langohr
Campground

Buckskin
Creek

Hyalite Creek

REFERENCE MAPS
P. 130

46.
**Langohr Loop
Accessible Trail**

To Hyalite
Reservoir

47. Lick Creek Loop to
BOZEMAN CREEK DIVIDE

Hiking distance: 8-mile loop
Hiking time: 4 hours
Elevation gain: 11,150 feet
Maps: U.S.G.S. Mount Ellis
        Beartooth Publishing: Bozeman, Big Sky, W. Yellowstone

map
page 141

Summary of hike: Lick Creek, a tributary of Hyalite Creek, forms in the far northwest slope of Palisade Mountain just northeast of Hyalite Reservoir. This hike follows Lick Creek Road, an abandoned logging road along the north side of the creek. The road continues past the creek's headwaters and meanders upward through a pristine forest to the Bozeman Creek Divide. Atop the divide are great views of the Hyalite peaks flanking the upper reaches of Hyalite Canyon. The trail connects with the Wild Horse Trail (which drops down to the South Fork of Bozeman Creek—Hike 39) and with the Hood Creek Trail (descending to Hyalite Reservoir—Hike 48).

Driving directions: From Main Street and 19th Avenue in Bozeman, drive south on 19th Avenue (which becomes South 19th Road) 7 miles to Hyalite Canyon Road on the left. Turn left and continue 8.4 miles to the unsigned dirt road on the left. It is located a half mile north of the History Rock Trail and 1.5 miles north of Hyalite Reservoir. Turn left and park in the small space on the left, staying clear of the gate.

For additional parking, large pullouts are on the creekside of Hyalite Canyon Road. They are located 0.2 miles on each side of the Lick Creek Road junction.

Hiking directions: Head up the unpaved road past the vehicle gate. Walk through open rolling meadows and pine forests. Pass through a cattle gate on the south edge of Lick Creek at 0.2 miles. At the top of the hill, just before a left bend in the road, is an old two-track roadbed on the right. Begin the loop, staying on the main road to the left. Steadily gain elevation, crossing several feeder streams. Pass a rocky road veering off to the left and stay straight, climbing the west wall of the gulch. Curve sharply to the left, then to the right, to open vistas across the entire Hyalite drainage. The mountainous panorama includes Palisade Mountain, Sleeping Giant Mountain, Hyalite Peak, Elephant Mountain, and Mount Blackmore. Descend a quarter mile to the bottom of the hill and a faint trail on the right at 2.8 miles—the return loop.

For now, continue straight ahead towards the divide. Near the summit, pass through an old logging area to a posted junction at the head of the Lick Creek drainage and the Bozeman Creek Divide. To the left, the Wild Horse Trail drops 1,300 feet over 1.5 miles to the South Fork of Bozeman Creek. Straight ahead, the Hood Creek Trail descends to Hyalite Reservoir (Hike 48).

Retrace your steps to the return trail junction, now on the left. Take the side path through a grassy clearing and descend to Lick Creek. Cross the creek and merge with an old roadbed, curving to the right. Traverse the south wall of the drainage, completing the loop. ■

48. Hood Creek Trail #436
to WILD HORSE CREEK

Hiking distance: 4.6 miles round trip
Hiking time: 2.5 hours
Elevation gain: 900 feet
Maps: U.S.G.S. Fridley Peak
       Beartooth Publishing: Bozeman, Big Sky, W. Yellowstone

map
page 143

Summary of hike: Hood Creek flows down Palisade Mountain, feeding Hyalite Reservoir at the foot of its western slope. The Hood Creek Trail (also known as the Wild Horse Trail) parallels Hood Creek, but the creek is never actually within sight or sound. The trailhead is located at Hood Creek Campground at Hyalite Reservoir. The trail then heads up the foothills of Palisade Mountain to great overlooks of the Hyalite Creek drainage, the East Fork of Hyalite Creek, Mount Blackmore, and Hyalite Reservoir (front cover photo). The trail continues to the Bozeman

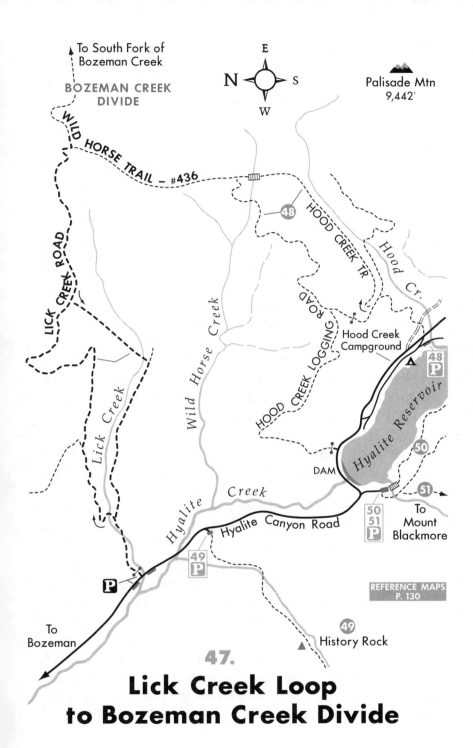

To South Fork of
Bozeman Creek

BOZEMAN CREEK
DIVIDE

E
N — S
W

Palisade Mtn
9,442'

WILD HORSE TRAIL – #436

48

HOOD CREEK TR

Hood Cr.

LICK CREEK ROAD

Wild Horse Creek

HOOD CREEK LOGGING ROAD

Hood Creek
Campground

48
P

Lick Creek

Hyalite Reservoir

50

Hyalite   Creek

DAM

Hyalite

Hyalite Canyon Road

50
51
P

51

To
Mount
Blackmore

REFERENCE MAPS
P. 130

P

49
P

To
Bozeman

47.

49

History Rock

Lick Creek Loop
to Bozeman Creek Divide

Creek drainage and Mystic Lake. This hike makes a return loop on an old logging road between Hood Creek and Wild Horse Creek. It is also part of an 8.5-mile loop with Lick Creek Road (Hike 47).

Driving directions: From Main Street and 19th Avenue in Bozeman, drive south on 19th Avenue (which becomes South 19th Road) 7 miles to Hyalite Canyon Road on the left. Turn left and continue 11 miles, crossing to the east side of Hyalite Reservoir, to the signed Trail 436 on the left. It is located 20 yards south of the Hood Creek boat ramp and picnic area turnoff. Parking is not available at the trailhead, so turn right into the picnic area. Bear left at the first turn, and park in the day-use parking area by campsite 20.

Hiking directions: Hike back up the campground road to the signed trailhead on the east side of the main road. Head uphill to the northeast through the forest, and cross an old jeep road. Wide, sweeping switchbacks weave up the hill to an overlook of Hyalite Reservoir and Mount Blackmore. At one mile the trail reaches an old unpaved road. Follow the road 0.1 mile to the left, and take the footpath to the right at the trail sign—the beginning of the loop.

Head uphill to an overlook of the East Fork and Main Fork of Hyalite Creek. Continue up the exposed northeast wall of the Hood Creek drainage, reaching the shade of the forest as the trail levels out. Cross a small bridge in a meadow over Wild Horse Creek at 2.3 miles, and head 50 yards to a junction. The right fork (straight ahead) leads to the Wild Horse Trail, Bozeman Creek, and Lick Creek (Hike 47). Go left on the old road and cross over Wild Horse Creek again. Slowly descend through meadows and evergreen pockets to a trail on the left with three large rocks and a blue cross-country ski diamond on a tree. The Hood Creek Logging Road to the right—a gated fire road—leads one mile to an alternative access near the dam. Bear left and traverse the hill, passing a trail gate. Complete the loop by the trail sign. Continue straight 0.1 miles and bear right, returning 1 mile downhill to the campground trailhead. ■

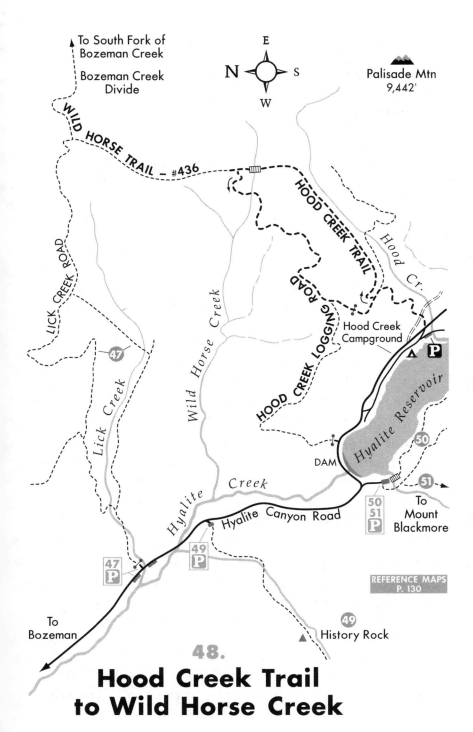

To South Fork of
Bozeman Creek

Bozeman Creek
Divide

N · E · S · W

Palisade Mtn
9,442'

WILD HORSE TRAIL – #436

HOOD CREEK TRAIL

Hood Cr.

LICK CREEK ROAD

HOOD CREEK LOGGING ROAD

Hood Creek
Campground

47

Wild Horse Creek

Lick Creek

Hyalite Reservoir

50

DAM

51

To
Mount
Blackmore

Hyalite Creek

Hyalite Canyon Road

50
51
P

49
P

47
P

To
Bozeman

49
History Rock

REFERENCE MAPS
P. 130

48.
Hood Creek Trail
to Wild Horse Creek

49. History Rock Trail

Hiking distance: 2.4 miles round trip
Hiking time: 1 hour
Elevation gain: 300 feet
Maps: U.S.G.S. Fridley Peak
U.S.F.S. Hyalite Drainage Map
Beartooth Publishing: Bozeman, Big Sky, W. Yellowstone
Crystal Bench Maps: Bozeman, Montana

Summary of hike: History Rock is a sandstone rock outcropping with natural and cultural history. Signatures and inscriptions by early settlers and hunters, dating back to the mid-1800s, are carved into the distinct outcropping. Current inscriptions are also present. The History Rock Trail begins a mile downstream of Hyalite Reservoir and gradually climbs through meadows and lodgepole pines, paralleling History Rock Creek to the natural rock monument. Beyond History Rock, the trail climbs to the divide and descends for several miles, linking the Hyalite drainage with South Cottonwood Creek. This trail can be hiked as a one-way, 11-mile shuttle, leaving a shuttle car at the South Cottonwood Creek Trailhead (Hike 43).

Driving directions: From Main Street and 19th Avenue in Bozeman, drive south on 19th Avenue (which becomes South 19th Road) 7 miles to Hyalite Canyon Road on the left. Turn left and continue 8.8 miles to the History Rock turnoff on the right, one mile before Hyalite Reservoir. Turn right and park 100 feet ahead in the trailhead parking area.

Hiking directions: From the parking area, follow the log-bordered trail southwest through the meadow. Beyond the meadow, enter a forest and begin ascending the mountain slope. At 1.2 miles, the distinct History Rock appears on the right. After studying the formation and etchings, return along the same path for a 2.4-mile round trip hike.

To extend the hike, climb two miles (gaining 1,000 feet) to the divide above South Cottonwood Creek. Descend two more

miles to South Cottonwood Creek Trail—Hike 43. For the sh
hike, reference the map for Hike 43. ■

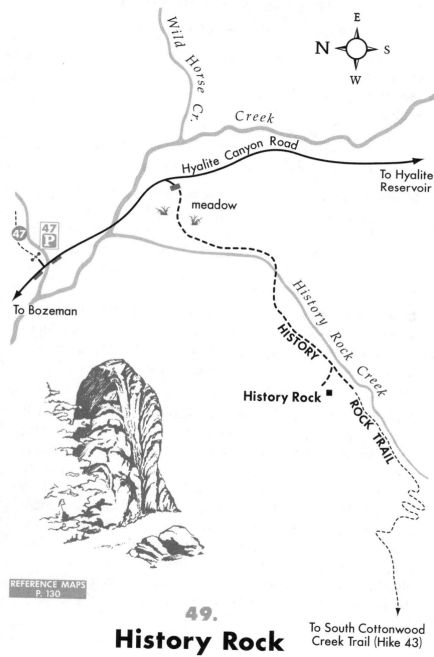

49.
History Rock

To South Cottonwood
Creek Trail (Hike 43)

50. Crescent Lake—
Hyalite Reservoir Loop

Hiking distance: 2.5-mile loop
Hiking time: 1.5 hours
Elevation gain: 240 feet
Maps: U.S.G.S. Fridley Peak
U.S.F.S. Hyalite Drainage Map
Beartooth Publishing: Bozeman, Big Sky, W. Yellowstone
Crystal Bench Maps: Bozeman, Montana

Summary of hike: Crescent Lake is a small, crescent-shaped tarn surrounded by picturesque mountains on the southwest corner of Hyalite Reservoir. The Crescent Lake Trail meanders through the forest on an easy grade to the lake. The return route on the West Shore Trail loops back along the entire western shoreline of Hyalite Reservoir.

Driving directions: From Main Street and 19th Avenue in Bozeman, drive south on 19th Avenue (which becomes South 19th Road) 7 miles to Hyalite Canyon Road on the left. Turn left and continue 9.9 miles to the trailhead parking area on the right. Hyalite Reservoir is to the left.

Hiking directions: The hike begins on the Blackmore Trail at the north end of the parking area. Take the trail to a log crossing over Blackmore Creek, a tributary of Hyalite Reservoir. Across the creek is a signed junction. The right fork continues on to Blackmore Lake—Hike 51. Take the left fork on the Crescent Lake Trail. Continue one mile through the forest to the north shore of Crescent Lake. The trail follows the northeast shore of the lake before heading to a pond at the southern tip of the reservoir. Head to the left on the West Shore Trail. The trail returns along the reservoir's west shore. Near the trailhead, cross over Blackmore Creek on a wooden bridge, completing the loop. ■

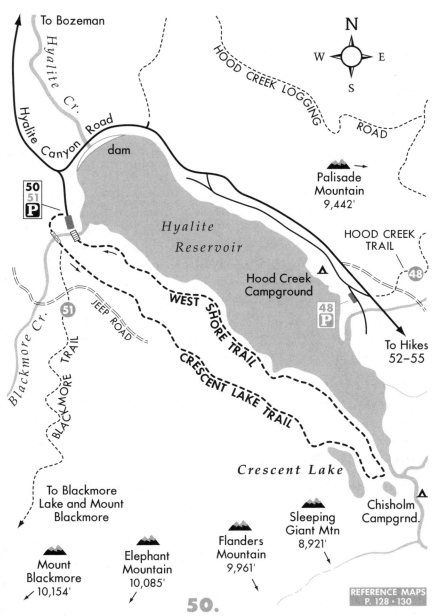

To Bozeman

Hyalite Cr.

Hyalite Cr.

Hyalite Canyon Road

HOOD CREEK LOGGING ROAD

N
W   E
S

dam

50
51
P

Hyalite Reservoir

Palisade
Mountain
9,442'

HOOD CREEK
TRAIL

48

Hood Creek
Campground

WEST SHORE TRAIL

48
P

To Hikes
52–55

51

JEEP ROAD

Blackmore Cr.

BLACKMORE TRAIL

CRESCENT LAKE TRAIL

Crescent Lake

Chisholm
Campgrnd.

To Blackmore
Lake and Mount
Blackmore

Sleeping
Giant Mtn
8,921'

Flanders
Mountain
9,961'

Mount
Blackmore
10,154'

Elephant
Mountain
10,085'

REFERENCE MAPS
P. 128 • 130

50.
Crescent Lake–
Hyalite Reservoir Loop
CRESCENT LAKE–WEST SHORE TRAILS

51. Blackmore Trail to Blackmore Lake

Hiking distance: 3.3 miles round trip
Hiking time: 2 hours
Elevation gain: 500 feet
Maps: U.S.G.S. Fridley Peak
U.S.F.S. Hyalite Drainage Map
Beartooth Publishing: Bozeman, Big Sky, W. Yellowstone
Crystal Bench Maps: Bozeman, Montana

Summary of hike: Blackmore Lake sits 600 feet above the west shore of Hyalite Reservoir at an elevation of 7,300 feet. A dense pine forest and meadow surround the lake beneath Mount Blackmore and Elephant Mountain. The 5-mile Blackmore Trail begins at the west shore of Hyalite Reservoir and leads to Blackmore Lake en route to the top of Mount Blackmore, high above on the divide between the South Cottonwood Creek and Hyalite Creek drainages. This trail can also be hiked as a one-way, 13-mile shuttle with the South Cottonwood Creek Trail, leaving a shuttle car at the South Cottonwood Creek trailhead (Hike 43).

Driving directions: From Main Street and 19th Avenue in Bozeman, drive south on 19th Avenue (which becomes South 19th Road) 7 miles to Hyalite Canyon Road on the left. Turn left and continue 9.9 miles to the trailhead parking area on the right. Hyalite Reservoir is to the left.

Hiking directions: From the north end of the parking area, take the signed Blackmore Trail to a log crossing over Blackmore Creek and a trail junction. The left fork leads to Crescent Lake—Hike 50. Stay on the Blackmore Trail to the right. At 0.4 miles, cross an old jeep road and zigzag uphill through the forest. As you near the lake, which is not yet within view, there is a short but steep descent that leads to the southeast corner of Blackmore Lake. The main trail continues along the east side of the lake into a meadow where Blackmore Creek flows placidly. This is the turn-around spot. Return along the same trail.

To hike farther, the Blackmore Trail continues another 3.5 miles and gains 2,800 feet to Mount Blackmore, then descends to South Cottonwood Creek. ■

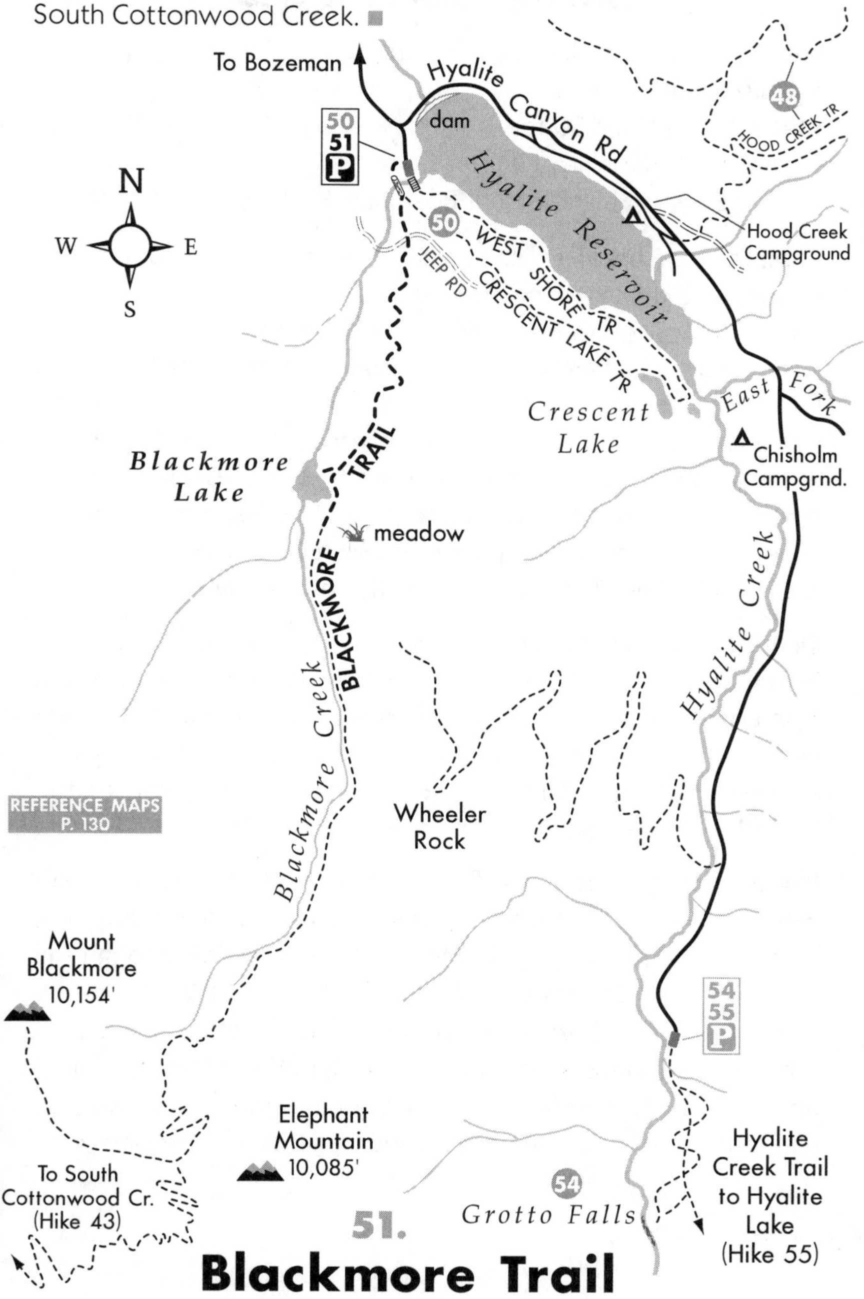

To Bozeman

Hyalite Canyon Rd

dam

48

HOOD CREEK TR

50
51
P

N
W   E
S

50

WEST SHORE TR

JEEP RD

CRESCENT LAKE TR

Hyalite Reservoir

Hood Creek Campground

BLACKMORE TRAIL

Crescent Lake

East Fork

Blackmore Lake

Chisholm Campgrnd.

meadow

Blackmore Creek

Hyalite Creek

REFERENCE MAPS
P. 130

Wheeler Rock

Mount Blackmore
10,154'

54
55
P

Elephant Mountain
10,085'

To South Cottonwood Cr.
(Hike 43)

54

Grotto Falls

Hyalite Creek Trail to Hyalite Lake
(Hike 55)

51.
Blackmore Trail

52. Palisade Falls
EAST FORK of HYALITE CREEK

Hiking distance: 1.2 miles round trip
Hiking time: 30 minutes
Elevation gain: 250 feet
Maps: U.S.G.S. Fridley Peak
　　　　Beartooth Publishing: Bozeman, Big Sky, W. Yellowstone

Summary of hike: Palisade Falls is a towering cataract that drops more than 80 feet off a vertical rock wall at the southern base of Palisade Mountain. The water pours from a notch in the scalloped columnar basalt, the result of an ancient lava flow. From the tree-lined ridge, the waterfall fans out in a mosaic of white cascades tumbling down the rocks. The forested trail is a paved, wheelchair-accessible path that sits 700 feet above the Hyalite Reservoir. The hike begins at the East Fork of Hyalite Creek, then follows the tributary creek for 0.6 miles to a bridge fronting the falls. There are picnic sites at the trailhead.

Driving directions: From Main Street and 19th Avenue in Bozeman, drive south on 19th Avenue (which becomes South 19th Road) 7 miles to Hyalite Canyon Road on the left. Turn left and continue 11.7 miles, crossing to the east side of Hyalite Reservoir, to a road fork. Take the left fork one mile to the Palisade Falls parking and picnic area on the left.

Hiking directions: Take the paved path past the posted trailhead, and weave through the forest on a gentle uphill grade. The jagged ridgeline of Palisade Mountain can be seen through the pine and fir trees. Pass a talus slope on the left at the first view of the falls. Cross a wooden bridge over the creek to the end of the trail at the base of Palisade Falls. Side paths to the right climb up the slippery hillside on loose gravel to additional views. Use caution and good judgement if venturing beyond the bridge. ■

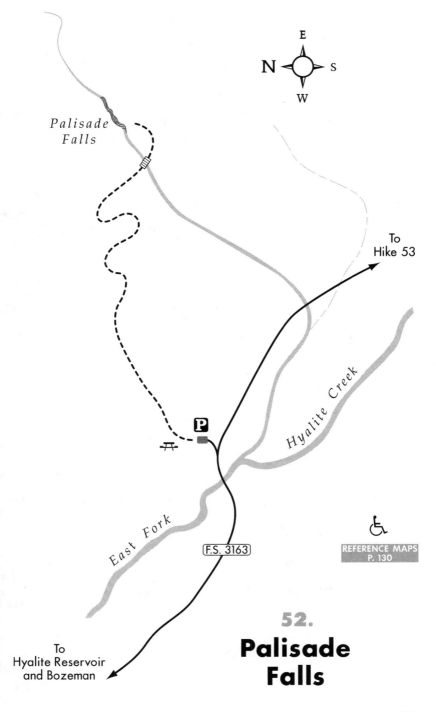

Palisade Falls

N E S W

To Hike 53

Hyalite Creek

P

East Fork

F.S. 3163

REFERENCE MAPS
P. 130

To
Hyalite Reservoir
and Bozeman

52.
Palisade Falls

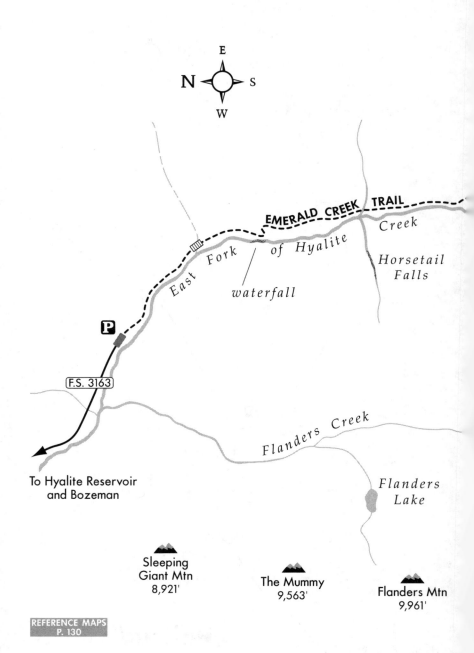

N E S W

EMERALD CREEK TRAIL

East Fork of Hyalite Creek

waterfall

Horsetail Falls

P

F.S. 3163

To Hyalite Reservoir and Bozeman

Flanders Creek

Flanders Lake

Sleeping Giant Mtn 8,921'

The Mummy 9,563'

Flanders Mtn 9,961'

REFERENCE MAPS P. 130

53. Emerald Lake Trail
EAST FORK of HYALITE CREEK

Hiking distance: 10 miles round trip
Hiking time: 5 hours
Elevation gain: 2,000 feet
Maps: U.S.G.S. Fridley Peak
U.S.F.S. Hyalite Drainage map
Beartooth Publishing: Bozeman, Big Sky, W. Yellowstone

Summary of hike: The Emerald Lake Trail (also called East Fork Hyalite Creek Trail) leads 5 miles up the creek to the head of the canyon, where Emerald Lake and Heather Lake sit in a mountainous alpine meadow. The towering rock walls of Mount Chisholm and Overlook Mountain

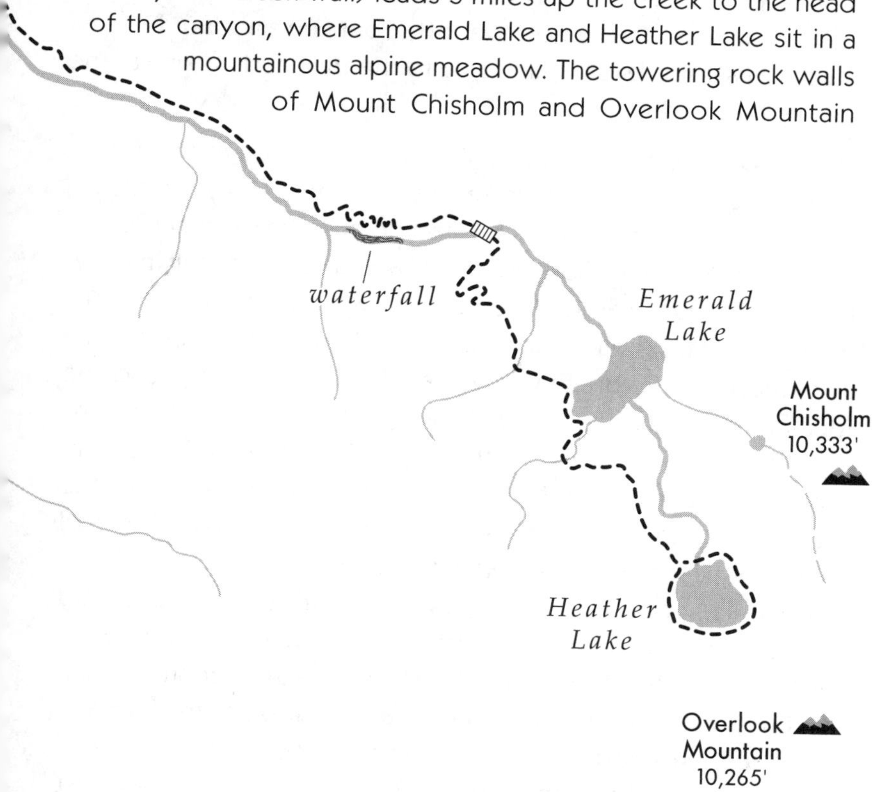

waterfall

Emerald Lake

Mount Chisholm
10,333'

Heather Lake

Overlook Mountain
10,265'

53.
Emerald Lake Trail
EAST FORK HYALITE CREEK

drop sharply to the shore, forming a dramatic cirque around the lakes. The trail passes Horsetail Falls, a long, narrow waterfall tumbling off the west canyon wall, and another 60-foot waterfall farther up the creek drainage. The trail follows the cascading creek through meadows and mixed forests of lodgepole pine, Engelmann spruce, subalpine fir, and whitebark pine.

Driving directions: From Main Street and 19th Avenue in Bozeman, drive south on 19th Avenue (which becomes South 19th Road) 7 miles to Hyalite Canyon Road on the left. Turn left and continue 11.7 miles, crossing to the east side of Hyalite Reservoir, to a road fork. Take the left fork one mile to the Palisade Falls parking and picnic area on the left. Continue another 1.1 miles past the Palisade Falls parking area to the trailhead parking at the end of the road.

Hiking directions: The trail heads south through the forest above the East Fork of Hyalite Creek, continuously paralleling the creek to its headwaters. Head up the drainage and cross a log bridge at 0.5 miles. Horsetail Falls, a series of tall, narrow braids of water, can be seen on the west canyon wall at 1.5 miles. At 3 miles, the trail reaches the banks of the creek in a small meadow. Across the canyon are Flanders Mountain and The Mummy. Ascend the hill, zigzagging up 10 switchbacks and gaining 400 feet in a half mile. At the edge of the cliff by the second switchback is the beautiful 60-foot waterfall. At the top of the switchbacks are great views back down the canyon. The trail levels out near the base of Mount Chisholm.

Cross a log bridge over the East Fork Hyalite Creek, and head through the high open meadow with stands of conifers. Four switchbacks lead to an array of wildflowers in a second meadow. Cross a culvert over a stream to an overlook of the lake and a trail split. The left fork follows the northeast shoreline and circles the lake. The right fork—the main trail—continues past the north end of Emerald Lake, reaching Heather Lake a half mile farther. The trail circles Heather Lake in a cirque at the base of 10,000-foot peaks. Return along the same route. ■

54. Grotto Falls
HYALITE CREEK

Hiking distance: 2.5 miles round trip
Hiking time: 1.25 hours
Elevation gain: 250 feet
Maps: U.S.G.S. Fridley Peak
U.S.F.S. Hyalite Drainage map
Beartooth Publishing: Bozeman, Big Sky, W. Yellowstone

map
page 156

Summary of hike: Grotto Falls is a wide and magnificent waterfall on Hyalite Creek. The cataract is in the forested canyon above Hyalite Reservoir beneath towering Flanders Mountain and Elephant Mountain. The shady 1.25-mile trail has a gradual grade and is wheelchair accessible. Along the gravel path are log benches that are placed at scenic vista points overlooking Hyalite Creek. This hike is the first section of the Hyalite Creek Trail (Hike 55), which passes ten additional waterfalls en route to Hyalite Lake.

Driving directions: From Main Street and 19th Avenue in Bozeman, drive south on 19th Avenue (which becomes South 19th Road) 7 miles to Hyalite Canyon Road on the left. Turn left and continue 11.7 miles, crossing to the east side of Hyalite Reservoir, to a road fork. Take the right fork 1.9 miles to the Hyalite Creek/Grotto Falls parking area at the end of the road.

Hiking directions: Hike south past the trailhead sign along the wide trail. A short distance ahead is a junction with the Hyalite Creek Trail. These two trails crisscross each other four times en route to the falls. Each junction is well marked. The Grotto Falls Trail is the wider trail which leads to the waterfall, where a log bench overlooks the beautiful falls.

To extend the hike, continue with Hike 55. The scenic path leads another 4 miles (gaining 1,800 feet) to Hyalite Lake and the Hyalite Basin. En route, the trail passes ten stair-stepping waterfalls. ■

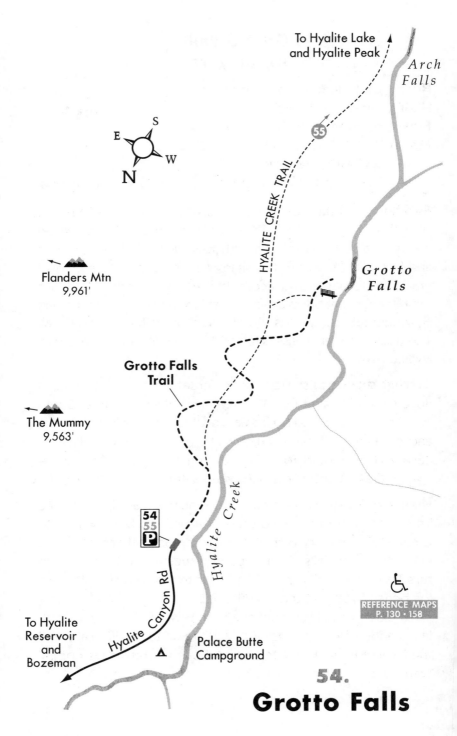

To Hyalite Lake
and Hyalite Peak

Arch
Falls

HYALITE CREEK TRAIL

55

Grotto
Falls

Flanders Mtn
9,961'

**Grotto Falls
Trail**

The Mummy
9,563'

Hyalite Creek

54
55
P

Hyalite Canyon Rd

To Hyalite
Reservoir
and
Bozeman

Palace Butte
Campground

REFERENCE MAPS
P. 130 • 158

54.
Grotto Falls

55. Hyalite Creek Trail to Hyalite Lake

Hiking distance: 11 miles round trip
Hiking time: 5 hours
Elevation gain: 1,900 feet

map
page 158

Maps: U.S.G.S. Fridley Peak, U.S.F.S. Hyalite Drainage map
    Beartooth Publishing: Bozeman, Big Sky, W. Yellowstone

Summary of hike: The Hyalite Creek Trail is considered the most spectacular hike in the Bozeman area. The trail passes eleven waterfalls in a deep canyon with massive cliff walls and majestic peaks. The hike leads to Hyalite Lake, an alpine glacial tarn in a horseshoe-shaped basin. The lake is surrounded by the craggy pinnacles of Fridley Peak and Hyalite Peak. Beyond the lake, the trail continues 2 miles (and gains 1,400 feet in elevation) to Hyalite Peak and the Gallatin Crest Trail.

Driving directions: From Main Street and 19th Avenue in Bozeman, drive south on 19th Avenue (which becomes South 19th Road) 7 miles to Hyalite Canyon Road on the left. Turn left and continue 11.7 miles, crossing to the east side of Hyalite Reservoir, to a road fork. Take the right fork 1.9 miles to the Hyalite Creek/Grotto Falls parking area at the end of the road.

Hiking directions: The Hyalite Creek Trail heads south on a wide path through the forest, paralleling the creek to its head-waters. The Grotto Falls Trail (Hike 54) begins on the same path but zigzags through the forest, crossing the Hyalite Creek Trail four times.

At the last junction, the left fork bypasses Grotto Falls and heads up the canyon. Twin Falls is on the west canyon wall to the south of Elephant Mountain, two adjacent waterfalls plunging off the sheer cliffs. At 1.4 miles, a signed side path leads to Arch Falls on the right, a falls with a natural rock arch. At 2.2 miles, a signed detour to the left leads to Silken Skein Falls. A short distance ahead on the right is an unnamed 20-foot waterfall in a rock bowl with a pool. At 3 miles, a short detour leads to Champagne Falls, an 80-foot waterfall in a narrow, fern-lined rock grotto. At 3.7 miles are three successive waterfalls—Chasm, Shower, and

Apex Falls. Cross a log footbridge over Hyalite Creek below the base of Apex Falls. Rock hop over Shower Creek, then loop back and recross the creek at a stunning cascade. Cross back to the east side of Hyalite Creek and pass S'il Vous Plait Falls. Recross the creek at the base of Alpine Falls, and traverse the cliff overlooking the entire U-shaped, glacier-carved canyon. A short distance ahead is a signed junction at 5.3 miles. Bear left to a second junction. The right fork leads to Hyalite Peak, 2 miles ahead. The left fork leads 100 yards to an overlook of Hyalite Lake at the base of Fridley Peak and Hyalite Peak. Descend to the shoreline in the dramatic mountain bowl. Return on the same trail. ■

The Mummy
9,563'

Mount Flanders
9,961'

Silken Skein
Falls

falls

54

GROTTO FALLS
TRAIL

54
55
P

HYALITE CREEK TRAIL

Hyalite

To
Hyalite Reservoir
and Bozeman

Grotto
Falls

Arch
Falls

falls

Maid of the Mist Cr.

Twin
Falls

Palace Butte
9,202'

55.

Hyalite Creek Trail to Hyalite Lake

Palace
Lake

Arden
Lake

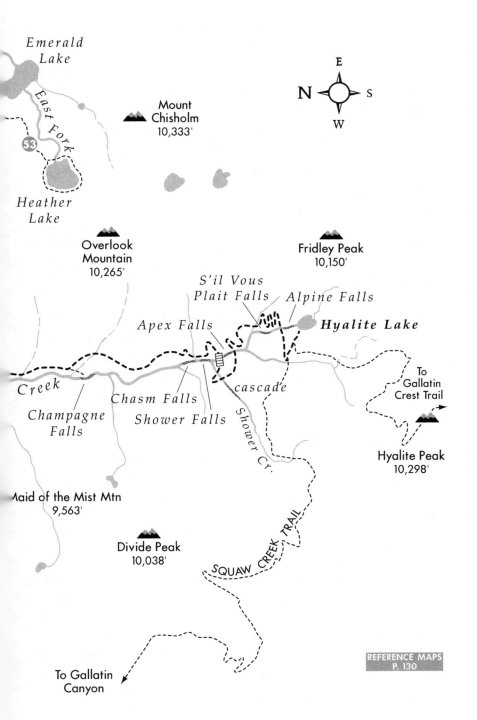

Emerald
Lake

East Fork

53

Heather
Lake

Mount
Chisholm
10,333'

N E S W

Overlook
Mountain
10,265'

Fridley Peak
10,150'

S'il Vous
Plait Falls

Alpine Falls

Apex Falls

Hyalite Lake

Creek

Chasm Falls

cascade

To
Gallatin
Crest Trail

Champagne
Falls

Shower Falls

Shower Cr.

Hyalite Peak
10,298'

Maid of the Mist Mtn
9,563'

Divide Peak
10,038'

SQUAW CREEK TRAIL

REFERENCE MAPS
P. 130

To Gallatin
Canyon

56. Bear Trap Canyon Trail

Hiking distance: 0.5 to 14 miles round trip
Hiking time: 30 minutes to all day
Elevation gain: 50 feet to 500 feet
Maps: U.S.G.S. Bear Trap Creek, Norris, Ennis Lake
U.S.F.S. Gallatin National Forest: West Half
BLM Bear Trap Canyon Wilderness Guide

Summary of hike: Bear Trap Canyon is a spectacular drainage encompassing 6,000 acres in the Lee Metcalf Wilderness within the Madison Range. The Madison River, its headwaters in Yellowstone National Park, rages through the remote, roadless canyon for 9 miles, from Ennis Lake to the Madison River Bridge. The canyon is a well known and popular fishing area between Bozeman and Norris. The trail hugs the east shore of the river, winding along sheer rock cliffs carved 2,000 feet deep by the river. The only hiking access is from the north, so solitude increases deeper into the canyon. The full length of the trail is seven miles. At the southern end is the powerhouse and dam holding back Ennis Lake. Hiking is prohibited around the dam.

Bear Trap Canyon has rattlesnakes. As a precaution, a snakebite kit is recommended.

Driving directions: From Bozeman, drive 9 miles west to Four Corners on Highway 191. Continue 20.7 miles west on Highway 84 to Bear Trap Road on the left. It is located by the Bear Trap Recreational Area sign, just before the bridge crossing the Madison River. Turn left and drive on the gravel road 3.2 miles along the east side of the river. The trailhead parking area is at the end of the road.

Hiking directions: From the parking area, hike south along the east bank of the Madison River. The wide trail soon becomes a footpath and follows the eastern edge of the cliffs. The coarse canyon continually becomes steeper and deeper below the 2,000-foot cliffs. The trail reaches the mouth of Bear Trap Creek at 3.5 miles. It is a level area with campsites and a good spot to take a break. The Madison Powerhouse is at 9 miles. Hike as deep into the rocky canyon as you choose, returning on the same path. ■

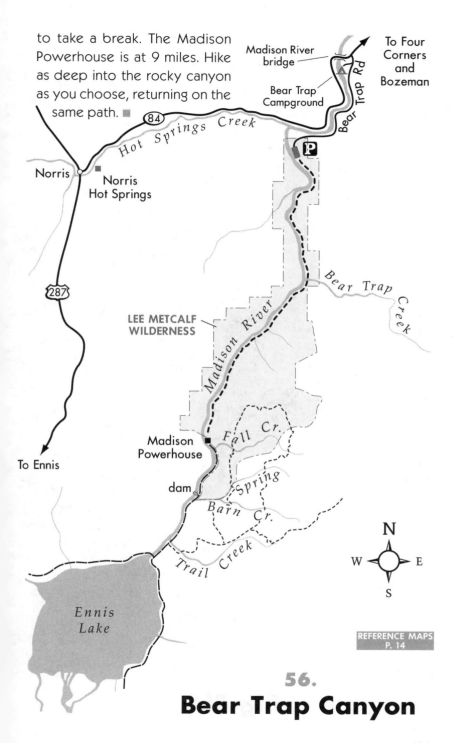

Madison River bridge

To Four Corners and Bozeman

Bear Trap Campground

Bear Trap Rd

84

Hot Springs Creek

Norris

Norris Hot Springs

287

LEE METCALF WILDERNESS

Madison River

Bear Trap Creek

To Ennis

Madison Powerhouse

dam

Fall Cr.

Spring

Barn Cr.

Trail Creek

N
W — E
S

Ennis Lake

REFERENCE MAPS
P. 14

56.
Bear Trap Canyon

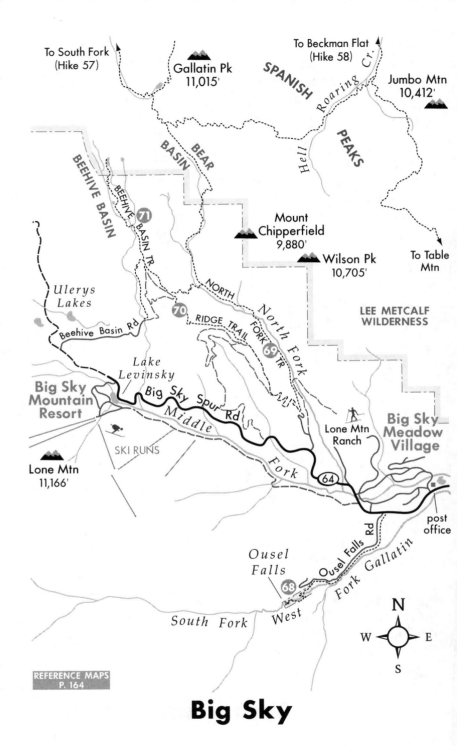

To South Fork
(Hike 57)

Gallatin Pk
11,015'

To Beckman Flat
(Hike 58)

SPANISH

Roaring Cr.

Jumbo Mtn
10,412'

BEEHIVE BASIN

BASIN

BEAR

PEAKS

Hell

71

Mount
Chipperfield
9,880'

Wilson Pk
10,705'

To Table
Mtn

*Ulerys
Lakes*

NORTH

70

RIDGE TRAIL

North Fork

LEE METCALF
WILDERNESS

Beehive Basin Rd

FORK TR

69

*Lake
Levinsky*

Big Sky Spur Rd

**Big Sky
Mountain
Resort**

Middle

Lone Mtn
Ranch

**Big Sky
Meadow
Village**

SKI RUNS

Fork

64

Lone Mtn
11,166'

post
office

*Ousel
Falls*

Ousel Falls Rd

West Fork Gallatin

68

South Fork

West

N

W   E

S

REFERENCE MAPS
P. 164

Big Sky

Gallatin Canyon

HIKES 57—75

The Gallatin Canyon is a narrow cleft that lies between the Gallatin Range and the Madison Range 14 miles southwest of Bozeman. The tumbling whitewater of the Gallatin River cascades through the serpentine gorge, splitting the mountain ranges. The river ultimately flows into the south end of the Gallatin Valley. US Highway 191 snakes alongside the Gallatin River, connecting Bozeman with Big Sky and West Yellowstone.

The Gallatin Range to the east of the canyon divides Gallatin Canyon from Paradise Valley. The 10,000-foot mountain range stretches from Bozeman to Yellowstone National Park. The diverse area has wide valleys, open meadows, numerous creeks, and the 26,000-acre Gallatin Petrified Forest, an ancient rock forest with preserved tropical trees.

The dramatic Madison Range to the west divides the Gallatin Canyon from Madison Valley. The range includes the 256,000-acre Lee Metcalf Wilderness and the landmark Spanish Peaks, a cluster of jagged, snow-capped peaks visible from Bozeman. The 60-mile Madison Range has 10,000- and 11,000-foot peaks. It is the second highest range in Montana (following the 12,000-foot Beartooth Mountains). The Madison Range is home to U-shaped glacial valleys, subalpine meadows, serrated ridges, thick forests, nearly 200 lakes, and a mosaic of trails that connect canyon drainages on both sides of the range.

The Spanish Peaks are accessed on the north from Hikes 57 and 58. Hikes 59—67 and 72—75 explore the east side of the Gallatin Valley from the Gallatin. Hike 60 is a level trail that hugs the cliffs parallel to the Gallatin River, while Hike 74 heads up to the vast pass straddling the Gallatin Divide. The Lava Lake Trail (Hike 61) is one of the most popular trails in the area. Hikes 68—71 are located in the area around Big Sky. Ousel Falls (Hike 68) is a beautiful waterfall just south of Big Sky.

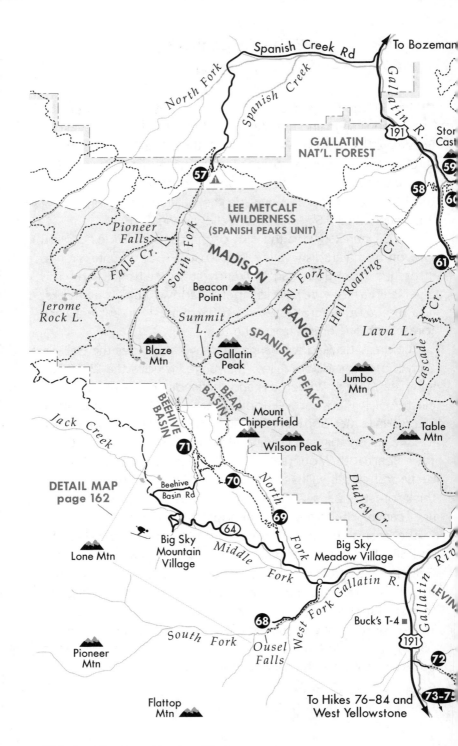

To Bozeman

Spanish Creek Rd

Spanish Creek

North Fork

Gallatin R.

191

Stor
Cast

GALLATIN
NAT'L. FOREST

59

60

57

58

LEE METCALF
WILDERNESS
(SPANISH PEAKS UNIT)

61

Pioneer
Falls

Falls Cr.

South Fork

MADISON

N. Fork

Hell Roaring Cr.

Lava L.

Beacon
Point

Jerome
Rock L.

Summit
L.

RANGE

SPANISH

Cascade Cr.

Blaze
Mtn

Gallatin
Peak

Jumbo
Mtn

PEAKS

Jack Creek

BEEHIVE
BASIN

BEAR
BASIN

Mount
Chipperfield

Table
Mtn

71

Wilson Peak

DETAIL MAP
page 162

Beehive
Basin Rd

70

North Fork

Dudley Cr.

69

Lone Mtn

Big Sky
Mountain
Village

64

Middle Fork

Big Sky
Meadow Village

Gallatin River

LEVIN

Pioneer
Mtn

South Fork

68

Ousel
Falls

West Fork Gallatin R.

Buck's T-4 ■

191

72

Flattop
Mtn

To Hikes 76–84 and
West Yellowstone

73–7

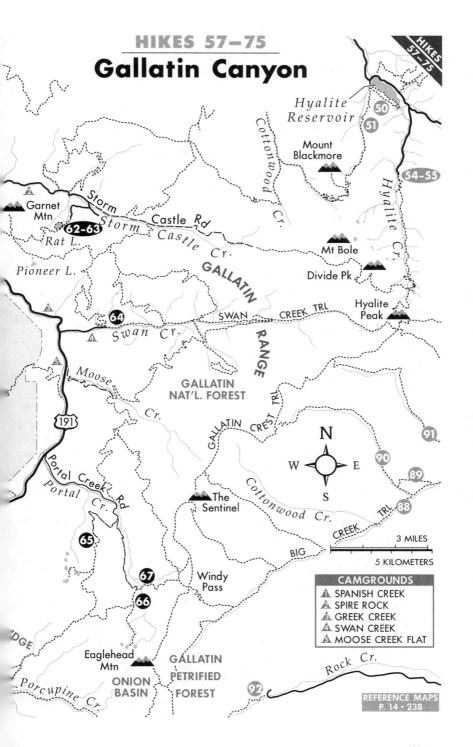

Gallatin Canyon

Hyalite
Reservoir

50

51

Cottonwood Cr.

Mount
Blackmore

54-55

Hyalite Cr.

Garnet
Mtn

Storm

Storm Castle Rd

62-63

Castle Cr.

Rat L.

Mt Bole

Pioneer L.

GALLATIN

Divide Pk

Hyalite
Peak

SWAN CREEK TRL

64

Swan Cr.

RANGE

GALLATIN
CREST
TRL

Moose

GALLATIN
NAT'L. FOREST

91

191

Cr.

N

90

W   E

89

S

Portal Creek Rd

The
Sentinel

Cottonwood Cr.

88

Portal Cr.

CREEK TRL

3 MILES

65

5 KILOMETERS

BIG

CAMGROUNDS

67

Windy
Pass

🏕 SPANISH CREEK
🏕 SPIRE ROCK
🏕 GREEK CREEK
🏕 SWAN CREEK
🏕 MOOSE CREEK FLAT

66

DGE

Eaglehead
Mtn

GALLATIN
PETRIFIED
FOREST

Rock Cr.

92

ONION
BASIN

Porcupine Cr.

REFERENCE MAPS
P. 14 · 238

57. Pioneer Falls
SOUTH FORK of SPANISH CREEK

Hiking distance: 7.5 miles round trip
Hiking time: 3.5 hours
Elevation gain: 800 feet
Maps: U.S.G.S. Beacon Point and Willow Swamp
Beartooth Publishing: Bozeman, Big Sky, W. Yellowstone
Rocky Mountain Surveys: Spanish Peaks

Summary of hike: Pioneer Falls is a full-bodied, 40-foot cascade on Falls Creek, a tributary of the South Fork of Spanish Creek. The trail heads into the Lee Metcalf Wilderness, part of the Spanish Peaks Unit of the Madison Range. The near-level trail parallels the South Fork of Spanish Creek beneath Gallatin Peak, Beacon Point, and Blaze Mountain. Several short, steep switchbacks ascend up the canyon along Falls Creek to Pioneer Falls. The Spanish Creek Road to the trailhead is a public access road through Ted Turner's Flying D Ranch. It is a scenic drive with great vistas along the North Fork of Spanish Creek.

Driving directions: From Four Corners 9 miles west of Bozeman, take Highway 191 south towards the Gallatin Canyon. Drive 13.1 miles to Spanish Creek Road on the right. Turn right and continue on Spanish Creek Road 9 miles, through the Flying D Ranch, to the Spanish Creek Campground and trailhead parking area.

From the Big Sky turnoff, drive 20.7 miles north on Highway 191 to Spanish Creek Road on the left.

Hiking directions: Take the trail to the west, crossing the bridge over the South Fork of Spanish Creek. Bear left and head upstream through lodgepole pines and Engelmann spruce on the South Fork Trail. At a half mile, enter the Lee Metcalf Wilderness, and cross several streams while staying close to the South Fork. At 3 miles is a posted junction with the Falls Creek Trail. Take the right fork along Falls Creek. Switchbacks continue for 0.75 miles, rising 450 feet to the brink of Pioneer Falls. Shortly before reaching the top, a side trail leads to a magnificent view of the waterfall. Return on the same trail.

To extend the hike, the Falls Creek Trail continues to Jerome Rock Lakes, just below the Madison Divide. The South Fork Trail continues south to Mirror Lake, Summit Lake, and Big Sky. ■

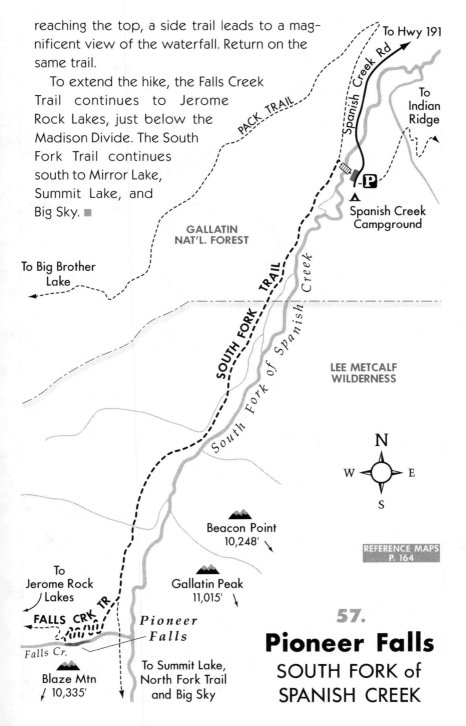

To Hwy 191

Spanish Creek Rd

To Indian Ridge

PACK TRAIL

P

Spanish Creek Campground

GALLATIN NAT'L. FOREST

To Big Brother Lake

SOUTH FORK TRAIL

South Fork of Spanish Creek

LEE METCALF WILDERNESS

N
W E
S

Beacon Point
10,248'

REFERENCE MAPS
P. 164

To Jerome Rock Lakes

FALLS CRK TR

Gallatin Peak
11,015'

Pioneer Falls

Falls Cr.

Blaze Mtn
10,335'

To Summit Lake, North Fork Trail and Big Sky

57.

Pioneer Falls
SOUTH FORK of SPANISH CREEK

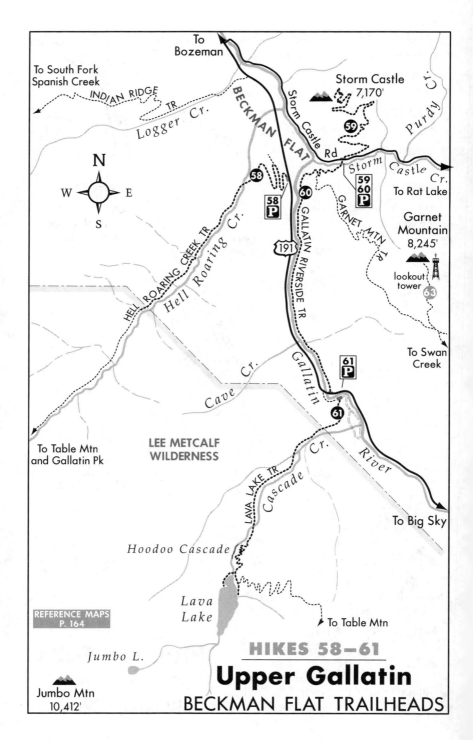

To
Bozeman

To South Fork
Spanish Creek

INDIAN RIDGE

Logger Cr. TR

BECKMAN FLAT

Storm Castle Rd

Storm Castle
7,170'

59

Purdy Cr.

Storm Castle Cr.

To Rat Lake

N
W E
S

58

58
P

60

191

GALLATIN RIVERSIDE TR

GARNET MTN TR

59
60
P

Garnet
Mountain
8,245'

lookout
tower

63

To Swan
Creek

HELL ROARING CREEK TR

Hell Roaring Cr.

Cave Cr.

Gallatin

61
P

61

To Table Mtn
and Gallatin Pk

LEE METCALF
WILDERNESS

Cascade Cr.

River

To Big Sky

LAVA LAKE TR

Hoodoo Cascade

To Table Mtn

REFERENCE MAPS
P. 164

Lava
Lake

Jumbo L.

HIKES 58–61

Upper Gallatin

BECKMAN FLAT TRAILHEADS

Jumbo Mtn
10,412'

58. Hell Roaring Creek Trail

Hiking distance: 5 miles round trip
Hiking time: 2.5 hours
Elevation gain: 500 feet
Maps: U.S.G.S. Garnet Mountain and Beacon Point
U.S.F.S. Lee Metcalf Wilderness
Beartooth Publishing: Bozeman, Big Sky, W. Yellowstone
Rocky Mountain Surveys: Spanish Peaks

map
page 170

Summary of hike: Hell Roaring Creek, a tributary of the Gallatin River, drains out of Hell Roaring Lake at the head of a steep, narrow drainage between Wilson Peak and Jumbo Mountain in the Spanish Peaks. The Hell Roaring Creek Trail begins at the south end of Beckman Flat along the Gallatin River and climbs past Hell Roaring Lake to Table Mountain. This hike follows the lower portion of the trail, paralleling the creek past a continuous display of tumbling whitewater with small waterfalls, cascades, and pools. The Hell Roaring Creek Trail accesses a network of other backcountry trails within the Spanish Peaks and the Lee Metcalf Wilderness.

Driving directions: From Four Corners 9 miles west of Bozeman, take Highway 191 south towards the Gallatin Canyon. Drive 18.4 miles to the Hell Roaring Creek trailhead parking area on the right, 1.7 miles past Squaw Creek Road.

From the Big Sky turnoff, drive 15.5 miles north on Highway 191 to the trailhead parking area on the left.

Hiking directions: From the north end of the parking area, head southwest into the forest. A series of switchbacks lead 0.6 miles to a ridge. At the junction midway through the switchbacks, take the hairpin switchback curving left. Once over the ridge, gradually descend to Hell Roaring Creek. Cross the log bridge over the creek, and head southwest up canyon. Continue along the north side of Hell Roaring Creek. At 2.5 miles, enter the Lee Metcalf Wilderness, the turn-around spot for a 5-mile hike.

To hike farther, the trail continues along the creek up to Hell Roaring Lake, Table Mountain, Gallatin Peak, and Summit Lake. ■

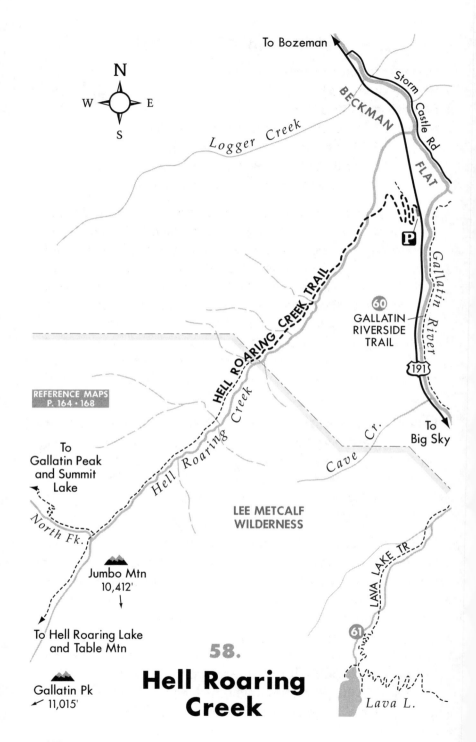

N
W · E
S

To Bozeman

Logger Creek

BECKMAN FLAT

Storm Castle Rd

P

HELL ROARING CREEK TRAIL

60
GALLATIN
RIVERSIDE
TRAIL

Gallatin River

191

To
Big Sky

Cave Cr.

REFERENCE MAPS
P. 164 • 168

To
Gallatin Peak
and Summit
Lake

Hell Roaring Creek

LEE METCALF
WILDERNESS

North Fk.

Jumbo Mtn
10,412'

To Hell Roaring Lake
and Table Mtn

LAVA LAKE TR

61

Gallatin Pk
11,015'

58.
Hell Roaring
Creek

Lava L.

59. Storm Castle Peak

Hiking distance: 5 miles round trip
Hiking time: 3 hours
Elevation gain: 2,300 feet
Maps: U.S.G.S. Garnet Mountain
      Beartooth Publishing: Bozeman, Big Sky, W. Yellowstone

map
page 173

Summary of hike: Storm Castle Peak is a rocky peak that rises to an elevation of 7,170 feet atop the east wall in Gallatin Canyon. The hike begins at Storm Castle Creek and climbs the south-facing mountain slope to the dramatic, multi-tiered summit, where there are sweeping 360-degree views of the adjacent mountains and valleys. En route to the summit, the trail zigzags up through meadows and stands of evergreens. The trail travels alongside some impressive vertical limestone fins. Throughout the hike are views of the surrounding mountains, including forested Garnet Mountain, the jagged Spanish Peaks in the Lee Metcalf Wilderness, the Hyalite Divide, Storm Castle Creek Canyon, Gallatin Canyon, and the Hell Roaring Creek drainage.

Driving directions: From Four Corners 9 miles west of Bozeman, take Highway 191 south towards the Gallatin Canyon. Drive 16.7 miles to Storm Castle Road (formerly Squaw Creek Road) on the left between mile markers 66 and 65. Turn left, cross Storm Castle Bridge over the Gallatin River, and curve to the right. Continue 1.9 miles to the posted trailhead parking area on the left.

From the Big Sky turnoff, drive 17.2 miles north on Highway 191 to Storm Castle Road on the right.

Hiking directions: Pass the trailhead sign on the north side of the road, and follow the path beneath the vertical rock wall. Traverse the mountain to the east, alternating between open meadows and forested pockets of juniper, lodgepole pines, and spruce. At 0.3 miles, switchback left and continue through the tree-dotted meadow. The great views span up and across Storm Castle Creek Canyon to forested Garnet Mountain. At 0.6 miles, after gaining 400 feet in elevation, is another switchback at an overlook across Gallatin Canyon to the Madison Range.

The trail temporarily levels out and passes through a lodgepole pine forest, then quickly resumes the climb. The views now include the serpentine canyon up to the Hyalite Divide, the fire lookout tower atop Garnet Mountain, Hell Roaring Creek Canyon, and the Spanish Peaks. Wind uphill on the cliff-hugging path with the aid of three more switchbacks, offering great close-up views of the limestone fins. Begin a series of short switchbacks, crossing talus slopes to the grassy saddle. Along the way, several steep shortcuts have become distinct paths. Whenever in doubt, take the lower route. From the saddle, veer left and follow the ridge through the forest to the craggy rock formations atop Storm Castle. On the left, a short side path leads to a natural arch, where there is a great view up the Storm Castle Creek drainage from the window beneath the arch. Just past the weather-carved window are flat rocks, perfect for sitting and savoring the views. Return by retracing your steps. ∎

60. Gallatin Riverside Trail

Hiking distance: 5.5 miles round trip
Hiking time: 2.5 hours
Elevation gain: 200 feet

map
page 175

Maps: U.S.G.S. Garnet Mountain
      Rocky Mountain Surveys: Spanish Peaks
      Beartooth Publishing: Bozeman, Big Sky, W. Yellowstone

Summary of hike: The Gallatin Riverside Trail parallels the eastern bank of the Gallatin on the lower west flank of Garnet Mountain. The mostly-level trail hugs the rocky cliffs through forests of lodgepole pines, Douglas fir, and Engelmann spruce, passing moss-covered rocks and small streams feeding the river. Kayakers and rafters are often seen working their way downstream. The trailhead is at Storm Castle Creek at the southern base of Storm Castle Peak. This trail may be hiked as a 2.25-mile, one-way shuttle by leaving a car south of the Highway 191

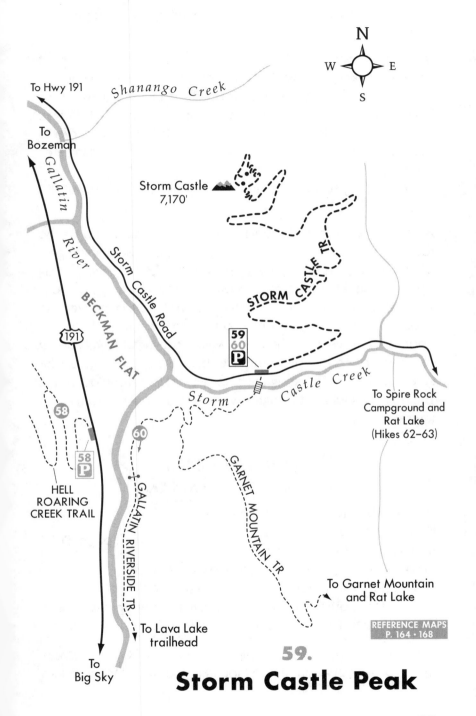

N
W   E
S

To Hwy 191

Shanango Creek

To
Bozeman

Gallatin River

BECKMAN FLAT

Storm Castle Road

191

Storm Castle
7,170'

STORM CASTLE TR.

59
60
P

Storm   *Castle Creek*

To Spire Rock
Campground and
Rat Lake
(Hikes 62–63)

58

58
P

HELL
ROARING
CREEK TRAIL

60

GALLATIN RIVERSIDE TR.

GARNET MOUNTAIN TR.

To Garnet Mountain
and Rat Lake

To Lava Lake
trailhead

To
Big Sky

REFERENCE MAPS
P. 164 · 168

59.
Storm Castle Peak

bridge over the Gallatin River, just beyond the Lava Lake trailhead (Hike 61).

Driving directions: From Four Corners 9 miles west of Bozeman, take Highway 191 south towards the Gallatin Canyon. Drive 16.7 miles to Storm Castle Road (formerly Squaw Creek Road) on the left between mile markers 66 and 65. Turn left, cross Storm Castle Bridge over the Gallatin River, and curve to the right. Continue 1.9 miles to the posted trailhead parking area on the left.

From the Big Sky turnoff, drive 17.2 miles north on Highway 191 to Storm Castle Road on the right.

Hiking directions: The trailhead is on the south side of the road. Cross the bridge over Storm Castle Creek, and head uphill 0.2 miles through the dense evergreen forest to a signed trail junction. The left fork climbs to Garnet Mountain and a lookout tower. Take the right fork, continuing on the Gallatin Riverside Trail. Zigzag through the forest to a grassy bench on the valley floor. A short distance ahead is a walk-through gate. Walk down to the river's edge. Follow the river bank along the edge of the steep, rocky cliffs, passing talus slopes and limestone outcrops. The trail ends where the highway crosses the river. Return along the same trail. ∎

61. Lava Lake Trail
CASCADE CREEK to LAVA LAKE

Hiking distance: 6 miles round trip
Hiking time: 3.5 hours
Elevation gain: 1,600 feet

map
page 177

Maps: U.S.G.S. Garnet Mountain and Hidden Lake
Rocky Mountain Surveys: Spanish Peaks
Beartooth Publishing: Bozeman, Big Sky, W. Yellowstone
Crystal Bench Maps: Bozeman, Montana

Summary of hike: The tumbling whitewater of Cascade Creek rushes down between Jumbo Mountain and Table Mountain into

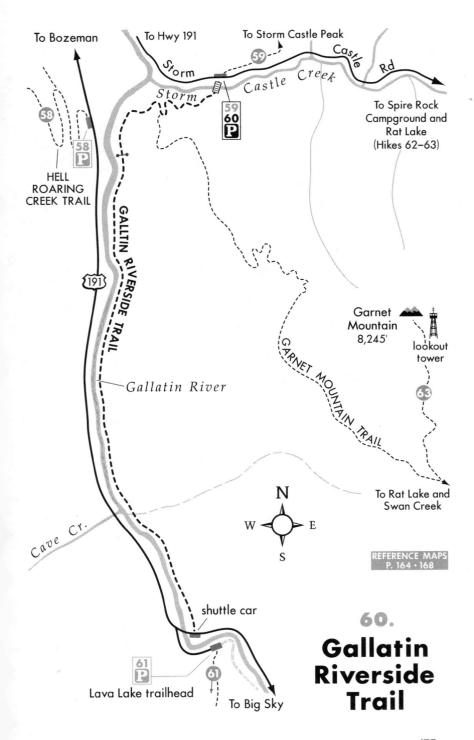

To Bozeman

To Hwy 191

To Storm Castle Peak

Storm

Castle Creek

Castle Rd

59

To Spire Rock Campground and Rat Lake (Hikes 62–63)

Storm

59
60
P

58

58
P

HELL ROARING CREEK TRAIL

191

GALLATIN RIVERSIDE TRAIL

Garnet Mountain 8,245'

lookout tower

Gallatin River

GARNET MOUNTAIN TRAIL

63

To Rat Lake and Swan Creek

Cave Cr.

N

W E

S

REFERENCE MAPS
P. 164 · 168

shuttle car

60.
Gallatin Riverside Trail

61
P

61

Lava Lake trailhead

To Big Sky

Lava Lake, a 40-acre tarn formed by a landslide damming the creek. The forest-lined lake sits in a small, steep valley surrounded by granite walls, with the Spanish Peaks rising in the distance. It is the only lake in the Lee Metcalf Wilderness that was not glacially formed.

The Lava Lake Trail (also called the Cascade Creek Trail) is one of the most popular trails in the Gallatin Canyon. The trail begins at the Gallatin River and climbs 1,600 feet along the frothy creek through a thick evergreen forest to the small lake-filled valley. En route, the trail passes turbulent Hoodoo Cascade and a few waterfalls.

Driving directions: From Four Corners 9 miles west of Bozeman, take Highway 191 south towards the Gallatin Canyon. Drive 20.3 miles to the Lava Lake trailhead parking area on the right, just north of the Gallatin River bridge. Turn right and continue 0.2 miles to the parking area.

From the Big Sky turnoff, the trailhead is 13.5 miles north on Highway 191. From this direction, you can not turn left to access the parking area. Continue to the first turnout and double back.

Hiking directions: Head south on the well-marked trail, immediately gaining elevation in the moist, shady forest of lodgepole pines. At 0.3 miles, the trail meets Cascade Creek and enters the Lee Metcalf Wilderness. Continue up the canyon, paralleling the noisy creek, and cross a bridge over a tributary stream at one mile. At 1.9 miles, enter a wet meadow. At the upper end of the meadow, cross a log footbridge to the east side of the creek. Climb a series of eight steep switchbacks alongside Hoodoo Cascade. At just under 3 miles, the path reaches the north end of Lava Lake, where there are great vistas of Jumbo Mountain, the U-shaped upper valley of Cascade Creek, and Table Mountain. A side path skirts the northwest shoreline to a rocky promontory.

To extend the hike, the main trail zigzags east, climbing more than 2,000 feet to the 9,840-foot summit of Table Mountain in the heart of the Spanish Peaks. Cairns mark the route above the timberline. ■

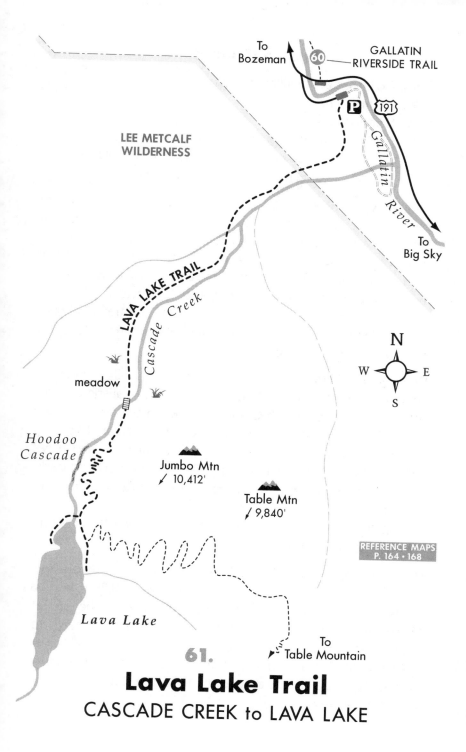

To
Bozeman

60

GALLATIN
RIVERSIDE TRAIL

P

191

Gallatin River

To
Big Sky

LEE METCALF
WILDERNESS

LAVA LAKE TRAIL

Cascade Creek

meadow

N
W   E
S

Hoodoo
Cascade

Jumbo Mtn
10,412'

Table Mtn
9,840'

REFERENCE MAPS
P. 164 · 168

Lava Lake

To
Table Mountain

61.

Lava Lake Trail
CASCADE CREEK to LAVA LAKE

62. Rat Lake

Hiking distance: 1.5 miles round trip
Hiking time: 1 hour
Elevation gain: 160 feet
Maps: U.S.G.S. Garnet Mountain
Beartooth Publishing: Bozeman, Big Sky, W. Yellowstone
Rocky Mountain Surveys: Spanish Peaks

Summary of hike: Rat Lake sits on the east slope of Garnet Mountain at 6,600 feet, just south of Storm Castle Creek. Rat Lake, affectionately named for the rodent, is a beautiful, forested lake that probably deserves a more attractive title. It is an ideal spot for fishing, picnicking, and strolling, with an easily accessible shoreline. The short, scenic hike to the lake is a good option for children. Beyond Rat Lake, the trail continues another 1,500 feet up to the Garnet Mountain Lookout Tower at an elevation of 8,245 feet—Hike 63.

Driving directions: From Four Corners 9 miles west of Bozeman, take Highway 191 south towards the Gallatin Canyon. Drive 16.7 miles to Storm Castle Creek Road (formerly Squaw Creek Road) on the left between mile markers 66 and 65. Turn left, cross Storm Castle Bridge over the Gallatin River, and curve to the right. Continue 6.8 miles to the Rat Lake trailhead parking area. Along the way are two road forks—take the right fork both times.

From Big Sky, drive 17.2 miles north on Highway 191 to Storm Castle Road on the right.

Hiking directions: Take the signed trail south on the old logging road, traversing the west canyon wall. At 0.35 miles is a posted junction. The left fork leads 3 miles up to the Garnet Mountain Lookout Tower (Hike 63). For this easier hike, go to the right and head up the slope. Curve left and descend to the north end of Rat Lake. Cross over the outlet stream to the banks of the lake. A trail loops around the wooded shoreline. Return along the same route.

To continue hiking, return to the junction and veer right, taking Hike 63 up to the Garnet Mountain Lookout Tower. The trail gains 1,700 feet in elevation over 3 miles to the summit. Garnet Mountain is also accessible from the Storm Castle Trailhead (Hike 60). ■

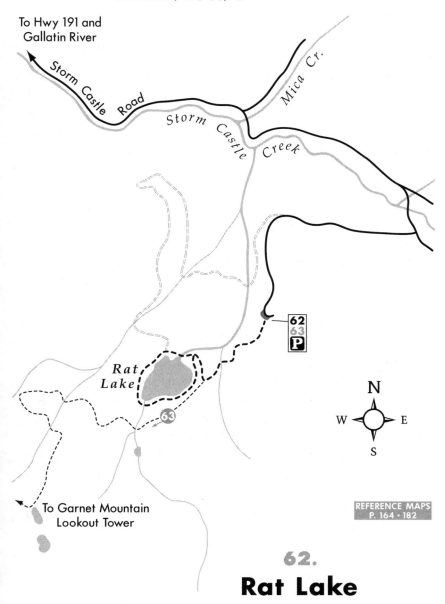

To Hwy 191 and
Gallatin River

Storm Castle Road

Storm Castle Creek

Mica Cr.

62
63
P

Rat
Lake

63

N
W · E
S

To Garnet Mountain
Lookout Tower

REFERENCE MAPS
P. 164 · 182

62.
Rat Lake

63. Garnet Mountain Lookout Tower from Rat Lake

Hiking distance: 7 miles round trip
Hiking time: 3.5 hours
Elevation gain: 1,850 feet
Maps: U.S.G.S. Garnet Mountain
　　　　Beartooth Publishing: Bozeman, Big Sky, W. Yellowstone

Summary of hike: Garnet Mountain sits on the west edge of the Gallatin Range, just south of Storm Castle Peak and high above the Gallatin Canyon. In 1930, a fire lookout tower was built on the 8,245-foot summit of the dome-shaped mountain. It was rebuilt in 1960. The tower is currently a two-story rental cabin. It is the only fire lookout for rent in the Gallatin National Forest inventory.

From the lookout are vast, unobstructed panoramas. The far-reaching views extend across the Gallatin Mountains and the Spanish Peaks of the Madison Range to the peaks of the Tobacco Root Mountains, the Bridger Range, and the Gallatin Valley. Two routes access the Garnet Mountain summit—the Storm Castle trailhead at the Gallatin River Valley (Hike 60) and this hike from Rat Lake. The trail passes Rat Lake on old logging roads through flower-filled meadows and pockets of forests.

Driving directions: From Four Corners 9 miles west of Bozeman, take Highway 191 south towards the Gallatin Canyon. Drive 16.7 miles to Storm Castle Creek Road (formerly Squaw Creek Road) on the left between mile markers 66 and 65. Turn left, cross Storm Castle Bridge over the Gallatin River, and curve to the right. Continue 6.8 miles to the Rat Lake trailhead parking area by 3 large boulders. Along the way are two road forks— take the right fork both times.

From Big Sky, drive 17.2 miles north on Highway 191 to Storm Castle Road on the right.

Hiking directions: Take the signed trail south on the old logging road, traversing the west canyon wall. At 0.35 miles is a posted junction. The right fork leads to the north shore of Rat Lake (Hike 62). For this hike, stay to the left. Curve around the east (left) side of Rat Lake, with views through the fir forest towards the lake. High above the south side of the lake, cross over the lake's inlet stream as the old road leaves Rat Lake behind. Stroll through the open forest, with small meadows and pockets of pines and firs, on a steady but gentle uphill grade. Pass an unnamed lake on the left as the trail bends to the right. As you approach the upper base of Garnet Mountain, make a horseshoe left bend by a trail sign at 2 miles. The trail begins a short, steep climb, then levels out. Descend through a lodgepole pine forest to a beautiful, flower-filled meadow with a pond on the left. Climb to a higher and larger meadow teaming with more flowers. Near the top of the slope is a posted junction. Pioneer Trail veers left, leading one mile to Pioneer Lakes. Continue straight 250 yards to another junction. The Garnet Mountain Trail goes left and descends 3 miles to the trailhead by the Storm Castle Road (Hikes 59—60).

For this hike, walk straight ahead as the grade gets steeper, gaining 400 feet over the next 0.3 miles to a gate. Pass through the gate as the lookout tower comes into view. Cross the sloping meadow, dotted with whitebark pine and subalpine fir, while enjoying the spectacular views of the Madison and Gallatin Ranges. At the ridge, bend left, following the broad dome to the tower atop the 8,245-foot peak. Climb the lookout steps to the deck that circles the perimeter of the tower. After taking in the panoramic views, return by retracing your steps.

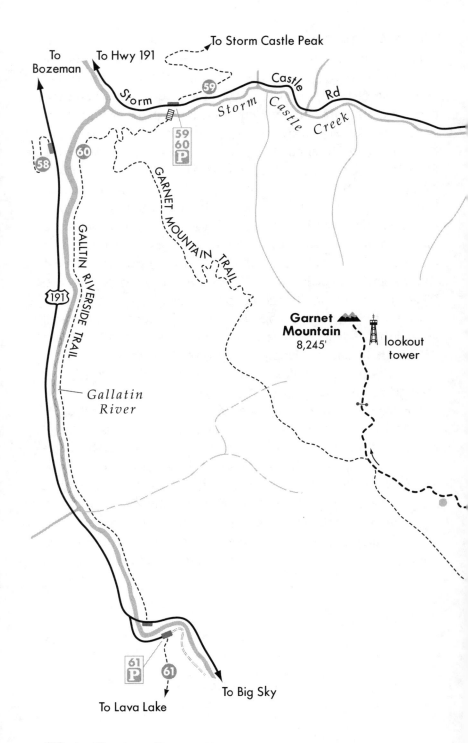

To Storm Castle Peak

To Bozeman

To Hwy 191

Storm

Castle

Rd

59

Storm Castle Creek

58

60

59 60 P

GARNET MOUNTAIN TRAIL

GALLATIN RIVERSIDE TRAIL

191

Gallatin River

Garnet Mountain 8,245'

lookout tower

61 P

61

To Lava Lake

To Big Sky

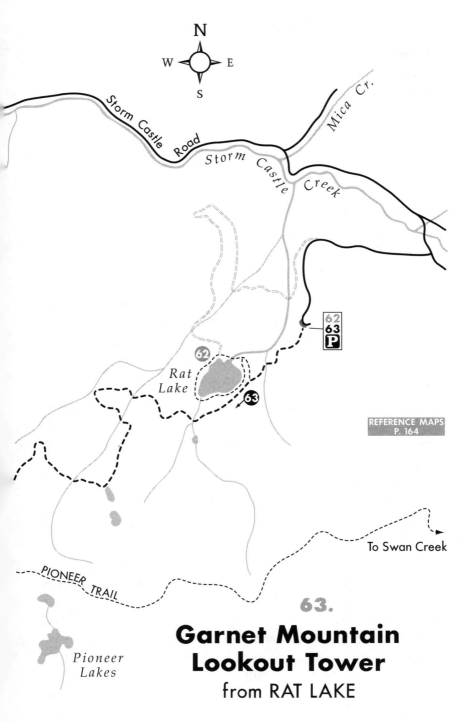

N
W   E
S

Storm Castle Road

Mica Cr.

Storm Castle Creek

62
63
P

62

Rat Lake

63

REFERENCE MAPS
P. 164

To Swan Creek

PIONEER TRAIL

63.

Garnet Mountain
Lookout Tower
from RAT LAKE

Pioneer Lakes

64. Swan Creek Trail

Hiking distance: 1 mile to 10 miles round trip
Hiking time: 30 minutes to 5 hours
Elevation gain: 100 feet to 1,000 feet
Maps: U.S.G.S. Hidden Lake, Garnet Mountain,
Mount Blackmore, The Sentinel
Beartooth Publishing: Bozeman, Big Sky, W. Yellowstone
Rocky Mountain Surveys: Spanish Peaks
Crystal Bench Maps: Bozeman, Montana

Summary of hike: The headwaters of Swan Creek begin at 9,400 feet on the upper west slope of Hyalite Peak. The creek drops 3,700 feet westward to the Gallatin River, tumbling over granite rock and meandering through meadows. The Swan Creek Trail follows the north side of the creek for 11 miles to Hyalite Peak at the Gallatin-Yellowstone Divide, where it connects with the Hyalite Creek Trail (Hike 55) and the Gallatin Crest Trail. This hike follows the lower portion of the trail, passing meadows, beaver ponds, and volcanic rock as it parallels the creek.

Driving directions: From Four Corners 9 miles west of Bozeman, take Highway 191 south towards the Gallatin Canyon. Drive 24.5 miles to the Swan Creek turnoff on the left. Turn left and continue 1.4 miles alongside Swan Creek to the trailhead parking area at the road's end.

From the Big Sky turnoff, drive 9.3 miles north on Highway 191 to the Swan Creek turnoff on the right.

Hiking directions: Head east on the wide path along the banks of Swan Creek. The trail quickly narrows to a footpath and enters the forest. Traverse the edge of the hillside while overlooking Swan Creek. At a half mile is a flower-filled meadow and a pond on the left, formed by the outlet stream from Lake of the Pines. Swan Creek winds through the meadow, pooled up by beaver dams. The trail rises and falls along the hillside, always within view of Swan Creek. Choose your own turn-around spot, and return along the same route. ■

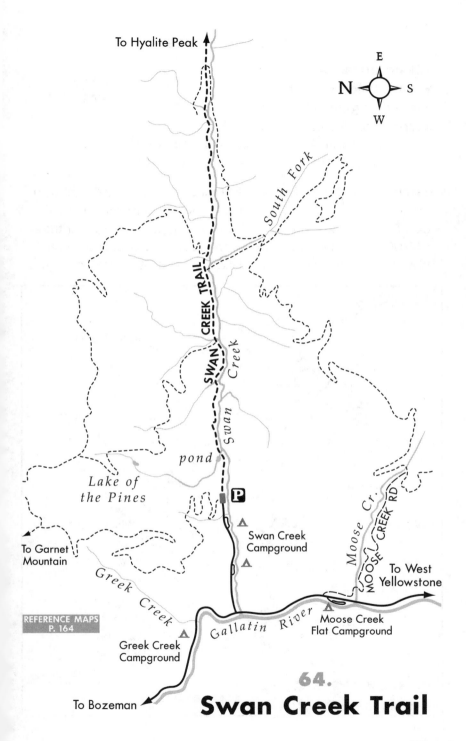

To Hyalite Peak

N E S W

SWAN CREEK TRAIL

South Fork

Swan Creek

pond

Swan Creek

Lake of the Pines

P

Swan Creek Campground

Moose Cr.

MOOSE CREEK RD

To Garnet Mountain

To West Yellowstone

Greek Creek

Gallatin River

Moose Creek Flat Campground

REFERENCE MAPS P. 164

Greek Creek Campground

To Bozeman

64.
Swan Creek Trail

65. Hidden Lakes

Hiking distance: 6 miles round trip
Hiking time: 3.5 hours
Elevation gain: 1,000 feet
Maps: U.S.G.S. Hidden Lake
        Beartooth Publishing: Bozeman, Big Sky, W. Yellowstone
        U.S.D.A. Gallatin National Forest West Half map

map page 188

Summary of hike: The Hidden Lakes are a series of eight high mountain lakes in the Gallatin Range between Bozeman and Big Sky. The chain of lakes, at the base of a ridge, rest at an altitude of 9,000 feet. Five of the lakes contain golden trout and/or rainbow trout. The upper, largest lake is tucked into a scenic cirque

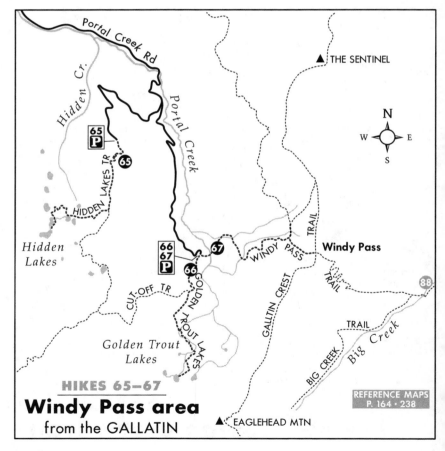

HIKES 65–67
Windy Pass area
from the GALLATIN

with mountains towering 800 feet along three sides of the lake. The Hidden Lakes Trail begins above 8,000 feet and follows a ridge with spectacular vistas. En route, the trail crosses streams, strolls through forests and meadows, and leads to the series of forested lakes.

Driving directions: From Four Corners 9 miles west of Bozeman, take Highway 191 south towards the Gallatin Canyon. Drive 28.6 miles to Portal Creek Road on the left between mile markers 54 and 53. Turn left and wind 3.8 miles up the canyon to a clearly marked Y-fork. Veer to the right and continue 2.25 bumpy miles to the Hidden Lakes trailhead parking area at the end of the road.

From the Big Sky turnoff, drive 5.2 miles north on Highway 191 to Portal Creek Road on the right.

Hiking directions: Pass the trailhead kiosk and head south into the forest. Follow the wide path on a gentle uphill grade. Within a quarter mile, begin weaving up the mountain with the aid of six switchbacks. Continue through lodgepole pines to the ridge. Stroll across the length of the ridge, with southwest views across the canyon of Levinski Ridge. Continue south and descend to an unsigned Y-fork. The left fork connects with the Golden Trout Lakes Trail (Hike 66) and the Porcupine Creek Trail (Hike 72).

For this hike, stay to the right on the Hidden Lakes Trail, the main trail. Pass a small spring in a meadow on the right. Drop down to a minor saddle and cross three streams. Climb the slope on the dirt and slab rock path to the north end of the two lower Hidden Lakes at 2.5 miles. The forested lakes sit beneath a vertical rock wall to their west. For a short detour, walk between the two lakes.

Back on the main trail, follow the north side of the lake. Leave the lake's edge and head up the hillside, following intermittent cairns. Steadily gain elevation to the northeast end of another lake. Follow the east side of the lake, crossing the outlet stream to the far end of the lake. Curve left and parallel the lake's inlet stream, reaching the largest of the Hidden Lakes. The lake is tucked into a massive, rock-walled cirque, where the trail ends. ▪

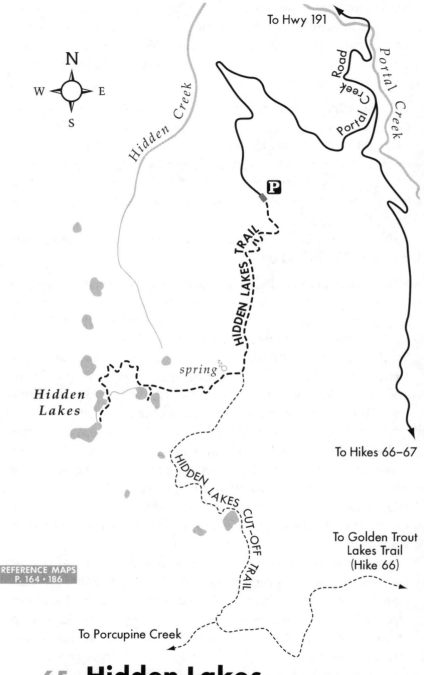

To Hwy 191

Portal Creek Road

Portal Creek

P

Hidden Creek

N
W E
S

HIDDEN LAKES TRAIL

spring

Hidden Lakes

To Hikes 66–67

HIDDEN LAKES CUT-OFF TRAIL

To Golden Trout Lakes Trail (Hike 66)

To Porcupine Creek

REFERENCE MAPS
P. 164 • 186

65. **Hidden Lakes**

66. Golden Trout Lakes

Hiking distance: 5 miles round trip

Hiking time: 3 hours

Elevation gain: 1,000 feet

Maps: U.S.G.S. Hidden Lake and Lone Indian Peak

Beartooth Publishing: Bozeman, Big Sky, W. Yellowstone

U.S.D.A. Gallatin National Forest West Half map

map
page 191

Summary of hike: The Golden Trout Lakes sit in a basin at an elevation of 9,050 feet. The high mountain lakes rest in a cirque on the northern slope of Eaglehead Mountain, a three-peaked mountain with a rounded, grassy ridge. The largest of the Golden Trout Lakes is surrounded by forest, with good campsites above the north and east shores. A couple of smaller lakes can be found above and to the west. The Golden Trout Lakes Trail climbs through a series of flower-filled meadows and a mixed forest of pine, spruce, and fir to the scenic lakes.

Driving directions: From Four Corners 9 miles west of Bozeman, take Highway 191 south towards the Gallatin Canyon. Drive 28.6 miles to Portal Creek Road on the left between mile markers 54 and 53. Turn left and wind 3.8 miles up the canyon to a clearly marked Y-fork. Veer to the left and continue 3 bumpy miles to the Upper Portal Trailhead parking area at the end of the public road.

From the Big Sky turnoff, drive 5.2 miles north on Highway 191 to Portal Creek Road on the right.

Hiking directions: Walk twenty yards past the parking area on the dirt road to the sign on the left for the Golden Trout Lakes. Veer left and head up the slope into a mixed forest of lodgepole pine, Engelmann spruce, and subalpine fir. Pass two ponds on the right, and climb the west canyon wall, overlooking the forested drainage. Cross an abandoned logging road at 0.6 miles. Zip up three switchbacks to a posted junction with the Hidden Lakes Cut-off Trail, which leads two miles west to the Hidden Lakes.

Stay to the left and continue south, meandering through a series of sloping meadows. Descend to a cascading stream, which drains the Golden Lakes, then climb a fairly steep grade up the north slope. As the path mercifully levels out, cross the outlet stream again. Pass through a meadow containing a large bog. Begin the last, steep climb along a rock-embedded path amid huge boulders. At 2.5 miles, emerge at the northeast shore of the largest of the Golden Trout Lakes. The lakes sit beneath the north flank of Eaglehead Mountain, rising 800 feet above the lake in a towering cirque. ■

67. Windy Pass Trail
(PORTAL CREEK TRAIL)

Hiking distance: 5 to 6.5 miles round trip
Hiking time: 3 to 4 hours
Elevation gain: 1,250 feet
Maps: U.S.G.S. Hidden Lake and The Sentinel
      Beartooth Publishing: Bozeman, Big Sky, W. Yellowstone

map page 193

Summary of hike: Windy Pass is a vast alpine meadow that straddles the Gallatin Crest between The Sentinel and Eaglehead Mountain. At an elevation of 9,250 feet, the open, windswept plateau feels like the top of the world. It is covered in wildflowers for a few short months. Atop the Gallatin Divide, the Windy Pass Trail (also known as Portal Creek Trail) intersects the Gallatin Crest Trail, which heads north along the ridge to The Sentinel and Hyalite Peak and south through the Gallatin Petrified Forest. Past the divide, the East Windy Pass Trail continues east into the next drainage, descending to Big Creek in Paradise Valley.

En route up to Windy Pass, this trail crosses Portal Creek, meanders through a few meadows with vistas of the Madison Range, and climbs to the broad expanse by the Windy Pass Cabin, a forest service rental cabin.

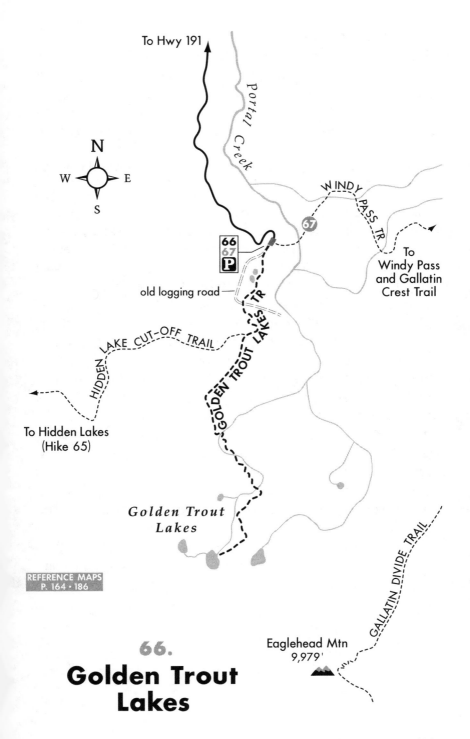

To Hwy 191

Portal Creek

WINDY PASS TR.

67

To
Windy Pass
and Gallatin
Crest Trail

66
67
P

old logging road

HIDDEN LAKE CUT-OFF TRAIL

GOLDEN TROUT LAKES TR.

To Hidden Lakes
(Hike 65)

*Golden Trout
Lakes*

GALLATIN DIVIDE TRAIL

REFERENCE MAPS
P. 164 · 186

Eaglehead Mtn
9,979'

N
W   E
S

66.
**Golden Trout
Lakes**

Driving directions: From Four Corners 9 miles west of Bozeman, take Highway 191 south towards the Gallatin Canyon. Drive 28.6 miles to Portal Creek Road on the left between mile markers 54 and 53. Turn left and wind 3.8 miles up the canyon to a clearly marked Y-fork. Veer to the left and continue 3 bumpy miles to the Upper Portal Trailhead parking area at the end of the public road.

From the Big Sky turnoff, drive 5.2 miles north on Highway 191 to Portal Creek Road on the right.

Hiking directions: The Windy Pass Trail begins by the kiosk for the Upper Portal Trailhead on the east side of the road. Pass the trail sign and enter the pine forest. Descend to Portal Creek at 0.2 miles. Cross downfall logs or wade across the creek. Slowly gain elevation and cross a tributary stream by a beautiful cascade. Cross a second tributary stream, which forms on Windy Pass, and pass through a few small meadows. Climb up a short, steep stretch to an overlook of the Madison Range. Steadily weave up the mountain through a mixed forest of Engelmann spruce, lodgepole pine, and subalpine fir. Pass a waterfall on the left. At 2.5 miles, emerge from the forest onto Windy Pass, a large open expanse dotted with pines. At a posted junction, detour left across the plateau towards the Forest Service cabin a quarter mile ahead. Cross the stream and head up the slope to the cabin.

Return to the junction and now take the other fork to Windy Pass. Follow the tree-lined meadow uphill for a half mile, topping out at the 9,270-foot Gallatin Divide and a signed junction with the Gallatin Crest Trail #96. This is our turn-around spot. After exploring the divide and the endless vistas, return along the same route. ■

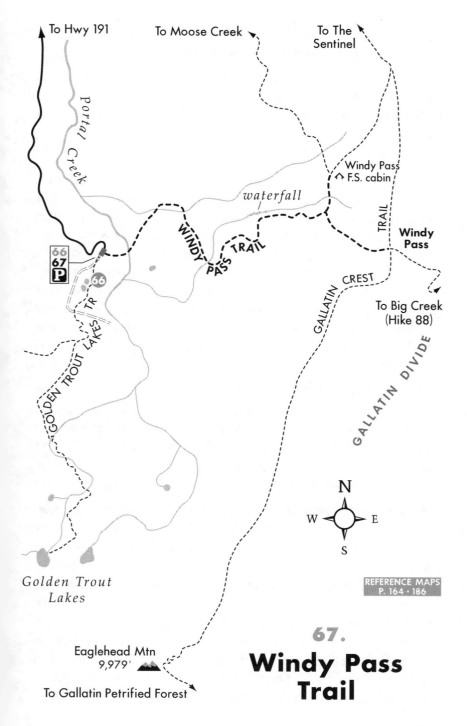

To Hwy 191

To Moose Creek

To The Sentinel

Portal Creek

waterfall

Windy Pass F.S. cabin

WINDY PASS TRAIL

TRAIL

Windy Pass

66
67 P

66

GALLATIN CREST

To Big Creek (Hike 88)

GOLDEN TROUT LAKES TR

GALLATIN DIVIDE

N
W — E
S

Golden Trout Lakes

REFERENCE MAPS
P. 164 · 186

Eaglehead Mtn
9,979'

To Gallatin Petrified Forest

67.
Windy Pass Trail

68. Ousel Falls
SOUTH FORK of the WEST FORK GALLATIN

Hiking distance: 1.6 miles round trip
Hiking time: 45 minutes
Elevation gain: 400 feet
Maps: U.S.G.S. Ousel Falls
　　　　Beartooth Publishing: Bozeman, Big Sky, W. Yellowstone

Summary of hike: Ousel Falls is a powerful 35-foot cataract that plunges off a moss-covered rock wall onto a granite shelf in an amazing display of whitewater. The waterfall is located in 29-acre Ousel Falls Park a short distance southwest of Big Sky Meadow Village. Ousel Falls is named after water ouzels, small gray birds often present in the nooks next to the waterfall. The interpretive trail parallels the South Fork of the West Fork of the Gallatin River through a forested gulch with three bridge crossings. The trail leads to three separate viewing areas of the falls. Interpretive signs describe the geology, wildlife, and vegetation.

Driving directions: From Four Corners 9 miles west of Bozeman, take Highway 191 south towards the Gallatin Canyon. Drive 33.8 miles to Big Sky Spur Road (Highway 64) at mile marker 48. Turn right and continue 2.9 miles to Ousel Falls Road by the posted Big Sky Town Center. Turn left and continue 1.8 miles to the signed Ousel Falls Park on the left. Turn left and park.

Hiking directions: From the trailhead, the left fork leads two miles back to the town center. Take the Yellow Mules Trail to the right. Descend on the wide gravel path, and enter a Douglas fir forest. Continue on the north wall of the stream-fed canyon. Three switchbacks zigzag down to a bridge crossing over the South Fork of the West Fork of the Gallatin. Ascend the south wall of the canyon, curving up the mountain contours. Cross a bridge over a tributary stream to a posted Y-fork. The Yellow Mules Trail veers left. Curve right towards Ousel Falls. Descend to the river via two switchbacks. Across the river is a vertical rock wall with seepage dripping through the fractured rock. Walk upstream along the South Fork Cascades and the sandstone formations. Cross a bridge over the river, and climb along the north side of the waterway. Two more switchbacks lead to a 4-way trail split. The right fork leads a short distance to the South Fork Overlook, with views of the river and falls from high above the river. The second trail to the right leads to the top of Ousel Falls on a natural footpath. The path straight ahead leads to a picnic area and a pool at the base of the waterfall. The left fork leads to a rock overlook of Ousel Falls. Return along the same path. ■

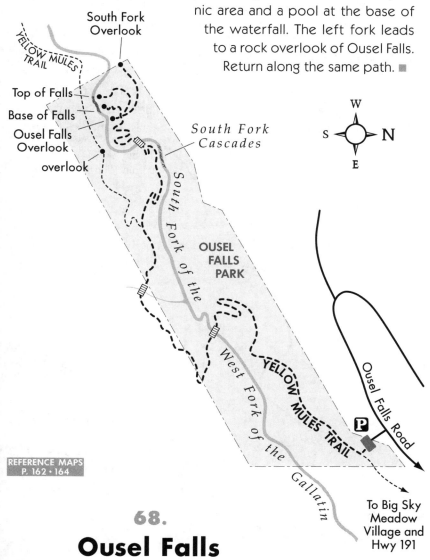

68.

Ousel Falls

69. North Fork Trail
NORTH FORK of the GALLATIN

Hiking distance: 6 miles round trip
Hiking time: 3 hours
Elevation gain: 600 feet
Maps: U.S.G.S. Gallatin Peak
       Beartooth Publishing: Bozeman, Big Sky, W. Yellowstone
       Rocky Mountain Surveys: Spanish Peaks

Summary of hike: The North Fork of the Gallatin River forms in
Bear Basin on the south flank of Gallatin Peak, merging with the
Middle Fork at Big Sky Meadow Village. The North Fork Trail follows the course of the river upstream into Bear Basin and passes
its headwaters to Summit Lake, then descends to the South Fork

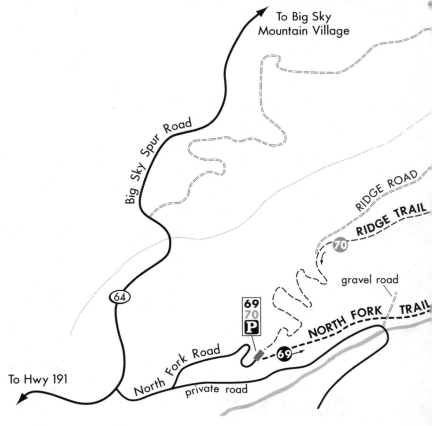

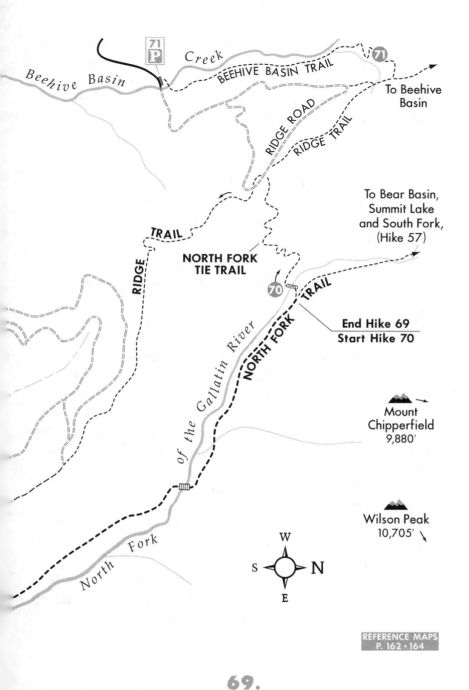

69.
North Fork Trail

of Spanish Creek on the opposite side of Gallatin Peak (Hike 57). This is a popular 16-mile overnight backpack trip. This shorter hike takes in the first three miles of the North Fork Trail to a crossing of the river below Mount Chipperfield and Wilson Peak. The trail continuously parallels the river.

Driving directions: From Four Corners 9 miles west of Bozeman, take Highway 191 south towards the Gallatin Canyon. Drive 33.8 miles to Big Sky Spur Road (Highway 64) at mile marker 48. Turn right and continue 4.8 miles to the North Fork Road on the right. Turn right and drive 0.8 miles to the posted trailhead parking area to the left.

Hiking directions: Head north on the wide, well-defined trail. Traverse the east-facing slope high above the North Fork of the Gallatin River. Gradually descend and cross a gravel road at 0.6 miles. Continue up the canyon, climbing gradually but steadily. On the right is the North Fork and towering mountains with jagged, weather-carved spires, including Wilson Peak and Mount Chipperfield. At 2 miles veer to the right and descend to the log bridge. Cross the bridge over the North Fork of the Gallatin River. Continue along the northeast side of the creek, passing flower-filled meadows, pockets of evergreens, and a series of cascades and small waterfalls formed by downfall logs. Climb a small rise to a posted junction at 3 miles. This is the turn-around spot.

To extend the hike, the North Fork Trail steadily climbs over 2 miles into Bear Basin while gaining 1,200 feet. After the basin, the trail steeply ascends the Spanish Peaks 3 more miles to Summit Lake at 9,500 feet, connecting to a network of trails in the Lee Metcalf Wilderness.

Hike 70 continues on the left fork—the North Fork Tie Trail. This route crosses back over the creek and climbs to the ridge, forming an 8.4-mile loop via the Ridge Trail. ■

70. North Fork—Ridge Trail Loop
NORTH FORK of the GALLATIN

Hiking distance: 8.4-mile loop
Hiking time: 4 hours
Elevation gain: 1,200 feet
Maps: U.S.G.S. Gallatin Peak and Lone Mountain
          Beartooth Publishing: Bozeman, Big Sky, W. Yellowstone
          Rocky Mountain Surveys: Spanish Peaks

map
page 200

Summary of hike: This hike continues from Hike 69, forming an 8.4-mile loop up through a river drainage and back down across a ridge. The trail follows the North Fork of the Gallatin River for the first three miles (Hike 69), crossing two bridges over the creek. This hike continues on the North Fork Tie Trail, heading up the west canyon wall to the ridge between Beehive Basin and the North Fork drainage. The hike then returns down the Ridge Trail, offering views of Lone Mountain, Gallatin Peak, the Spanish Peaks, and Bear Basin.

Driving directions: From Four Corners 9 miles west of Bozeman, take Highway 191 south towards the Gallatin Canyon. Drive 33.8 miles to Big Sky Spur Road (Highway 64) at mile marker 48. Turn right and continue 4.8 miles to the North Fork Road on the right. Turn right and drive 0.8 miles to the posted trailhead parking area to the left.

Hiking directions: Head north on the wide, well-defined trail. Traverse the east-facing slope high above the North Fork of the Gallatin River. Gradually descend and cross a gravel road at 0.6 miles. Continue up the canyon, climbing gradually but steadily. On the right is the North Fork and towering mountains with jagged, weather-carved spires, including Wilson Peak and Mount Chipperfield. At 2 miles veer to the right and descend to the log bridge. Cross the bridge over the North Fork of the Gallatin River. Continue along the northeast side of the creek, passing flower-filled meadows, pockets of evergreens, and a series of cascades and small waterfalls formed by downfall logs. Climb a small rise to a posted junction at 3 miles.

Bear left on the North Fork Tie Trail, and descend to the North Fork of the Gallatin River. Cross the one-log bridge and head up the hillside. Climb a series of 11 switchbacks. The awesome vistas include Bear Basin, Gallatin Peak, the jagged spine of the Spanish Peaks, and the North Fork drainage. Continue climbing to the ridge. Follow the ridge north and curve west through a tree-rimmed meadow to a junction by the unpaved Ridge Road. The right fork leads to Beehive Basin (Hike 71). Bear left on the Ridge Trail. Cross and recross the dirt road, following the Ridge Trail signs. Descend through the forest and skirt the ridge, with alternating views of Beehive Basin and the North Fork Canyon. Descend the west wall of the North Fork drainage, and steadily descend to the Ridge Road. Bear left on the forested dirt road, and continue 1.7 miles downhill, completing the loop at the trailhead. ▪

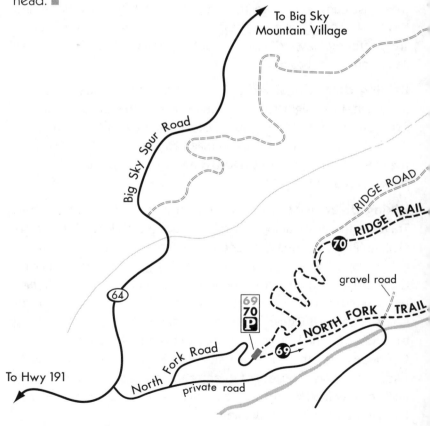

To Big Sky
Mountain Village

Big Sky Spur Road

RIDGE ROAD

RIDGE TRAIL

70

gravel road

64

69
70
P

NORTH FORK TRAIL

69

North Fork Road

To Hwy 191

private road

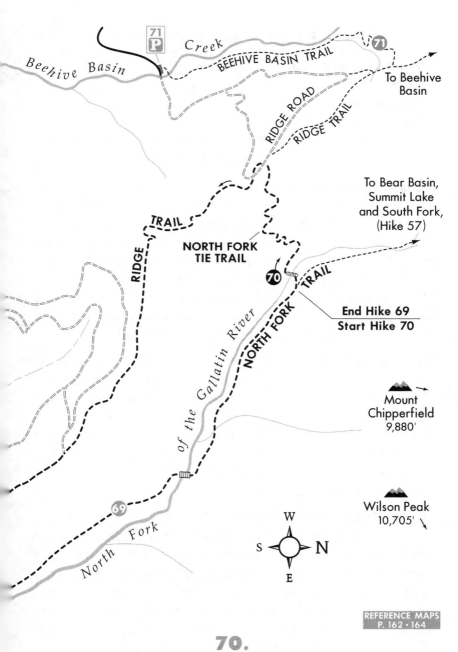

70.
North Fork–
Ridge Trail Loop

71. Beehive Basin Trail

Hiking distance: 6.5 miles round trip
Hiking time: 4 hours
Elevation gain: 1,200 feet
Maps: U.S.G.S. Lone Mountain
      Beartooth Publishing: Bozeman, Big Sky, W. Yellowstone
      Rocky Mountain Surveys: Spanish Peaks

Summary of hike: Beehive Basin sits in a bowl surrounded on three sides by 10,000-foot mountains in the Spanish Peaks Primitive Area. The picturesque basin is a glacial cirque with a small lake. The lake sits beneath the rock walls of Blaze Mountain, Gallatin Peak, and Mount Chipperfield at 9,200 feet. This top-of-the-world hike includes alpine meadows covered with wildflowers, a tumbling creek, and tall stands of Engelman spruce and subalpine fir. At the trail's end is a lake and wide open vistas into the Lee Metcalf Wilderness. Moose frequent the area.

Driving directions: From Four Corners 9 miles west of Bozeman, take Highway 191 south towards the Gallatin Canyon. Drive 33.8 miles to Big Sky Spur Road (Highway 64) at mile marker 48. Turn right and continue 10.1 miles to Beehive Basin Road on the right. (It is located 1.3 miles beyond the Big Sky Mountain Village turnoff and 30 yards before the Moonlight Basin Ranch entrance.) Turn right and drive 1.6 miles to the posted trailhead parking area on the left.

Hiking directions: Walk north to Beehive Creek. Cross a primitive log bridge over the creek, and head up the grassy meadow rimmed with evergreens. Cross the east slope of the meadow, overlooking the serpentine creek and Blaze Mountain along the jagged ridge of the Spanish Peaks. Cross a fork of the creek, and zigzag up three switchbacks on the open slope. The vistas extend down canyon to pyramid-shaped Lone Mountain, The Sphinx, and the Madison Range. The path reaches a posted T-junction at one mile. The right fork leads two miles to the North Fork Trail (Hike 70).

    Bear left into a large meadow and three creek crossings. After the third crossing, begin a second ascent to another meadow and a pond, passing limestone rock formations. After crossing the second meadow, begin the final ascent. The trail flattens out at an unnamed, crescent-shaped lake in a steep-walled cirque, surrounded by a grassy basin marbled with streams. The views are breathtaking. Return on the same trail. ■

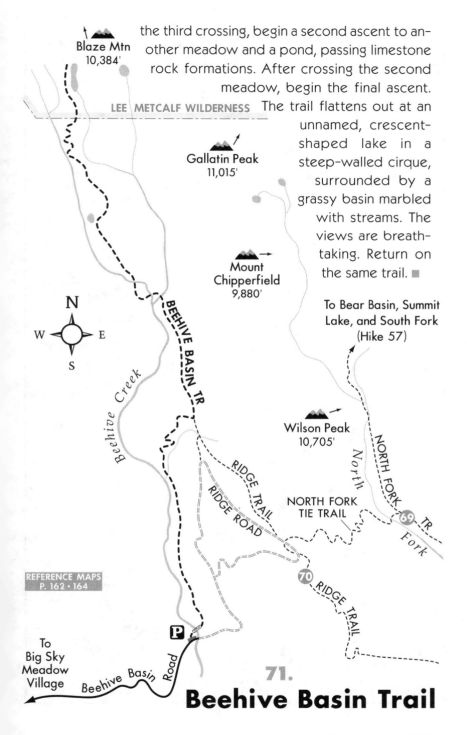

Blaze Mtn
10,384'

LEE METCALF WILDERNESS

Gallatin Peak
11,015'

Mount
Chipperfield
9,880'

To Bear Basin, Summit
Lake, and South Fork
(Hike 57)

N
W E
S

BEEHIVE BASIN TR

Beehive Creek

Wilson Peak
10,705'

North Fork

NORTH FORK TR

RIDGE TRAIL

RIDGE ROAD

NORTH FORK
TIE TRAIL

69

70 RIDGE TRAIL

REFERENCE MAPS
P. 162 · 164

P

To
Big Sky
Meadow
Village

Beehive Basin Road

71.
Beehive Basin Trail

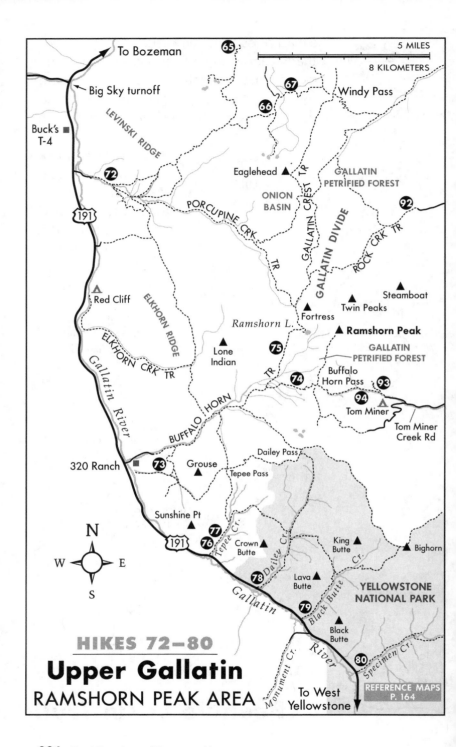

To Bozeman

Big Sky turnoff

Buck's T-4

LEVINSKI RIDGE

5 MILES
8 KILOMETERS

Windy Pass

65
67
66

Eaglehead ▲

GALLATIN CREST TR

GALLATIN PETRIFIED FOREST

ONION BASIN

92

72

191

PORCUPINE CRK TR

GALLATIN DIVIDE

ROCK CRK TR

Red Cliff ⌂

ELKHORN RIDGE

Fortress ▲

Ramshorn L.

Twin Peaks ▲

Steamboat ▲

▲ Ramshorn Peak

GALLATIN PETRIFIED FOREST

ELKHORN CRK TR

Lone Indian ▲

75

TR

74

Buffalo Horn Pass

93

Gallatin River

BUFFALO HORN

94 ⌂
Tom Miner

Tom Miner Creek Rd

320 Ranch ▪ 73

Grouse ▲

Dailey Pass

Tepee Pass

Sunshine Pt ▲

191

N
W · E
S

76 77

Tepee Cr.

Crown Butte ▲

78

Dailey Cr.

King Butte ▲

Bighorn ▲

Lava Butte ▲

YELLOWSTONE NATIONAL PARK

Gallatin

79

Black Butte Cr.

Black Butte ▲

80

Specimen Cr.

HIKES 72–80
Upper Gallatin
RAMSHORN PEAK AREA

Monument Cr.

River

To West Yellowstone

REFERENCE MAPS
P. 164

72. Porcupine Creek—First Creek Loop

Hiking distance: 6.5-mile loop
Hiking time: 3.5 hours
Elevation gain: 650 feet
Maps: U.S.G.S. Lone Indian Peak

map
page 207

       Beartooth Publishing: Bozeman, Big Sky, W. Yellowstone

Summary of hike: The Porcupine Creek Trail begins near the Gallatin River and climbs 9 miles up to its headwaters in Onion Basin at the Gallatin–Yellowstone Divide. En route, the trail gains more than 3,000 feet to the basin and Gallatin Crest Trail along the ridge. Connecting trails lead to the Gallatin Petrified Forest, Eaglehead Mountain, Fortress Mountain, and into Paradise Valley. The first two miles of the trail follow a gentle grade along Porcupine Creek and lead into the Porcupine Elk Preserve. The large, rolling meadows are a vital winter range for elk and home to many coyotes. After the snow melts, moose and deer are frequently spotted in the meadows.

    To continue around a loop, the trail follows First Creek (a tributary of Porcupine Creek), which drains a minor canyon to the north. The First Creek Trail parallels the creek up a scenic, forested canyon. The trail returns through high meadows with spectacular 360-degree vistas of the surrounding mountains, including Lone Mountain at Big Sky Resort.

Driving directions: From Four Corners 9 miles west of Bozeman, take Highway 191 south towards the Gallatin Canyon. Drive 36.5 miles to Porcupine Creek Road on the left, between mile markers 45 and 46. (The turnoff is 2.7 miles south of Big Sky.) Turn left (east) and drive 0.5 miles, passing the log cabins to the trailhead parking area at the end of the road.

Hiking directions: From the left (north) side of the parking area, walk over a fork of Porcupine Creek. Walk through the forested grassland, and pass a cabin on the left. Cross a bridge over Porcupine Creek and head upstream on the south slope of Levinski Ridge. Parallel the creek through open sage brush meadows dotted with pine trees. Traverse the hillside on the old dirt road above the creek. The views span in every direction. Continue through the open meadow to a Y-fork at 0.8 miles.

Begin the loop to the right, and cross a bridge over Porcupine Creek. Within 50 feet is another junction. Take the left fork and ascend the 200-foot slope. On the ridge, Porcupine Creek can be seen placidly flowing through the large, scenic meadow. Descend into the meadow, and cross a bridge over a feeder stream to a junction by a wood post at 1.5 miles. The Porcupine Creek Trail continues east to the right.

For this hike, veer left and rock-hop over the creek. Follow the watercourse upstream a short distance to a 3-way split. The right fork parallels Second Creek. The left fork returns for a shorter and easier 3.4-mile loop. Take the middle fork straight ahead, passing "trail" signs up the First Creek drainage. Follow the banks of First Creek up canyon, crossing the creek two times. After the second crossing, bend left and climb the hill to the highest point of the hike at 6,830 feet. Cross the upper meadow with its dramatic 360-degree vistas. Slowly but steadily descend, losing 600 feet over the next 1.4 miles. Complete the loop by the bridge. Return to the trailhead 0.8 miles to the right. ■

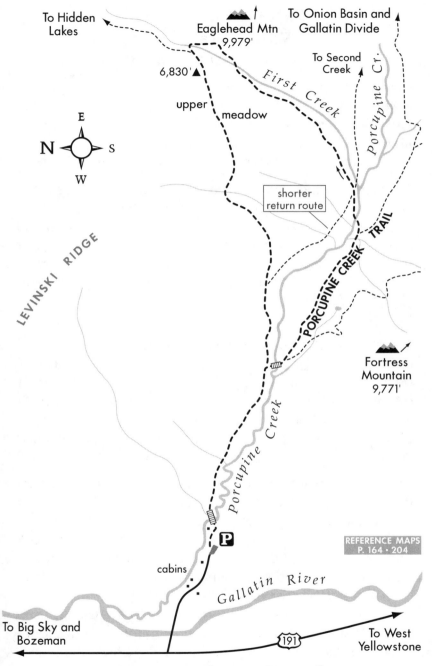

To Hidden Lakes

Eaglehead Mtn
9,979'

To Onion Basin and
Gallatin Divide

To Second
Creek

First Creek

6,830'▲

upper meadow

Porcupine Cr.

N
E
S
W

shorter
return route

LEVINSKI RIDGE

PORCUPINE CREEK TRAIL

Fortress
Mountain
9,771'

Porcupine Creek

REFERENCE MAPS
P. 164 · 204

P

cabins

Gallatin River

To Big Sky and
Bozeman

191

To West
Yellowstone

72. Porcupine Creek

73. Buffalo Horn Creek— Wilson Draw Loop
from the GALLATIN VALLEY

Hiking distance: 4 mile loop
Hiking time: 2 hours
Elevation gain: 700 feet
Maps: U.S.G.S. Sunshine Point
                Beartooth Publishing: Bozeman, Big Sky, W. Yellowstone

Summary of hike: Wilson Draw is a forested, stream-fed canyon south of Buffalo Horn Canyon on the western slope of Grouse Mountain. The draw joins with the Gallatin River and Buffalo Horn Creek by the 320 Guest Ranch. The historic guest ranch, dating back to 1898, sits at the mouth of both canyons. This hike forms a loop along the banks of Buffalo Horn Creek, climbs across the foothills of Grouse Mountain, and returns through Wilson Draw.

Driving directions: From Four Corners 9 miles west of Bozeman, take Highway 191 south towards the Gallatin Canyon. Drive 46 miles to the posted 320 Ranch turnoff on the left at mile marker 36. (The turnoff is 12 miles south of Big Sky.) Turn left and continue 1.1 mile into the mouth of the canyon to the upper trailhead parking area at the end of the road. En route, the road curves left and passes the 320 Ranch cabins.

Hiking directions: From the far end of the parking area, pass the trailhead gate and follow the south side of Big Horn Creek up the canyon. Stroll through the open forest and meadows between the creek on the left and multi-colored, vertical rock walls on the right. At 0.4 miles is a posted junction. The Buffalo Horn Trail continues straight ahead, following the creek to Buffalo Horn Pass and Ramshorn Lake (Hikes 74 and 75).

For this hike, veer right towards Wilson Draw. Gently climb up the hillside through a mixed evergreen forest to overlooks of Buffalo Horn Canyon and the meandering creek. The scenic, curvy path climbs to a 7,200-foot saddle on the west slope of

Grouse Mountain, where the trail levels out. Cross the saddle through a tree-dotted grassland teeming with wildflowers to an unsigned fork. The main trail, straight ahead, leads farther up into Wilson Draw and 3 more miles to Tepee Pass.

For this hike, bear right on the narrow footpath. Descend the south-facing slope into Wilson Draw. At the base of the draw, curve right and head down the forested canyon. Continue descending, losing 500 feet in elevation over the next mile. At the mouth of the canyon near the Gallatin River, curve right. Walk north on the 320 Ranch road, passing cabins along the way. Rejoin the trailhead access road, completing the loop at the trailhead. ■

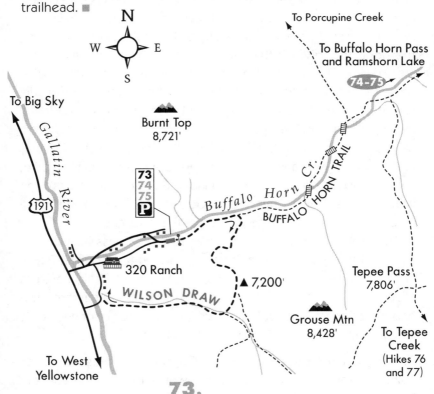

73.
Buffalo Horn Creek–
Wilson Draw Loop
from the GALLATIN VALLEY

74. Buffalo Horn Trail to Buffalo Horn Pass
from the GALLATIN VALLEY

Hiking distance: 13 miles round trip
Hiking time: 6—7 hours
Elevation gain: 1,900 feet
Maps: U.S.G.S. Sunshine Point, Lone Indian Peak, Ramshorn Peak
    Beartooth Publishing: Bozeman, Big Sky, W. Yellowstone

map
page 212

Summary of hike: Ramshorn Peak, the highest mountain in the Gallatin Range at 10,296 feet, is located along the Gallatin Divide near the northwest corner of Yellowstone National Park. Buffalo Horn Pass rests on a saddle south of the bald peak, straddling the ridge that divides the Gallatin and Yellowstone Rivers. The Buffalo Horn Trail, which climbs to the 8,523-foot pass, begins just past the 320 Guest Ranch near the valley floor along the Gallatin. En route, the trail passes through sagebrush, grassland meadows, alpine tundra, and a mixed forest of pine, fir, and spruce. Atop the ridge is the 26,000-acre Gallatin Petrified Forest. Fifty million years ago, volcanic mudflows buried ancient forests of pine, spruce, and deciduous trees. Groundwater silica seeped into the wood pores, transforming the wood into solid rock. Petrified logs and stumps are scattered across the landscape.

The fantastic, 360-degree views from the pass include the forested Buffalo Horn Creek valley, the jagged Spanish Peaks in the Madison Range, cone-shaped Ramshorn Peak, Fortress Mountain, and the dramatic peaks and alpine summits of the Absaroka Range. Over Buffalo Horn Pass, the trail continues east into Tom Miner Basin in Paradise Valley (Hike 96).

Driving directions: From Four Corners 9 miles west of Bozeman, take Highway 191 south towards the Gallatin Canyon. Drive 46 miles to the posted 320 Ranch turnoff on the left at mile marker 36. (The turnoff is 12 miles south of Big Sky.) Turn left and continue 1.1 mile into the mouth of the canyon to the upper trailhead parking area at the end of the road. En route, the road curves left and passes the 320 Ranch cabins.

Hiking directions: Head east past the trailhead gate. Follow the south side of Buffalo Horn Creek up canyon on the Buffalo Horn Trail. Stroll through the open forest and meadows between the creek on the left and multi-colored, vertical rock walls on the right. At 0.4 miles is a posted junction. The right fork leads to Wilson Draw (Hike 73) and Tepee Pass. Stay on the canyon bottom along the creek on the Bufffalo Horn Trail. At just under a mile, cross a bridge over Buffalo Horn Creek and continue up canyon. Cross another bridge over the creek, and meander through the tree-dotted grassland. Cross the creek again on a third bridge to a posted junction at 2 miles. The left fork leads 2 miles to Elkhorn Creek and 8 miles to Porcupine Creek.

Continue straight ahead, staying on the Buffalo Horn Trail as Fortress Mountain and Ramshorn Peak come into view. Drop into Cow Flats, a vast meadow, and cross a bridge over the creek. Walk through the open flats, passing a junction on the right that leads 2.5 miles to Tepee Pass (Hike 76). Rock hop over the creek and head up the hillside. Follow a minor ridge and moderately climb, passing the Buffalo Horn Lakes Trail on the right. Cross a bridge over a fork of Buffalo Horn Creek and climb through a meadow to a Y-fork. To the left, the Ramshorn Lake Trail leads two miles to the lake—Hike 75.

Take the right fork and continue east through the meadow. Buffalo Horn Pass can be seen straight ahead. Continue uphill at a gentle grade, crossing several feeder streams of Buffalo Horn Creek. The last half mile steeply climbs to Buffalo Horn Pass. Atop the pass are scattered whitebark pines, unobstructed world-class panoramas, and a 4-way junction.

To hike farther, the right fork heads south into Yellowstone National Park at Dailey Pass, 2.5 miles ahead (Hike 78). The left (north) fork heads 2 miles to Ramshorn Peak. Straight ahead (east), the route descends 2.3 miles along Trail Creek to Tom Miner Campground in Paradise Valley (Hike 96). ▪

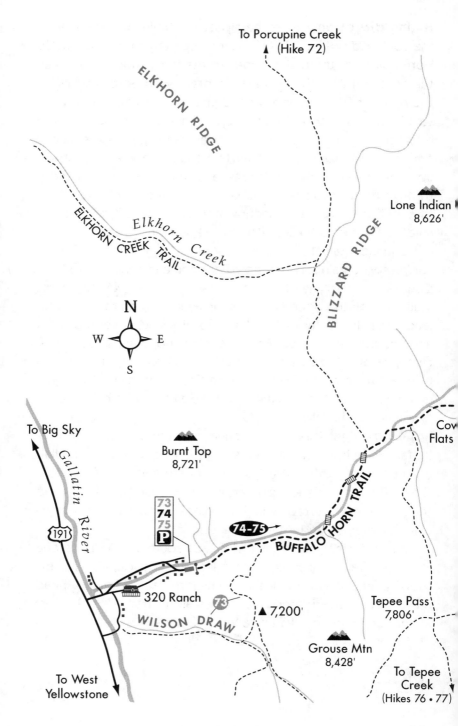

To Porcupine Creek
▲ (Hike 72)

ELKHORN RIDGE

Lone Indian
8,626'

Elkhorn Creek

ELKHORN CREEK TRAIL

BLIZZARD RIDGE

N
W   E
S

To Big Sky

Gallatin River

Burnt Top
8,721'

Cov
Flats

73
74
75
P

74-75

BUFFALO HORN TRAIL

191

320 Ranch

73

▲ 7,200'

Tepee Pass
7,806'

WILSON DRAW

Grouse Mtn
8,428'

To West
Yellowstone

To Tepee
Creek
(Hikes 76 • 77)

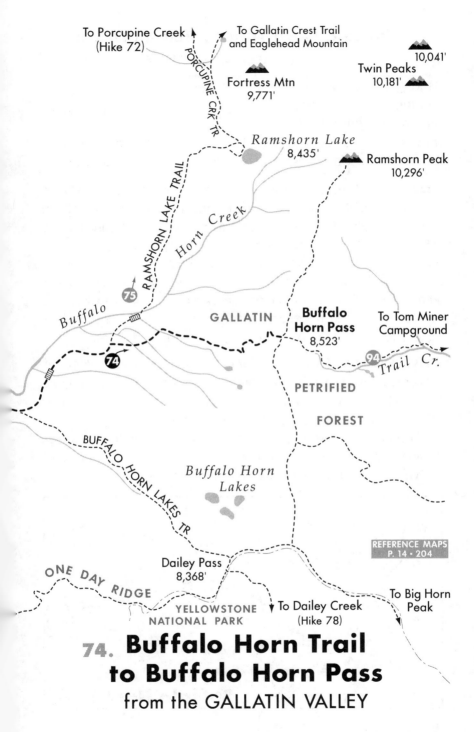

To Porcupine Creek
(Hike 72)

To Gallatin Crest Trail
and Eaglehead Mountain

PORCUPINE CRK TR

Fortress Mtn
9,771'

10,041'
Twin Peaks
10,181'

Ramshorn Lake
8,435'

Ramshorn Peak
10,296'

RAMSHORN LAKE TRAIL

Horn Creek

75

Buffalo

GALLATIN

**Buffalo
Horn Pass**
8,523'

To Tom Miner
Campground

94

Trail Cr.

74

PETRIFIED

FOREST

BUFFALO HORN LAKES TR

*Buffalo Horn
Lakes*

REFERENCE MAPS
P. 14 • 204

Dailey Pass
8,368'

ONE DAY RIDGE

YELLOWSTONE
NATIONAL PARK

To Dailey Creek
(Hike 78)

To Big Horn
Peak

74. **Buffalo Horn Trail
to Buffalo Horn Pass**
from the GALLATIN VALLEY

75. Buffalo Horn Trail to Ramshorn Lake
from the GALLATIN VALLEY

Hiking distance: 13 miles round trip
Hiking time: 6—7 hour
Elevation gain: 1,800 feet

> map
> page 216

Maps: U.S.G.S. Sunshine Point, Lone Indian Peak, Ramshorn Peak
　　　　Beartooth Publishing: Bozeman, Big Sky, W. Yellowstone

Summary of hike: Ramshorn Lake sits at the base of Fortress Mountain and Ramshorn Peak, the highest mountain in the Gallatin Range at 10,289 feet. The circular lake, rimmed with pines, rests 1,800 feet below the towering peaks. It is a popular fishing spot with cutthroat and golden trout. A few undeveloped campsites are located around the lake. The hike begins near the 320 Guest Ranch and follows Buffalo Horn Creek most of the way. The trail passes through lush meadows, spruce and lodgepole pine forests, and conglomerate boulder fields to the lakeshore.

Driving directions: From Four Corners 9 miles west of Bozeman, take Highway 191 south towards the Gallatin Canyon. Drive 46 miles to the posted 320 Ranch turnoff on the left at mile marker 36. (The turnoff is 12 miles south of Big Sky.) Turn left and continue 1.1 mile into the mouth of the canyon to the upper trailhead parking area at the end of the road. En route, the road curves left and passes the 320 Ranch cabins.

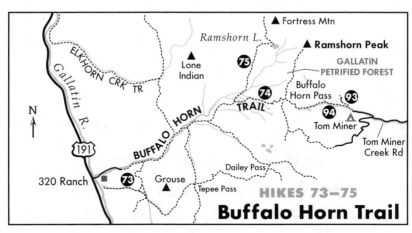

Hiking directions: Head east past the trailhead gate. Follow the south side of Buffalo Horn Creek up canyon on the Buffalo Horn Trail. Stroll through the open forest and meadows between the creek on the left and multi-colored, vertical rock walls on the right. At 0.4 miles is a posted junction. The right fork leads to Wilson Draw (Hike 73) and Tepee Pass. Stay on the canyon bottom along the creek on the Buffalo Horn Trail. At just under a mile, cross a bridge over Buffalo Horn Creek and continue up canyon. Cross another bridge over the creek, and meander through the grassland. Cross the creek again on a third bridge to a posted junction at 2 miles. The left fork leads 2 miles to Elkhorn Creek and 8 miles to Porcupine Creek.

Continue straight ahead, staying on the Buffalo Horn Trail as Fortress Mountain and Ramshorn Peak come into view. Drop into Cow Flats, a vast meadow, and cross a bridge over the creek. Walk through the open flats, passing a junction on the right that leads 2.5 miles to Tepee Pass (Hike 76). Rock hop over the creek and head up the hillside. Follow a minor ridge and moderately climb, passing the Buffalo Horn Lakes Trail on the right. Cross a bridge over a fork of Buffalo Horn Creek and climb through a meadow to a Y-fork. The right fork leads 2 miles to Buffalo Horn Pass and the Gallatin Petrified Forest—Hike 74.

Go left on the Ramshorn Lake Trail, and cross a bridge over a fork of Buffalo Horn Creek. Cross two more log bridges, and rock-hop over the creek. Pass a seasonal pond on the left. Climb through the meadow, with Ramshorn Peak and Fortress Mountain looming over the trail. Curve east, weaving through the forest as the grade gets steeper. Walk through a meadow to a Y-fork. Both forks lead to Ramshorn Lake. For this hike, veer left and descend to the base of Fortress Mountain's jagged vertical wall. Pass horse corrals to a junction. The Porcupine Creek Trail goes left (north) towards Eaglehead Mountain. Bear right and descend to the north end of circular Ramshorn Lake. After enjoying the lakeside area, return by retracing your steps. ▪

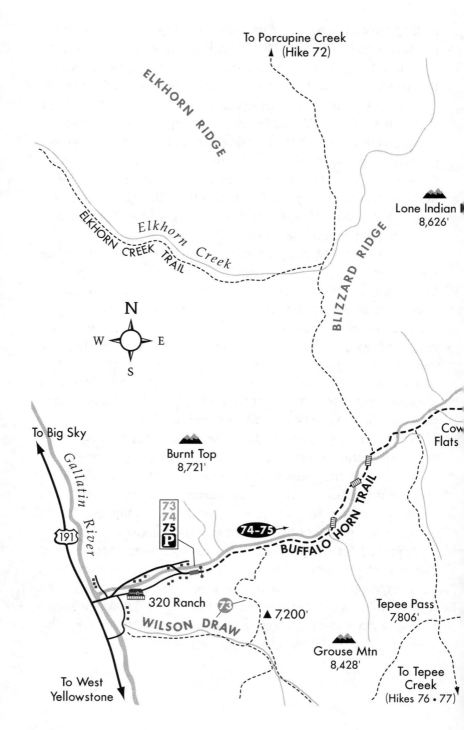

To Porcupine Creek
▲ (Hike 72)

ELKHORN RIDGE

Elkhorn Creek

ELKHORN CREEK TRAIL

BLIZZARD RIDGE

Lone Indian ▲
8,626'

N
W — E
S

To Big Sky

Gallatin River

191

Burnt Top
8,721'

73
74
75
P

74-75 ▶

Cow Flats

BUFFALO HORN TRAIL

320 Ranch

WILSON DRAW

73

▲ 7,200'

Tepee Pass
7,806'

Grouse Mtn
8,428'

To Tepee Creek
(Hikes 76 • 77)

To West Yellowstone

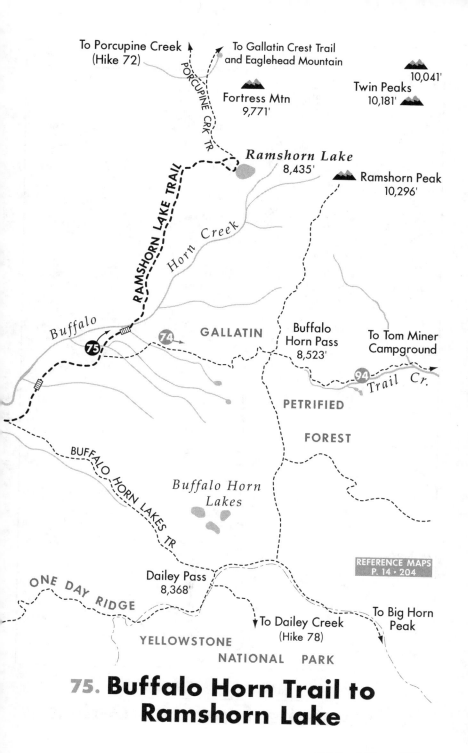

To Porcupine Creek
(Hike 72)

To Gallatin Crest Trail
and Eaglehead Mountain

PORCUPINE CRK TR

Fortress Mtn
9,771'

10,041'

Twin Peaks
10,181'

Ramshorn Lake
8,435'

Ramshorn Peak
10,296'

RAMSHORN LAKE TRAIL

Horn Creek

Buffalo

75

74

GALLATIN

Buffalo
Horn Pass
8,523'

To Tom Miner
Campground

94

Trail Cr.

PETRIFIED

FOREST

BUFFALO HORN LAKES TR

Buffalo Horn
Lakes

REFERENCE MAPS
P. 14 · 204

ONE DAY RIDGE

Dailey Pass
8,368'

To Big Horn
Peak

YELLOWSTONE

To Dailey Creek
(Hike 78)

NATIONAL PARK

**75. Buffalo Horn Trail to
Ramshorn Lake**

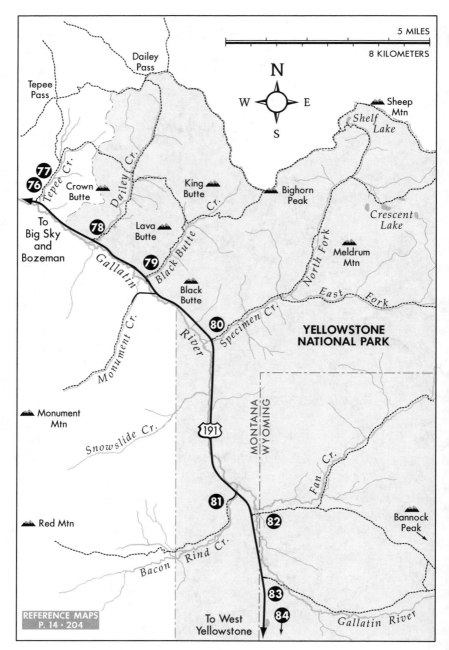

HIKES 76–84

Yellowstone from the Gallatin

Yellowstone National Park from the Upper Gallatin Valley

HIKES 76—84

The headwaters of the Gallatin River begin from the northwest corner of Yellowstone National Park. The area is filled with verdant valleys, alpine meadows, and crystal clear streams fed by alpine springs and snowmelt. These hikes branch off from the Gallatin River and climb up stream-fed valleys surrounded by the peaks of the Gallatin and Madison Ranges. All of the trails in this remote region of the park follow creeks through open, grassy slopes with rock escarpments and forests of aspen, Douglas fir, and lodgepole pine. The trails interconnect with the Hebgen Lake area, the Madison Range, the northern end of the Gallatin Range to Bozeman, Paradise Valley, and to Mammoth in the park.

Hikes 76—80 head northeast along three upper tributaries of the Gallatin. The trails eventually connect with Skyline Ridge, which forms the northwest Yellowstone Park boundary. The hikes take in the first 2—4 miles of the trails along quiet, gentle inclines, but the hikes can easily be extended for a longer outing.

The Bacon Rind Trail—Hike 81—is the only hike in Yellowstone that enters the Madison Range to the west and connects with the Lee Metcalf Wilderness. The lush valleys just north of the Madison River are included in Hikes 82—84.

The vast, open terrain and sweeping landscape throughout this region offers great scenery. The wildlife is abundant, including bear, moose, elk, and many species of birds.

76. Tepee Creek Trail to Tepee Pass

Hiking distance: 6 miles round trip
Hiking time: 3 hours
Elevation gain: 900 feet
Maps: U.S.G.S. Sunshine Point

Summary of hike: The Tepee Creek Trail follows the watercourse of Tepee Creek through expansive grasslands to Tepee Pass at the head of the verdant valley. From the pass are tremendous sweeping views down the wide valley and beyond, from the Madison Range to the Gallatin Range.

Driving directions: From Four Corners 9 miles west of Bozeman, take Highway 191 south towards the Gallatin Canyon. Drive 49.8 miles (16 miles south of the Big Sky turnoff) to the signed trail on the left by mile marker 32. Turn left and park 100 yards ahead by the trailhead.

From West Yellowstone, the trailhead is 33 miles north on Highway 191.

Hiking directions: Head northeast up the wide grassy draw between Sunshine Point and Crown Butte. Follow the trail along Tepee Creek to a signed junction with the Tepee Creek Cutoff Trail at 1.1 mile. The right fork crosses Tepee Creek and leads eastward into Yellowstone (Hike 77). Take the left fork towards Tepee Pass and Buffalo Horn Divide. Climb a small hill, then traverse the hillside above the valley. Continue past the prominent Grouse Mountain and stands of aspens and pines. After numerous dips and rises along the rolling ridges, the trail begins a half-mile ascent to Tepee Pass. At the top of the valley, near a dense stand of evergreens, is a signed 4-way junction on Tepee Pass. The right fork leads 200 yards to a flat area above the saddle with great views. This is the turn-around spot.

To hike farther, the east trail continues two miles to the Yellowstone National Park boundary, then on to Dailey Pass. The north trail from Tepee Pass descends for 2.5 miles to Buffalo Horn Creek (Hikes 74—75). The west trail from Tepee Pass leads down Wilson Draw to the Gallatin River (Hike 73). ∎

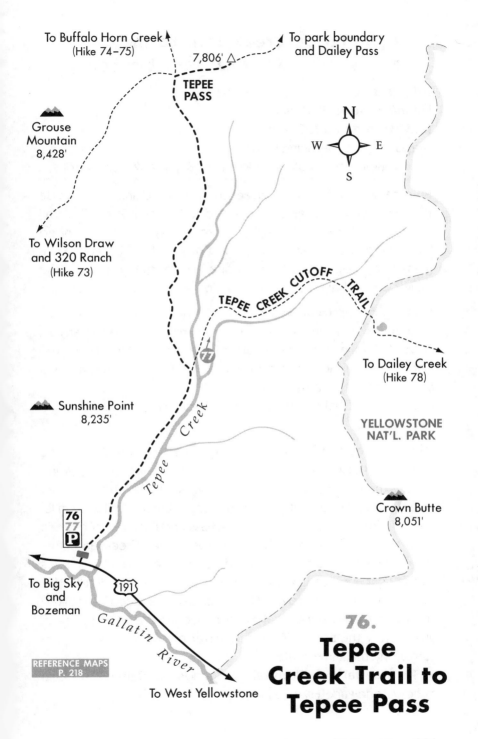

To Buffalo Horn Creek
(Hike 74–75)

7,806'

To park boundary
and Dailey Pass

TEPEE
PASS

N
W   E
S

Grouse
Mountain
8,428'

To Wilson Draw
and 320 Ranch
(Hike 73)

TEPEE CREEK CUTOFF TRAIL

To Dailey Creek
(Hike 78)

Sunshine Point
8,235'

YELLOWSTONE
NAT'L. PARK

Tepee Creek

Crown Butte
8,051'

76
77
P

To Big Sky
and
Bozeman

191

Gallatin River

To West Yellowstone

REFERENCE MAPS
P. 218

76.
Tepee
Creek Trail to
Tepee Pass

77. Tepee Creek Trail to the Yellowstone National Park boundary

Hiking distance: 4.6 miles round trip
Hiking time: 2.5 hours
Elevation gain: 700 feet
Maps: U.S.G.S. Sunshine Point
Beartooth Publishing: Bozeman, Big Sky, W. Yellowstone

Summary of hike: The Tepee Creek Trail begins just outside the northwest corner of Yellowstone National Park. The trail crosses gentle slopes through a broad, grassy valley surrounded by mountains and dense, tree-lined ridges. The hike ends on a grassy ridgetop at the Yellowstone boundary overlooking the Dailey Creek drainage, the next drainage to the east (Hike 78).

Driving directions: From Four Corners 9 miles west of Bozeman, take Highway 191 south towards the Gallatin Canyon. Drive 49.8 miles (16 miles south of the Big Sky turnoff) to the signed trail on the left by mile marker 32. Turn left and park 100 yards ahead by the trailhead.

From West Yellowstone, the trailhead is 33 miles north on Highway 191.

Hiking directions: Hike northeast past the hitching posts, and cross the grassy slopes along the base of Sunshine Point. Follow the open expanse along the west side of Tepee Creek to a signed junction with the Tepee Creek Cutoff Trail at 1.1 mile. The left fork heads north to Tepee Pass and Buffalo Horn Creek (Hikes 74—75). Take the right fork across Tepee Creek, and continue up the hillside on the east side of the creek. The trail curves to the right and heads east up a narrow drainage surrounded by mountains and tree groves. Near the top of a meadow, follow the ridge to the signed Yellowstone boundary on the saddle. Just below the saddle is a pond. After enjoying the views, return along the same route.

To hike farther, the trail descends to Dailey Creek in Yellowstone Park (Hike 78). ■

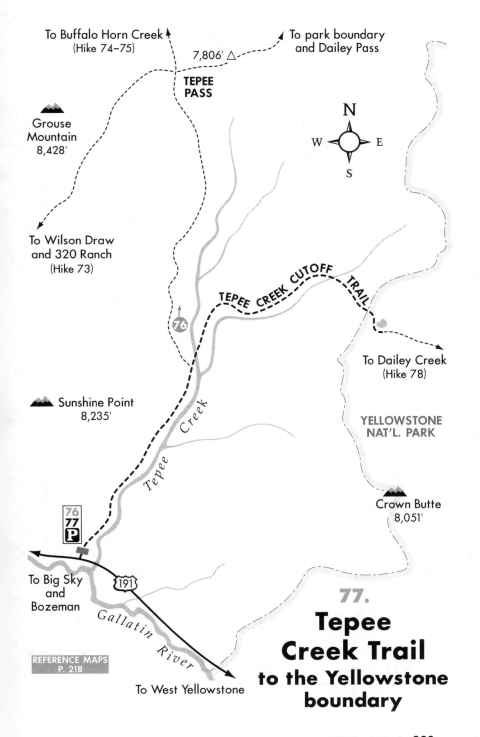

To Buffalo Horn Creek
(Hike 74–75)

To park boundary
and Dailey Pass

7,806' △

**TEPEE
PASS**

Grouse
Mountain
8,428'

N

W   E

S

To Wilson Draw
and 320 Ranch
(Hike 73)

TEPEE CREEK CUTOFF TRAIL

To Dailey Creek
(Hike 78)

Sunshine Point
8,235'

Tepee Creek

YELLOWSTONE
NAT'L. PARK

Crown Butte
8,051'

76
77
P

To Big Sky
and
Bozeman

191

Gallatin River

REFERENCE MAPS
P. 218

To West Yellowstone

77.

Tepee
Creek Trail
to the Yellowstone
boundary

78. Dailey Creek Trail

Hiking distance: 5.2 miles round trip
Hiking time: 2.5 hours
Elevation gain: 350 feet
Maps: U.S.G.S. Sunshine Point and Big Horn Peak
       Beartooth Publishing: Bozeman, Big Sky, W. Yellowstone
       Trails Illustrated: Mammoth Hot Springs

Summary of hike: Dailey Creek is the northernmost drainage in Yellowstone National Park. This backcountry hike makes a gradual ascent up the scenic valley, crossing the rolling sagebrush meadows and open hillsides parallel to Dailey Creek. The hillsides are fringed with aspens and Douglas fir. The impressive Crown Butte, Lava Butte, and King Butte formations are prominent throughout the hike. To the northeast is the Sky Rim Ridge that forms the northeast boundary of Yellowstone.

Driving directions: From Four Corners 9 miles west of Bozeman, take Highway 191 south towards the Gallatin Canyon. Drive 51.4 miles (17.6 miles south of the Big Sky turnoff) to the signed trail on the left between mile markers 30 and 31. Turn left and park in the lot.

From West Yellowstone, the trailhead is 31.4 miles north on Highway 191.

Hiking directions: Head northeast, skirting around the right side of the embankment parallel to Dailey Creek. At a quarter mile, cross the log footbridge over Dailey Creek. To the north, on the Yellowstone Park boundary, is the Crown Butte formation. King Butte rises high in the northeast. Climb the rolling ridge along the east side of the drainage through stands of lodgepole pines. Watch for a vernal pool on the right. At one mile, climb a small hill and cross a couple of streams to a great profile view of Crown Butte, now to the west. Continue through the open meadows past a signed junction with the Black Butte Cutoff Trail on the right at 1.8 miles. The well-defined trail straight ahead reaches the Tepee Creek Cutoff Trail junction at 2.6 miles. This is the turn-around point.

To hike farther, the north trail (straight ahead) climbs three additional miles to Dailey Pass at the park's northern boundary on Sky Rim Ridge. The left fork heads west, over the ridge and into the Tepee Creek valley (Hikes 76 and 77). The Black Butte Cutoff Trail heads over the ridge to the east to the Black Butte Creek drainage—Hike 79. ■

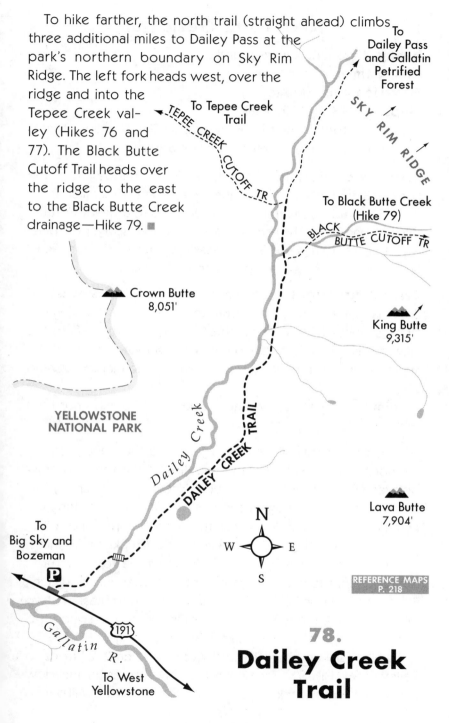

To Dailey Pass and Gallatin Petrified Forest

SKY RIM RIDGE

To Tepee Creek Trail

TEPEE CREEK CUTOFF TR

To Black Butte Creek (Hike 79)

BLACK BUTTE CUTOFF TR

Crown Butte
8,051'

King Butte
9,315'

YELLOWSTONE NATIONAL PARK

Dailey Creek

DAILEY CREEK TRAIL

Lava Butte
7,904'

N
W · E
S

REFERENCE MAPS
P. 218

To Big Sky and Bozeman

P

To West Yellowstone

Gallatin R.

191

78.
Dailey Creek Trail

79. Black Butte Creek Trail

Hiking distance: 4 miles round trip
Hiking time: 2 hours
Elevation gain: 600 feet
Maps: U.S.G.S. Big Horn Peak
       Beartooth Publishing: Bozeman, Big Sky, W. Yellowstone
       Trails Illustrated: Mammoth Hot Springs

Summary of hike: The Black Butte Creek Trail begins at the base of Black Butte in the Gallatin Valley. The trail parallels Black Butte Creek up a beautiful forested drainage to a meadow at the base of King Butte. The narrow valley has aspen, lodgepole pine, and Douglas fir. This trail is an access route up to Big Horn Peak, Shelf Lake, and the summit of Sheep Mountain.

Driving directions: From Four Corners 9 miles west of Bozeman, take Highway 191 south towards the Gallatin Canyon. Drive 53 miles (19.2 miles south of the Big Sky turnoff) to the signed trail on the left. Park on the right, 50 yards south of the signed trail, in the parking area between mile markers 28 and 29.

From West Yellowstone, the trailhead is 29.8 miles north on Highway 191.

Hiking directions: Cross the highway to the signed trail on the north side of Black Butte Creek. Hike up the forested draw between Black Butte and Lava Butte. Head gradually uphill, following the creek through meadows and pine groves along the creek drainage. Meander across the various slopes and rolling hills while remaining close to Black Butte Creek. At 1.5 miles, the trail enters a dense, old growth lodgepole forest. After a quarter mile, the path breaks out into an open meadow. King Butte and Big Horn Peak tower above to the northeast. At two miles, in the meadow at the base of King Butte, is a signed trail junction. This is the turn-around spot.

To hike farther, the left (northwest) fork leads 2.1 miles to Dailey Creek (Hike 78). The right (east) fork crosses the meadow along Black Butte Creek. After crossing the creek, the trail begins

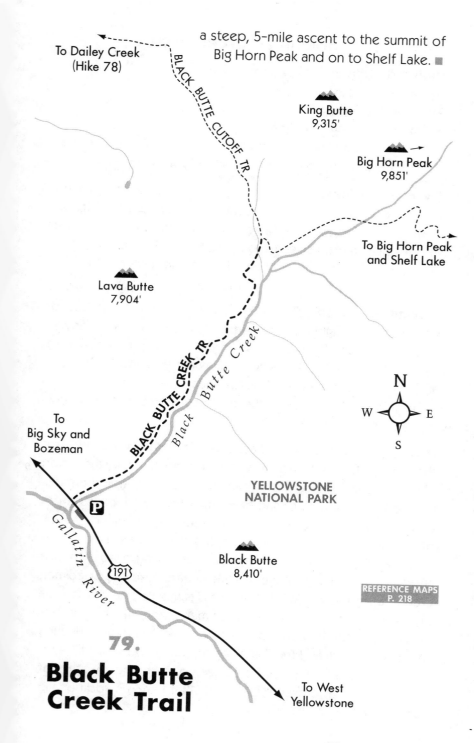

To Dailey Creek
(Hike 78)

BLACK BUTTE CUTOFF TR.

a steep, 5-mile ascent to the summit of
Big Horn Peak and on to Shelf Lake. ▪

King Butte
9,315'

Big Horn Peak
9,851'

To Big Horn Peak
and Shelf Lake

Lava Butte
7,904'

BLACK BUTTE CREEK TR.

Black Butte Creek

To
Big Sky and
Bozeman

N
W ← → E
S

YELLOWSTONE
NATIONAL PARK

P

Gallatin River

191

Black Butte
8,410'

REFERENCE MAPS
P. 218

79.
**Black Butte
Creek Trail**

To West
Yellowstone

80. Specimen Creek Trail

Hiking distance: 4.2 miles round trip
Hiking time: 2 hours
Elevation gain: 240 feet
Maps: U.S.G.S. Big Horn Peak
      Beartooth Publishing: Bozeman, Big Sky, W. Yellowstone
      Trails Illustrated: Mammoth Hot Springs

Summary of hike: The nearly flat Specimen Creek Trail follows Specimen Creek up the canyon through a mature forest dominated by lodgepole pines. This beautiful drainage crosses bridges over feeder streams to an open meadow at the confluence of the North Fork and East Fork of Specimen Creek. The meadow is frequented by elk and moose.

Driving directions: From Four Corners 9 miles west of Bozeman, take Highway 191 south towards the Gallatin Canyon. Drive 55.3 miles (21.5 miles south of the Big Sky turnoff) to the signed trail on the left between mile markers 25 and 26. Turn left and park by the trailhead 30 yards ahead.

From West Yellowstone, the trailhead is 27.5 miles north on Highway 191.

Hiking directions: Head east along Specimen Creek through the lodgepole pine forest. Pass talus slopes on the northern side of the narrow drainage. As the canyon widens, the trail alternates between stands of pines and open meadows. At 1.3 miles, cross a footbridge over a stream. Traverse the forested hillside to another footbridge over a stream and a signed trail split at two miles. The right fork follows the Sportsman Lake Trail to High Lake and Sportsman Lake, 6 and 8 miles ahead. Take the Specimen Creek Trail to the left. Within minutes is campsite WE1. The campsite sits in an open meadow by Specimen Creek, which meanders through the meadow. A short distance ahead is the confluence of the North Fork and the East Fork, the turn-around spot.

To hike farther, the trail continues up to the headwaters of the North Fork at Crescent Lake and Shelf Lake, an additional 5 miles ahead. ■

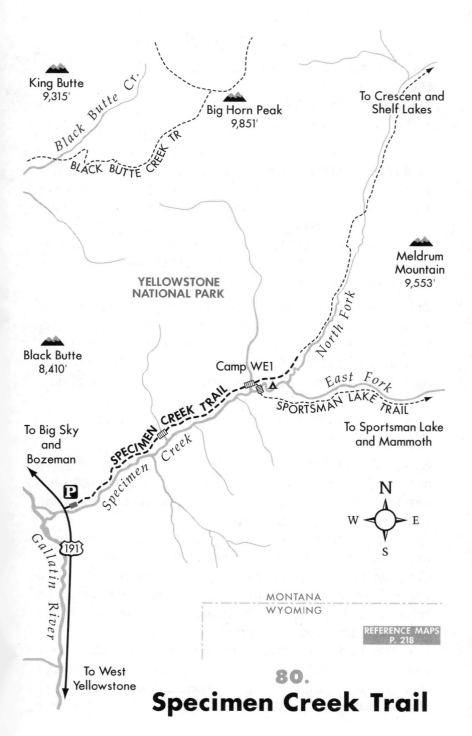

King Butte
9,315'

Black Butte Cr.

Big Horn Peak
9,851'

To Crescent and
Shelf Lakes

BLACK BUTTE CREEK TR.

YELLOWSTONE
NATIONAL PARK

Meldrum
Mountain
9,553'

Black Butte
8,410'

Camp WE1

North Fork

East Fork

SPECIMEN CREEK TRAIL

SPORTSMAN LAKE TRAIL

To Big Sky
and
Bozeman

Specimen Creek

To Sportsman Lake
and Mammoth

P

To West
Yellowstone

Gallatin River

191

N
W E
S

MONTANA
WYOMING

REFERENCE MAPS
P. 218

80.
Specimen Creek Trail

81. Bacon Rind Creek Trail

Hiking distance: 4.2 miles round trip
Hiking time: 2 hours
Elevation gain: 200 feet
Maps: U.S.G.S. Divide Lake
Trails Illustrated: Mammoth Hot Springs

Summary of hike: The Bacon Rind Creek Trail is the only hike inside Yellowstone that heads west from the Gallatin Valley. The flat, easy trail parallels the meandering Bacon Rind Creek through a valley surrounded by high mountain peaks. Moose, elk, and grizzly bears frequent the meadow. Beyond the western park boundary, the trail enters the Lee Metcalf Wilderness in the Gallatin National Forest.

Driving directions: From Four Corners 9 miles west of Bozeman, take Highway 191 south towards the Gallatin Canyon. Drive 59.3 miles (25.5 miles south of the Big Sky turnoff) to the trailhead sign on the right between mile markers 22 and 23. Turn right on the unpaved road, and drive 0.3 miles to the parking area.

From West Yellowstone, the trailhead is 23.5 miles north on Highway 191.

Hiking directions: Head south past the trail sign along the north side of Bacon Rind Creek. Follow the drainage upstream through beautiful stands of pine and fir. The path remains close to the riparian watercourse for the first 0.7 miles, where the valley opens to the Gallatin River. Bacon Rind Creek flows placidly through the wide valley between the forested hillsides. Continue up the draw to the head of the valley and cross a stream. Evergreens enclose the top of the meadow at the signed Yellowstone National Park boundary. This is the turn-around point. To return, reverse your route.

To hike farther, the trail enters the Lee Metcalf Wilderness, crosses Migration Creek, and eventually ascends to Monument Mountain (8 miles from the park boundary) and Cone Peak (7 miles from the park boundary). ■

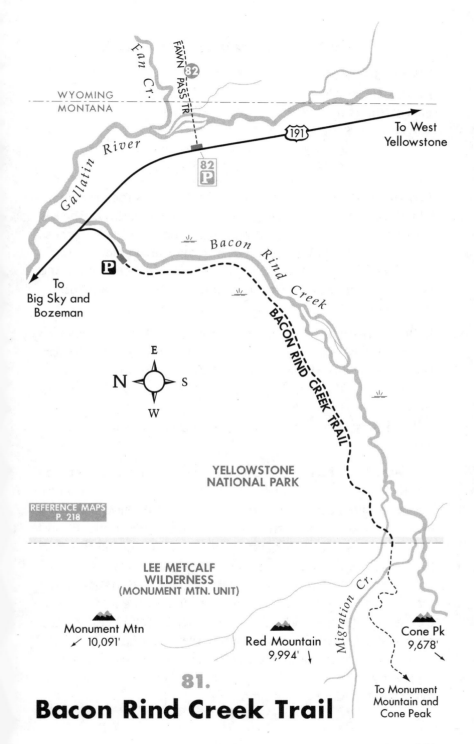

FAWN PASS TR.

82

WYOMING
MONTANA

Fan Cr.

Gallatin River

191

To West
Yellowstone

82
P

To
Big Sky and
Bozeman

P

Bacon Rind Creek

BACON RIND CREEK TRAIL

E

N · S

W

YELLOWSTONE
NATIONAL PARK

REFERENCE MAPS
P. 218

LEE METCALF
WILDERNESS
(MONUMENT MTN. UNIT)

Migration Cr.

Monument Mtn
10,091'

Red Mountain
9,994'

Cone Pk
9,678'

To Monument
Mountain and
Cone Peak

81.
Bacon Rind Creek Trail

82. Fawn Pass Trail to Fan Creek

Hiking distance: 3 miles round trip
Hiking time: 1.5 hours
Elevation gain: 200 feet
Maps: U.S.G.S. Divide Lake
Beartooth Publishing: Bozeman, Big Sky, W. Yellowstone
Trails Illustrated: Mammoth Hot Springs

Summary of hike: The Fawn Pass Trail to Fan Creek is an easy hike through forested, rolling hills and scenic meadows. The Fan Creek Trail (not shown on the U.S.G.S. map) is a fishing access trail established in the early 1980s. From the junction with the Fawn Pass Trail, the Fan Creek Trail heads northeast along the creek through Fan Creek meadow. Moose and elk frequent this beautiful meadow.

Driving directions: From Four Corners 9 miles west of Bozeman, take Highway 191 south towards the Gallatin Canyon. Drive 60 miles (26.2 miles south of the Big Sky turnoff) to the signed trail on the left, just south of mile marker 22. Turn left and park in the trailhead parking area.

From West Yellowstone, the trailhead is 22.8 miles north on Highway 191.

Hiking directions: Head east down a short flight of steps on the Fawn Pass Trail. After the trail register, cross the meadow marbled with meandering streams that form the upper Gallatin River. A series of wooden footbridges cross the wetlands and various lucid streams. Ascend the slope and enter the forested hillside. Cross the gently rolling hills to a signed trail split at 1.4 miles. The Fawn Pass Trail bears right to the Big Horn Pass Cutoff Trail and Fawn Pass. Take the Fan Creek Trail to the left. The trail descends into the wide open meadow to Fan Creek. At the creek is a wonderful picnic spot and place to rest.

To hike farther, the trail follows Fan Creek through the mountain valley for another 6 miles to the Sportsman Lake Trail, wading across Fan Creek three times. ■

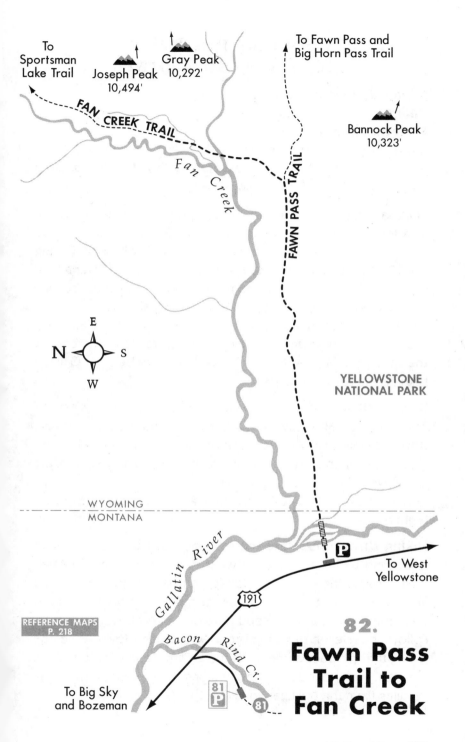

To
Sportsman
Lake Trail

Joseph Peak
10,494'

Gray Peak
10,292'

To Fawn Pass and
Big Horn Pass Trail

Bannock Peak
10,323'

FAN CREEK TRAIL

Fan Creek

FAWN PASS TRAIL

E
N S
W

YELLOWSTONE
NATIONAL PARK

WYOMING
MONTANA

P

To West
Yellowstone

Gallatin River

191

Bacon

Rind Cr.

81
P

81

To Big Sky
and Bozeman

REFERENCE MAPS
P. 218

82.
**Fawn Pass
Trail to
Fan Creek**

83. Big Horn Pass Trail
along the UPPER GALLATIN RIVER

Hiking distance: 1 to 12 miles round trip
Hiking time: Variable
Elevation gain: 150 feet
Maps: U.S.G.S. Divide Lake and Joseph Peak
Beartooth Publishing: Bozeman, Big Sky, W. Yellowstone
Trails Illustrated: Mammoth Hot Springs

Summary of hike: The Upper Gallatin Valley is a vast, open meadow that stretches along the Upper Gallatin River for many miles, making it easy to choose your own hiking distance. The Big Horn Pass Trail parallels the upper end of the Gallatin River all the way up to its headwaters. The relaxing hike through the scenic, treeless valley offers excellent trout fishing and wildlife viewing. The trail eventually leads over Big Horn Pass and Bannock Peak, which can be seen looming in the distance at the end of the valley. The headwaters of the Gallatin River begin at Gallatin Lake just south of the pass.

Driving directions: From Four Corners 9 miles west of Bozeman, take Highway 191 south towards the Gallatin Canyon. Drive 61.5 miles (27.7 miles south of the Big Sky turnoff) to the signed trail on the left between mile markers 20 and 21. Turn left and drive 0.2 miles to the parking area.

From West Yellowstone, the trailhead is 21.3 miles north on Highway 191.

Hiking directions: Take the trail southeast past the hitching posts and trail sign along the west edge of the Gallatin River. Walk through the stands of lodgepole pines, heading upstream along the winding river. At a quarter mile, cross the log bridge over the river. Continue southeast on the well-defined path. Follow the river through the broad, grassy meadows while enjoying the spectacular views of the Gallatin Valley stretching to the east. Turn around at any point along the trail. Big Horn Pass is 12 miles from the trailhead. ■

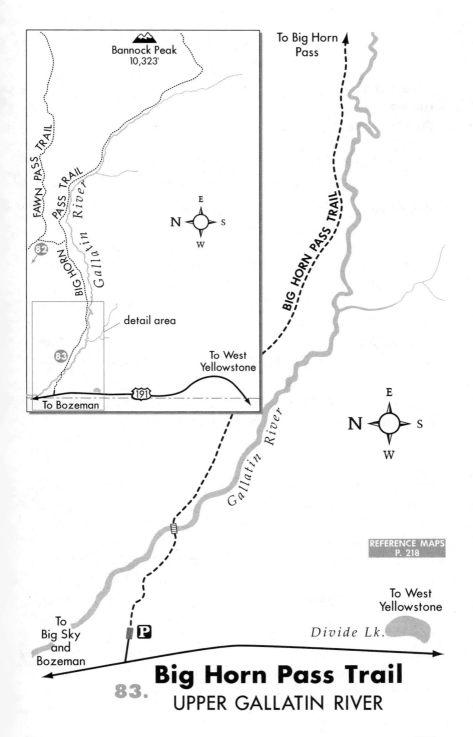

Bannock Peak
10,323'

To Big Horn
Pass

FAWN PASS TRAIL

PASS TRAIL

Gallatin River

BIG HORN

82

detail area

83

To West
Yellowstone

191

To Bozeman

BIG HORN PASS TRAIL

Gallatin River

REFERENCE MAPS
P. 218

To West
Yellowstone

Divide Lk.

To
Big Sky
and
Bozeman

P

Big Horn Pass Trail
83. UPPER GALLATIN RIVER

84. Gneiss Creek Trail
from the GALLATIN

Hiking distance: 3.6 miles round trip
Hiking time: 2 hours
Elevation gain: 300 feet
Maps: U.S.G.S. Richards Creek
       Beartooth Publishing: Bozeman, Big Sky, W. Yellowstone
       Trails Illustrated: Mammoth Hot Springs

Summary of hike: This hike follows the first section of the Gneiss Creek Trail from the northwest trailhead in the Gallatin. The 14-mile trail leads through the Madison Valley, crossing several creeks en route to the southern trailhead at the Madison River bridge (see inset map). This hike is an easy walk through the beautiful open terrain to Campanula Creek, a tributary of Gneiss Creek. The valley is abundant with wildlife.

Driving directions: From Four Corners 9 miles west of Bozeman, take Highway 191 south towards the Gallatin Canyon. Drive 72.2 miles (38.4 miles south of the Big Sky turnoff) to the signed trail on the left between mile markers 9 and 10. Turn left and park in the area straight ahead, past Fir Ridge Cemetery.

From West Yellowstone, the trailhead is 10.6 miles north on Highway 191.

Hiking directions: Follow the old, grassy two-track road east through aspen and pine groves. Cross a small rise and parallel the signed Yellowstone Park boundary. At 0.3 miles, the trail enters the park at a sign-in register. Continue along the ridge above Duck Creek and Richards Creek to the south. Head east along the rolling hills. The trail gradually loses elevation past the forested slopes of Sandy Butte to the right. At the east end of Sandy Butte, descend into the draw to Campanula Creek. Follow the creek upstream a short distance to the creek crossing, the turnaround point for this hike.

To hike farther, cross the creek and continue southeast through the open, flat valley along Gneiss Creek. ■

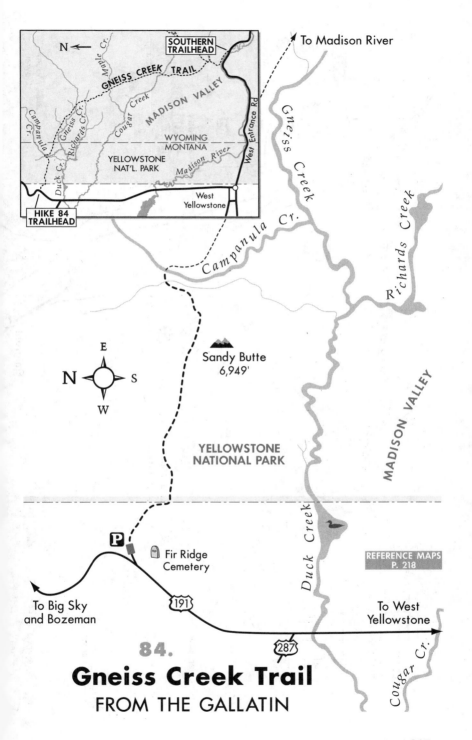

To Madison River

SOUTHERN TRAILHEAD

N ←

GNEISS CREEK TRAIL

Maple Cr.

Cougar Creek

MADISON VALLEY

WYOMING
MONTANA

YELLOWSTONE
NAT'L. PARK

Madison River

Campanula Cr.

Gneiss Cr.

Richards Cr.

Duck Cr.

West Entrance Rd

HIKE 84
TRAILHEAD

West
Yellowstone

Gneiss Creek

Richards Creek

Campanula Cr.

Sandy Butte
6,949'

N
E
S
W

YELLOWSTONE
NATIONAL PARK

MADISON VALLEY

Duck Creek

REFERENCE MAPS
P. 218

P

Fir Ridge
Cemetery

191

To Big Sky
and Bozeman

To West
Yellowstone

287

Cougar Cr.

84.
Gneiss Creek Trail
FROM THE GALLATIN

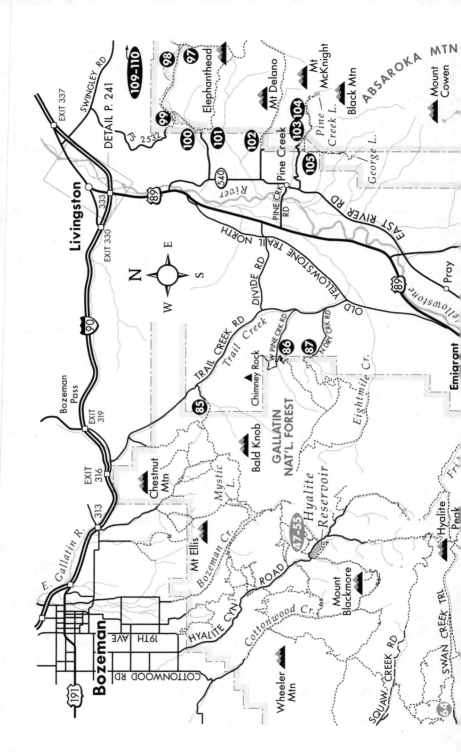

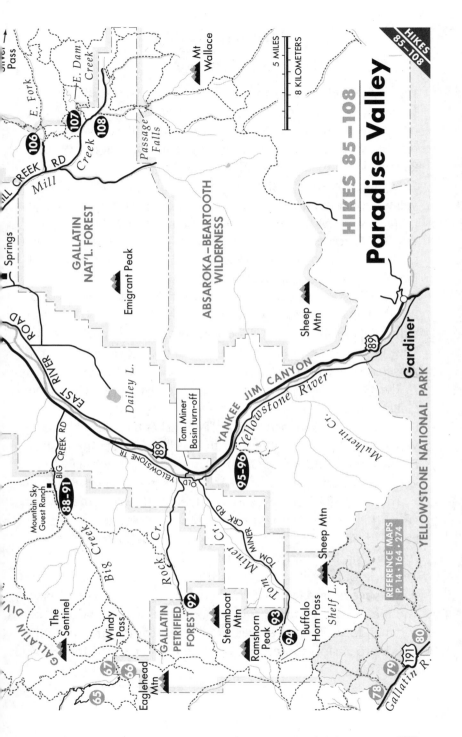

Mt
Wallace

5 MILES

8 KILOMETERS

107

108

106

E. Fork

E. Dam Creek

ILL CREEK RD

Mill Creek

Passage Falls

GALLATIN NAT'L. FOREST

ABSAROKA–BEARTOOTH WILDERNESS

Emigrant Peak

Springs

Sheep Mtn

YANKEE JIM CANYON

89

Gardiner

Yellowstone River

Mulherin Cr.

YELLOWSTONE NATIONAL PARK

EAST RIVER ROAD

Dailey L.

Tom Miner Basin turn-off

89

OLD YELLOWSTONE TR.

95-96

BIG CREEK RD

88-91

Mountain Sky Guest Ranch

Big Creek

Rock Cr.

Tom Miner

TOM MINER CRK RD

GALLATIN PETRIFIED FOREST

92

Steamboat Mtn

Ramshorn Peak

93

94

Buffalo Horn Pass

Sheep Mtn

Shelf L.

REFERENCE MAPS
P. 14 • 164 • 274

GALLATIN DIVIDE

The Sentinel

Windy Pass

Eaglehead Mtn

67

66

65

78

79

80

191

Gallatin R.

Paradise Valley

HIKES 85—108

Paradise Valley is known as the Valley of the Yellowstone River. The river flows through the valley from the north end of Yellowstone National Park to Livingston. It is a wide, scenic valley bordered on the east by the steep, craggy Absaroka Range and on the west by the Gallatin Range.

Highway 89 follows the course of the river through the broad valley, connecting Livingston with Gardiner and Yellowstone. Livingston sits at the head of the verdant valley in the north. The town of Gardiner is located at the other end of the valley by the northern entrance to Yellowstone Park. It is the only approach into the park that is open all year.

The hikes in this section are divided into the west side of Paradise Valley—heading into the Gallatin Range—and the east side of Paradise Valley—heading into the Absaroka Range. The hikes access a vast network of trails in the Gallatins, the Absaroka–Beartooth Wilderness, and Yellowstone Park.

The Gallatin Mountain Range separates Paradise Valley from Gallatin Canyon. The 10,000-foot Gallatin Range runs from Bozeman to Yellowstone National Park. Hikes 84—92 head westward from Paradise Valley into the Gallatins. Atop the Gallatin Divide is the 26,000-acre Gallatin Petrified Forest, an ancient forest of petrified pine, spruce, and tropical trees (Hikes 89—90).

The 930,584-acre Absaroka–Beartooth Wilderness, the second largest wilderness area in Montana, lies to the east of Paradise Valley. The Absaroka Range and the Beartooth Range run through the wilderness. Hikes 93—107 are located on the east side of Paradise Valley. The trails travel through steep, forested valleys amongst the craggy peaks of the Absaroka Range. The area is known for heavily wooded slopes and high ridge-top meadows. The Absarokas and the Beartooths stretch southward into Yellowstone, forming an integral part of the park's ecosystem.

Livingston

85. Trail Creek Trail
(Newman Trail)
GALLATIN RANGE from PARADISE VALLEY

Hiking distance: 4 miles round trip
Hiking time: 2 hours
Elevation gain: 400 feet
Maps: U.S.G.S. Bald Knob
U.S.D.A. Gallatin National Forest East Half map
Beartooth Publishing: Bozeman, Big Sky, West Yellowstone

Summary of hike: Trail Creek is located at the north end of the Gallatin Range in Paradise Valley. The trail along the creek is part of a trail system linking Bozeman with the upper end of Paradise Valley. The pastoral trail (also known as the Newman Trail) follows a section of Trail Creek, with surroundings ranging from open, rolling grassland with magnificent vistas to intimate pine forests. The hike leads to the Trail Creek cabin, a forest service rental cabin at an elevation of 6,200 feet. The cabin has a wood stove, a horse corral, and an outhouse. A portion of the trail crosses private land, so stay on the designated route. Past the cabin, the trail continues west over the divide to the Bear Lakes, Mystic Lake, and Bear Canyon.

Driving directions: FROM BOZEMAN: From Bozeman, drive 7 miles east on I-90 to the Trail Creek Road exit atop Bozeman Pass (Exit 316). It is the second exit east of Bozeman. Turn right on Trail Creek Road, and drive 7.7 scenic miles to signed Newman Road. Turn right and continue 1.1 mile to the trailhead parking area on the right at the end of the public road.

FROM PARADISE VALLEY: From Livingston at the I-90 and Highway 89 junction (Exit 333), drive 8.5 miles south on Highway 89 to the signed Divide Road. (A group of large green dumpsters are at the Divide Road junction.) Turn right on Divide Road, and drive 0.7 miles to a Y-fork. Veer left on the Old Yellowstone Trail and go 0.1 mile, then turn right on Divide Road again. Continue 4.2

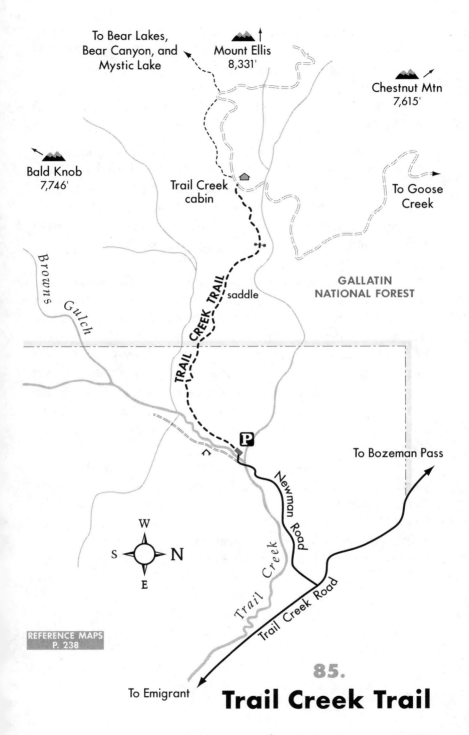

To Bear Lakes,
Bear Canyon, and
Mystic Lake

Mount Ellis
8,331'

Chestnut Mtn
7,615'

Bald Knob
7,746'

Trail Creek
cabin

To Goose
Creek

Browns Gulch

GALLATIN
NATIONAL FOREST

TRAIL CREEK TRAIL

saddle

To Bozeman Pass

P

Newman Road

W

S — N

E

Trail Creek

Trail Creek Road

REFERENCE MAPS
P. 238

85.
Trail Creek Trail

To Emigrant

miles to a T-junction with Trail Creek Road. Turn right and drive 5.5 miles to the signed Newman Road. Turn left and continue 1.1 mile to the trailhead parking area on the right at the end of the public road.

Divide Road is 13.4 miles north of Emigrant and 43 miles north of Gardiner.

Hiking directions: Pass the trailhead kiosk and head up the rise above cascading Trail Creek. Traverse the northwest slope through flower-filled grasslands dotted with aspen and pines while overlooking the creek. Follow the gentle uphill grade while enjoying the sweeping vistas across the rolling valley to Bald Knob, Mount Ellis, and Chestnut Mountain. Round the southern tip of the mountain, curving into a wide side canyon of Trail Creek. Head west up the canyon, and enter the Gallatin National Forest, leaving the private property easement. Cross the open, sloping meadow, where there are great views in every direction. At 1.5 miles, leave the national forest and reenter the private land. Descend through the flower-filled meadow. Cross a minor saddle and enter the pine forest. Pass through a trail gate, and weave through the forest with small dips and rises. Emerge into a large meadow by an old dirt road and the Trail Creek Cabin on the right. After exploring the area, return by retracing your steps.

To extend the hike, the trail continues west—located sixty yards up the road to the left. This route leads over the divide to Bear Lakes and Mystic Lake. The trail also connects with the Bear Canyon Trail (Hike 30). To the right, the unpaved, vehicle-restricted road skirts the northeast base of Chestnut Mountain 5.3 miles to the Goose Creek Trailhead, located off of Trail Creek Road. ∎

86. West Pine Creek Trail
GALLATIN RANGE from PARADISE VALLEY

Hiking distance: 5 miles round trip
Hiking time: 3 hours
Elevation gain: 1,400 feet
Maps: U.S.G.S. Bald Knob and Big Draw

map page 247

   U.S.D.A. Gallatin National Forest East Half map
   Beartooth Publishing: Absaroka Beartooth Wilderness

Summary of hike: The West Pine Creek Trail traverses high above West Pine Creek at the upper end of the Gallatins. The trail zigzags up an eastern mountain slope through open meadows and groves of pines to amazing overlooks. Along the way, and atop the 7,834-foot summit, are 360-degree vistas of the Gallatin Range, the Absaroka Range, Paradise Valley, the snow-capped peaks within Yellowstone National Park, and Chimney Rock. Chimney Rock is the distinct smokestack-shaped formation to the north.

Driving directions: FROM BOZEMAN: From Bozeman, drive 7 miles east on I-90 to the Trail Creek Road exit atop Bozeman Pass (Exit 316). It is the second exit east of Bozeman. Turn right on Trail Creek Road, and drive 15.2 scenic miles to signed West Pine Creek Road. Turn right and continue 3.2 miles to a posted fork. Curve left onto F.S. Road 976 (signed for the West Pine Trailhead), and wind 1.4 miles up the narrow, curving road to the trailhead at the end of the road.

FROM PARADISE VALLEY: From Livingston at the I-90 and Highway 89 junction (Exit 333), drive 8.5 miles south on Highway 89 to the signed Divide Road. (A group of large green dumpsters are at the Divide Road junction.) Turn right on Divide Road, and drive 0.7 miles to a Y-fork. Veer left on the Old Yellowstone Trail and go 0.1 mile, then turn right on the Divide Road again. Continue 4.2 miles to a T-junction with Trail Creek Road. Turn left and drive 2 miles to the signed West Pine Creek Road. Turn right and continue 3.2 miles to a posted fork. Curve left onto F.S. Road 976 (signed for the West Pine Trailhead), and wind 1.4 miles up the narrow, curving road to the trailhead at the end of the road.

Divide Road is 13.4 miles north of Emigrant and 43 miles north of Gardiner.

Hiking directions: Walk up the open grassland slope with great views of the surrounding mountains. Chimney Rock can be seen to the north. Wind up the mountain through the sloping flower-filled meadows and pockets of pines. Continue climbing through a skeleton forest, remnants from the Fridley Fire in the summer of 2001. Zigzag up seven switchbacks to the upper south slope of West Pine Creek Canyon. (At the fourth switchback are beautiful lava rock outcrops.) After the seventh switchback, the path reaches a large grassy knoll overlooking Paradise Valley and the Absaroka Range. A view spans up Mill Creek Canyon on the other side of Paradise Valley. Walk through the massive, sloping meadow, and pass through a trail gate. Traverse the mountain to a 7,350-foot saddle and curve left. Follow the ridge uphill among pockets of scattered pines. Near the summit, in a lava rock bed, are pink-colored bitterroot flowers, the Montana state flower. The scenic overlook sits atop a rounded, grassy knoll marked with a 3-foot cairn. This is our turn-around spot.

To extend the hike, the trail follows the ridge from peak to peak, reaching a T-junction with the North Dry Divide Trail just east of the Gallatin Divide at 5 miles. ■

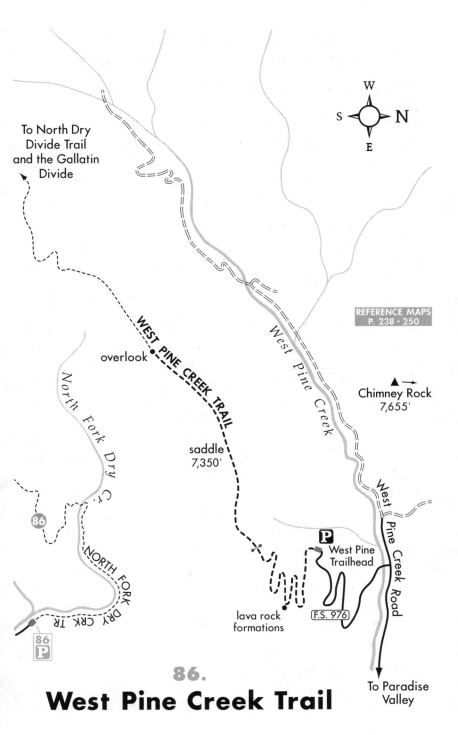

To North Dry
Divide Trail
and the Gallatin
Divide

West Pine Creek

overlook

WEST PINE CREEK TRAIL

North Fork Dry Cr.

saddle
7,350'

REFERENCE MAPS
P. 238 · 250

Chimney Rock
7,655'

West Pine Creek

86

NORTH FORK DRY CRK TR

86 P

P West Pine
Trailhead

West Pine Creek Road

F.S. 976

lava rock
formations

To Paradise
Valley

86.
West Pine Creek Trail

87. North Fork Dry Creek Trail
GALLATIN RANGE from PARADISE VALLEY

Hiking distance: 6 miles round trip
Hiking time: 3 hours
Elevation gain: 1,100 feet
Maps: U.S.G.S. Big Draw
U.S.D.A. Gallatin National Forest East Half map
Beartooth Publishing: Absaroka Beartooth Wilderness

Summary of hike: The North Dry Creek Trail is in the foothills of the upper Gallatin Range on the west side of Paradise Valley. The trail is a vehicle-restricted, two-track grassy road that winds up the mountain at a gentle grade. The route travels through an open, tree-rimmed canyon and pine forests to phenomenal panoramic views of Paradise Valley and the Absaroka Mountains.

Driving directions: FROM BOZEMAN: From Bozeman, drive 7 miles east on I-90 to the Trail Creek Road exit atop Bozeman Pass (Exit 316). It is the second exit east of Bozeman. Turn right on Trail Creek Road, and drive 16.8 scenic miles to signed North Dry Creek Road. Turn right and continue 3.1 miles to the circular trailhead parking area at the end of the road.

FROM PARADISE VALLEY: From Livingston at the I-90 and Highway 89 junction (Exit 333), drive 8.5 miles south on Highway 89 to the signed Divide Road. (A group of large green dumpsters are at the Divide Road junction.) Turn right on Divide Road, and drive 0.7 miles to a Y-fork. Veer left on the Old Yellowstone Trail and go 0.1 mile, then turn right on Divide Road again. Continue 4.2 miles to a T-junction with Trail Creek Road. Turn left and drive 3.6 miles to the signed North Dry Creek Road. Turn right and continue 3.1 miles to the signed trailhead parking area at the end of the road.

Divide Road is 13.4 miles north of Emigrant and 43 miles north of Gardiner.

Hiking directions: Head 100 yards up the grassy, two-track road to a road gate. To the left of the locked gate is a trail gate. Pass through and gently gain elevation up the open, tree-lined

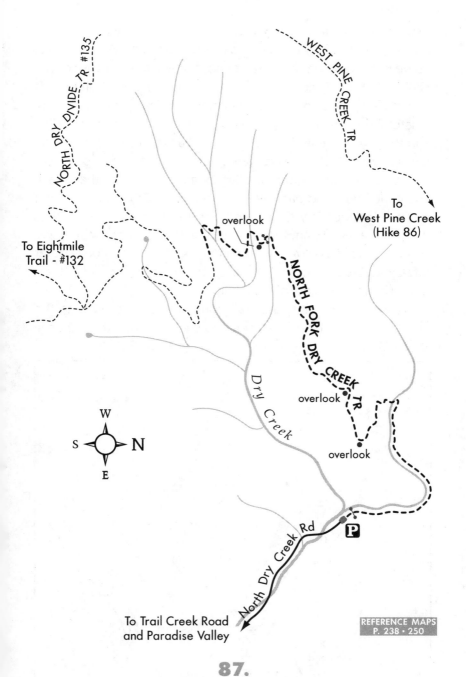

NORTH DRY DIVIDE TR #135

WEST PINE CREEK TR

To
West Pine Creek
(Hike 86)

overlook

NORTH FORK DRY CREEK TR

To Eightmile
Trail - #132

Dry Creek

overlook

W
S — N
E

overlook

North Dry Creek Rd

P

To Trail Creek Road
and Paradise Valley

REFERENCE MAPS
P. 238 · 250

87.
North Fork Dry Creek Trail

canyon surrounded by mountains. Steadily climb as the canyon narrows, and follow the east side of the drainage. At a half mile, curve left on a wide U-shaped bend, following the course of the seasonal North Fork of Dry Creek. At one mile, by a sharp left switchback, cross over the ephemeral drainage. Curve left by a natural rock wall to an overlook with vistas of Paradise Valley and the jagged peaks of the Absaroka Range. Traverse the ridge, leaving the meadows and views, and enter a dense pine forest as the trail levels out. Stroll through the quiet of the forest, and gently descend past lava rock outcrops. Cross over the first of four forks of Dry Creek, and bend left to a trail gate. Pass through the gate to another overlook of the Absaroka Mountains. Descend and cross over the second fork of the creek on another left bend. Cross two more forks on two more left bends. This is the turn-around spot for a six-mile hike.

To extend the hike, the trail continues east, traversing the mountain slope. The trail connects to the south with the Eightmile Trail and to the west with the North Dry Divide Trail. ■

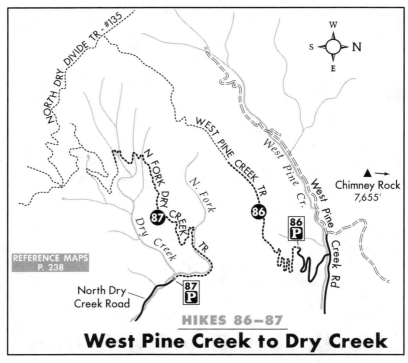

HIKES 86—87
West Pine Creek to Dry Creek

88. Big Creek Trail
GALLATIN RANGE from PARADISE VALLEY

Hiking distance: 4.6 miles round trip
Hiking time: 2.5 hours
Elevation gain: 300 feet
Maps: U.S.G.S. Lewis Creek
U.S.F.S. Gallatin National Forest: East Half
Beartooth Publishing: Absaroka Beartooth Wilderness

map
page 253

Summary of hike: The headwaters of Big Creek begin near the crest of the Gallatin Divide on the east slope of Eaglehead Mountain. The creek travels more than 14 miles eastward en route to the Yellowstone River in Paradise Valley. The Big Creek Trail parallels the creek up to Windy Pass, Porcupine Pass, and the Gallatin Crest Trail. This hike takes in the first segment of the trail with little elevation gain, passing meadows, rock cliffs, talus slides, and creekside wetlands. The Big Creek Trail provides eastern access to a number of trails that lead up to the Gallatin Crest Trail. The access trails follow several creek drainages up to the divide between Eaglehead Mountain and Hyalite Peak.

Driving directions: From Livingston at the I-90 and Highway 89 junction (Exit 333), drive 28.6 miles south on Highway 89 to the Big Creek Road on the right (west) between mile markers 24 and 25. Turn right and continue 6 miles to the posted trailhead parking area on the left at the end of the road. (At 3.6 miles is a road fork with Hyalite Creek Road—stay to the left.)

Big Creek Road is 6.7 miles south of Emigrant and 23 miles north of Gardiner.

Hiking directions: Climb a short hill, where the dirt road narrows to a footpath. Pass through the trail gate to a 3-way trail split. To the left, a forested path leads down the hill to meadows along the north bank of Big Creek. The right fork leads up to Cooper Bench. Walk straight ahead on the Big Creek Trail, and slowly descend on the north canyon wall high above Big Creek. Pass additional side paths leading down to the meadows along the creek. Gradually drop down the hillside to the edge of Big

Creek. Follow the wide creek upstream to a signed junction at 0.6 miles. The Cliff Creek Trail (Hike 90) veers right. Continue straight, staying on the Big Creek Trail in a spruce and fir forest. Cross a wooden bridge over cascading Cliff Creek and traverse the mountain, perched on the cliffs above Big Creek. Pass massive lava rock formations with caves and overhangs. Curve right, heading around a knob in the mountain. Bend left and descend to the banks of Cottonwood Creek above its confluence with Big Creek, the turn-around spot for a 4.6-mile, round-trip hike.

To extend the hike, wade across wide Cottonwood Creek, returning to Big Creek. Follow Big Creek upstream and ascend the south-facing slope. The trail continues for 12 miles, climbing to Porcupine Pass (just south of Eaglehead Mountain) and terminating at the Gallatin Crest Trail. The trail also connects to 9,200-foot Windy Pass on the Gallatin Divide. ■

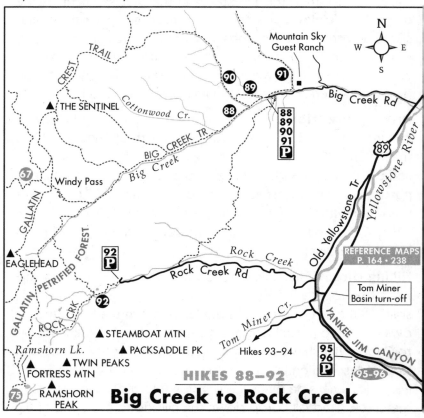

HIKES 88—92
Big Creek to Rock Creek

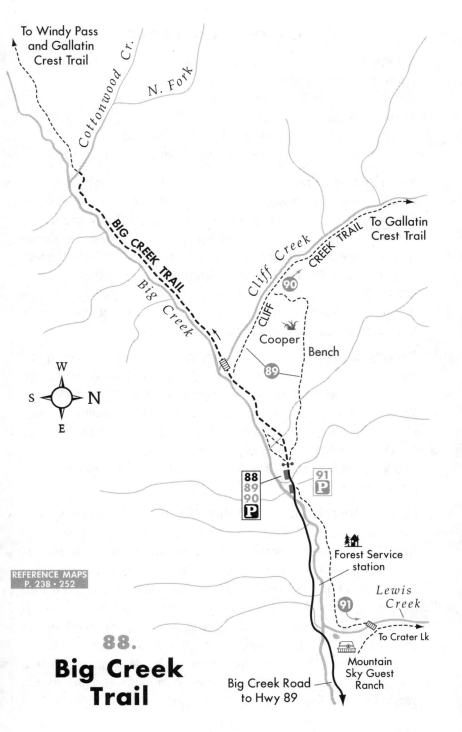

To Windy Pass and Gallatin Crest Trail

Cottonwood Cr.

N. Fork

BIG CREEK TRAIL

Big Creek

Cliff Creek

CREEK TRAIL

To Gallatin Crest Trail

90

CLIFF

Cooper Bench

89

W N S E

88
89
90
P

91
P

Forest Service station

91

Lewis Creek

To Crater Lk

Mountain Sky Guest Ranch

Big Creek Road to Hwy 89

88.
Big Creek Trail

89. Cooper Bench Loop

Hiking distance: 2.8-mile loop
Hiking time: 1.5 hours
Elevation gain: 500 feet
Maps: U.S.G.S. Lewis Creek
U.S.D.A. Gallatin National Forest: East Half
Beartooth Publishing: Bozeman, Big Sky, W. Yellowstone

Summary of hike: Cooper Bench is a massive, sloping meadow on the north canyon wall of Big Creek. The bench, rich with wildflowers, sits at 6,400 feet between the Cliff Creek and Lewis Creek drainages, tributaries of Big Creek. From the expansive meadow are 360-degree vistas that span from Big Creek Canyon to the Gallatin Crest and across Paradise Valley to the Absaroka Range. This scenic loop hike begins on the Big Creek Trail, climbs up a forested side canyon along Cliff Creek, and returns through the heart of the meadow atop Cooper Bench.

Driving directions: From Livingston at the I-90 and Highway 89 junction (Exit 333), drive 28.6 miles south on Highway 89 to Big Creek Road on the right (west) between mile markers 24 and 25. Turn right and continue 6 miles to the posted trailhead parking area on the left at the end of the road. (At 3.6 miles is a road fork with Hyalite Creek Road—stay to the left.)
Big Creek Road is 6.7 miles south of Emigrant and 23 miles north of Gardiner.

Hiking directions: Climb a short hill, where the dirt road narrows to a footpath. Pass through the trail gate to a 3-way trail split. To the left, a forested path leads down the hill to meadows along the north bank of Big Creek. The right fork leads up to Cooper Bench, our return route. Begin the loop straight ahead on the Big Creek Trail. Slowly descend on the north canyon wall high above Big Creek. Pass additional side paths leading down to the meadows along the creek. Gradually drop down the hillside to the edge of Big Creek. Follow the wide creek upstream to a signed junction at 0.6 miles. Hike 88 continues straight ahead, staying on the Big Creek Trail. (For a short detour to view Cliff

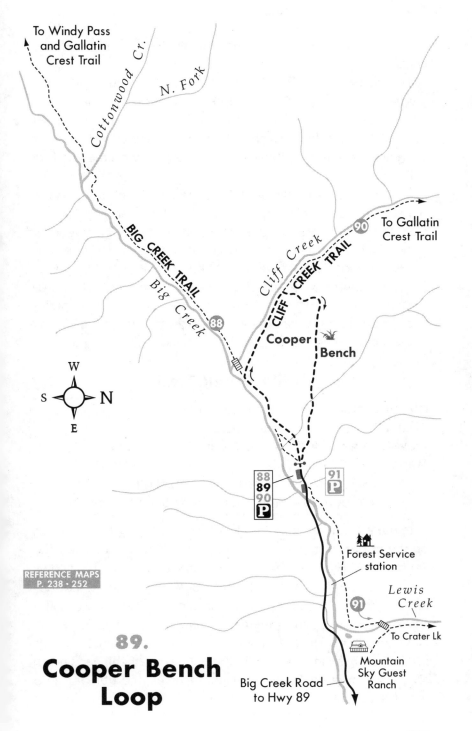

To Windy Pass
and Gallatin
Crest Trail

Cottonwood Cr.

N. Fork

BIG CREEK TRAIL

Big Creek

88

Cliff Creek

CLIFF CREEK TRAIL

90

To Gallatin
Crest Trail

Cooper Bench

W
S ✦ N
E

88
89
90
P

91 P

Forest Service
station

Lewis Creek

91

To Crater Lk

Mountain
Sky Guest
Ranch

REFERENCE MAPS
P. 238 · 252

Big Creek Road
to Hwy 89

89.
Cooper Bench Loop

Creek, walk 40 yards straight ahead to a bridge crossing over the creek.)

For this hike, veer right on the Cliff Creek Trail, and follow the gentle upward slope. Parallel cascading Cliff Creek, staying near its east bank past small meadows and moss-covered rocks. At one mile is a distinct, unsigned fork that is marked with a cairn. The Cliff Creek Trail continues up the waterway on the left fork (Hike 90).

For this hike, head right and leave the Cliff Creek Trail and the waterway. Steeply climb the forested east canyon wall. Emerge from the forest onto Cooper Bench, where there are sweeping vistas in all directions. Cross the sloping meadow while marveling at the landscape. At the far east end of the bench, begin the descent. Return to the forest and wind down the pristine area among gorgeous lava rock formations and a narrow, lush drainage. Return to Big Creek Canyon and traverse the south-facing slope, completing the loop at the trailhead gate. ■

90. Cliff Creek Trail

Hiking distance: 3 to 18 miles round trip
Hiking time: 1.5 to 9 hours
Elevation gain: 400 to 3,300 feet
Maps: U.S.G.S. Lewis Creek
U.S.D.A. Gallatin National Forest: East Half
Beartooth Publishing: Bozeman, Big Sky, W. Yellowstone

Summary of hike: Cliff Creek, a tributary of Big Creek, forms on the upper east slope near the Gallatin Divide between The Sentinel and Hyalite Peak. The Cliff Creek Trail closely follows the entire length of the waterway, beginning from its confluence with Big Creek and ending atop the Gallatin Divide. The trail steadily climbs the stream-fed canyon, gaining 3,300 feet in elevation over 8.5 miles to the Gallatin Crest Trail. This hike begins on the south-facing wall of Big Creek Canyon, then heads north up the narrow Cliff Creek drainage. At times, the trail dips into the creek along the canyon bottom.

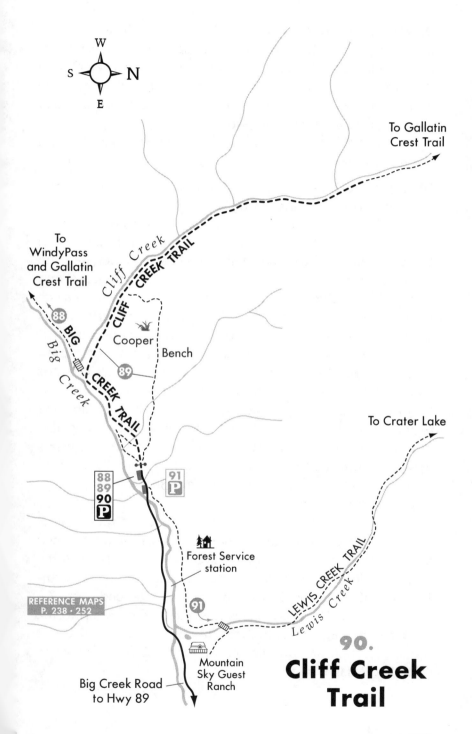

W N S E

To Gallatin
Crest Trail

To
WindyPass
and Gallatin
Crest Trail

Cliff Creek

CLIFF CREEK TRAIL

88

BIG

Big Creek

CLIFF

Cooper
Bench

89

CREEK TRAIL

To Crater Lake

88
89
90
P

91
P

Forest Service
station

LEWIS CREEK TRAIL

Lewis Creek

91

REFERENCE MAPS
P. 238 · 252

Mountain
Sky Guest
Ranch

Big Creek Road
to Hwy 89

90.
**Cliff Creek
Trail**

Driving directions: From Livingston at the I-90 and Highway 89 junction (Exit 333), drive 28.6 miles south on Highway 89 to Big Creek Road on the right (west) between mile markers 24 and 25. Turn right and continue 6 miles to the posted trailhead parking area on the left at the end of the road. (At 3.6 miles is a road fork with Hyalite Creek Road—stay to the left.)

Big Creek Road is 6.7 miles south of Emigrant and 23 miles north of Gardiner.

Hiking directions: Climb a short hill, where the dirt road narrows to a footpath. Pass through the trail gate to a 3-way trail split. To the left, a forested path leads down the hill to meadows along the north bank of Big Creek. The right fork leads up to Cooper Bench. Walk straight ahead on the Big Creek Trail, and slowly descend on the north canyon wall high above Big Creek. Pass additional side paths leading down to the meadows along the creek. Gradually drop down the hillside to the edge of Big Creek. Follow the wide creek upstream to a signed junction at 0.6 miles. Hike 88 continues straight ahead, staying on the Big Creek Trail. (For a short detour to view Cliff Creek, walk 40 yards straight ahead to a bridge crossing over the creek.)

For this hike, veer right on the Cliff Creek Trail, and follow the gentle upward slope. Parallel cascading Cliff Creek, staying near its east bank past small meadows and mossy rocks. At one mile is a distinct, unsigned fork that is marked with a cairn. To the right, a path leaves the creek and steeply climbs the east canyon wall to Cooper Bench (Hike 89).

For this hike veer left, staying close to Cliff Creek. Follow the east edge of the creek through lush riparian vegetation and moss-covered boulders. Pass massive lava rock cliffs along the creek-hugging path. Continue up canyon, staying on the northeast side of the creek. Choose your own turn-around spot.

The Cliff Creek Trail continues following the creek up to the Gallatin Crest Trail, 9 miles from the trailhead. The trail gains 3,300 feet in elevation, steeply climbing out of the Cliff Creek Canyon up to the Gallatin Divide. ∎

91. Lewis Creek Trail

Hiking distance: 4.8 miles round trip
Hiking time: 2.5 hours
Elevation gain: 400 feet
Maps: U.S.G.S. Lewis Creek
      U.S.D.A. Gallatin National Forest: East Half
      Beartooth Publishing: Bozeman, Big Sky, W. Yellowstone

*map
page 260*

Summary of hike: Lewis Creek, a tributary of Big Creek, forms near the Gallatin Divide at Crater Lake. The Lewis Creek Trail closely parallels the creek for 9.5 miles, from its terminus at Big Creek to the Gallatin Crest Trail by Crater Lake. This hike begins on the banks of Big Creek and follows Lewis Creek up the forested canyon. The footpath crosses the creek several times (which must be waded across) and weaves through lush riparian vegetation. This hike takes in the first 2.4 miles of the trail.

Driving directions: From Livingston at the I-90 and Highway 89 junction (Exit 333), drive 28.6 miles south on Highway 89 to Big Creek Road on the right (west) between mile markers 24 and 25. Turn right and continue 5.9 miles to the posted trailhead on the right, located just after crossing the bridge over Big Creek. Park in the grassy pullout on the left. (At 3.6 miles is a road fork with Hyalite Creek Road—stay to the left.)

Big Creek Road is 6.7 miles south of Emigrant and 23 miles north of Gardiner.

Hiking directions: From the posted trailhead on the north side of Big Creek Road, walk through the grassland to the bank of Big Creek. Head east up the hillside, with views of Big Creek and the forested canyon walls. Descend through meadows and pockets of spruce and fir. At 0.8 miles, curve left and head north up the Lewis Creek drainage while skirting the Mountain Sky Guest Ranch. Traverse the west canyon wall of Lewis Creek Canyon and descend to the creek. Cross a footbridge over the creek at 1.4 miles to a trail split. The right fork enters the private guest ranch land. Veer left and stroll through the lush riparian vegetation, staying close to the creek. Wind through the forest along

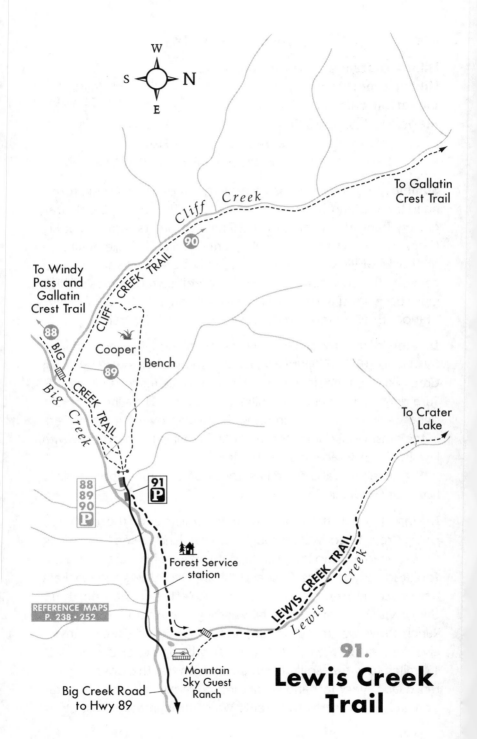

To Gallatin
Crest Trail

Cliff Creek

90

To Windy
Pass and
Gallatin
Crest Trail

88

BIG

CREEK TRAIL

Big Creek

Cooper

89

Bench

To Crater
Lake

88
89
90
P

91
P

Forest Service
station

LEWIS CREEK TRAIL

Lewis Creek

REFERENCE MAPS
P. 238 · 252

Mountain
Sky Guest
Ranch

Big Creek Road
to Hwy 89

91.
**Lewis Creek
Trail**

the watercourse. The trail crosses the creek three times—at 1.4 miles, 1.8 miles, and 2.4 miles. You will need to wade across the creek. This fourth crossing is the turn-around point for a 4.8-mile, round-trip hike.

To extend the hike, the trail follows the drainage closely, gaining 3,000 feet over the next 7 miles to Crater Lake and an unsigned junction with the Gallatin Crest Trail. ■

92. Rock Creek Trail
GALLATIN RANGE from PARADISE VALLEY

Hiking distance: 6 miles round trip
Hiking time: 3.5 hours
Elevation gain: 1,000 feet

map page 263

Maps: U.S.G.S. Ramshorn Peak
U.S.D.A. Gallatin National Forest East Half map
Beartooth Publishing: Bozeman, Big Sky, West Yellowstone

Summary of hike: Rock Creek, a tributary of the Yellowstone River, forms near the Gallatin Divide in a cirque of three mountains along the highest point of the divide: Fortress Mountain, Ramshorn Peak, and Twin Peaks. The Rock Creek Trail parallels the cascading creek, leading 4.5 miles to the Gallatin Crest Trail atop the divide near Fortress Mountain. This hike follows the first three miles of the trail to an overlook of a scenic, grassy valley beneath towering Fortress Mountain (back cover photo). En route, the trail passes the Meadows Trail, a 3.5-mile connector route to Big Creek. This trail is heavily used by hunters in the fall.

Driving directions: From Livingston at the I-90 and Highway 89 junction (Exit 333), drive 37 miles south on Highway 89 to the signed Tom Miner Basin turnoff on the right (west) between mile markers 16 and 17. Drive 0.4 miles on Tom Miner Creek Road, crossing a bridge over the Yellowstone River, to a junction. Turn right on the Old Yellowstone Trail, and go 0.3 miles to Rock Creek Road. Turn left and continue 5.8 miles to an unsigned Y-fork, just after crossing a cattle guard. Take the left fork and drive 2.5 miles to the posted trailhead on the left. Park off the road.

The Tom Miner Basin turnoff is 15 miles south of Emigrant and 16 miles north of Gardiner.

Hiking directions: Head up the footpath past the trailhead sign, and enter a pine forest. Traverse the north canyon slope above Rock Creek and below the lower slope of Steamboat Mountain. Cross a series of tributary streams and a small pond on the left. At 1.3 miles, on the crest of a slope, is a Y-fork. The 3.5-mile Meadows Trail veers right and ascends a ridge before dropping down to Big Creek.

For this hike, stay to the left and descend into a vast meadow surrounded by mountains. Stroll through the meadow and hop over a tributary of Rock Creek. Then cross a log or rock-hop over the main Rock Creek. Head southwest, following the course of the rocky creek. Cross the creek again and climb the slope, utilizing a log bridge over a wetland. Continue climbing at a moderate grade. The trail levels out at 2.5 miles in a tree-dotted meadow, where there are vistas across the drainage to Steamboat Mountain and Packsaddle Peak. Cross a feeder stream and pass through the meadow with pockets of trees. Continue to a posted trail fork a quarter mile ahead. The right fork leads 2 miles and another 1,000 feet in elevation to the Gallatin Crest, just north of Fortress Mountain. Continue straight—on the left fork—100 yards to an overlook of the valley beneath Fortress Mountain. After enjoying this scenic area, return by retracing your steps. ▪

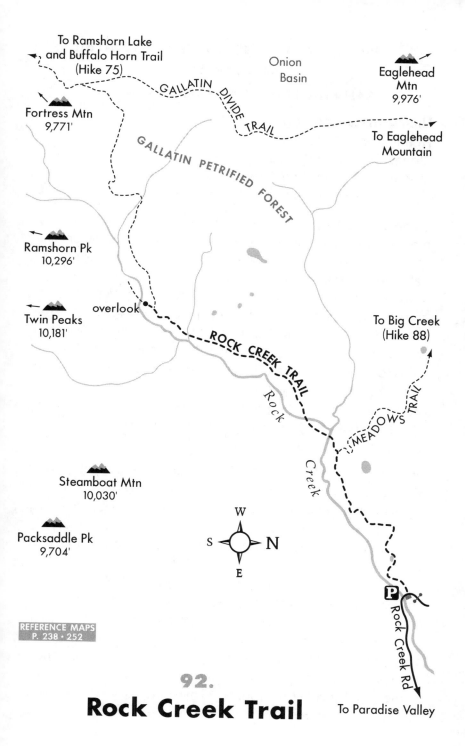

To Ramshorn Lake
and Buffalo Horn Trail
(Hike 75)

Onion
Basin

Eaglehead
Mtn
9,976'

GALLATIN DIVIDE TRAIL

Fortress Mtn
9,771'

To Eaglehead
Mountain

GALLATIN PETRIFIED FOREST

Ramshorn Pk
10,296'

Twin Peaks
10,181'

overlook

ROCK CREEK TRAIL

To Big Creek
(Hike 88)

Rock

Creek

MEADOWS TRAIL

Steamboat Mtn
10,030'

Packsaddle Pk
9,704'

W
S ✦ N
E

REFERENCE MAPS
P. 238 · 252

P

Rock Creek Rd

92.
Rock Creek Trail

To Paradise Valley

93. Petrified Forest Interpretive Trail

TOM MINER BASIN

GALLATIN RANGE from PARADISE VALLEY

Hiking distance: 2 miles round trip
Hiking time: 1 hour
Elevation gain: 600 feet
Maps: U.S.G.S. Ramshorn Peak
U.S.F.S. Gallatin National Forest: East Half

Summary of hike: The Gallatin Petrified Forest encompasses more than 40 square miles on the crest of the Gallatin Mountains. The fossilized forest extends from the northwest corner of Yellowstone National Park to Windy Pass north of Eaglehead Mountain. The petrified trees are the result of ancient volcanic activity that buried the vast forests 55 million years ago. The Petrified Forest Interpretive Trail begins on the lower slopes of Ramshorn Peak and Buffalo Horn Pass in Tom Miner Basin. The trail leads to a line of sculpted volcanic cliffs and caves interspersed with petrified trees and fossil remains. In one cave, a rock tree protrudes from the ceiling. Interpretive panels describe the geological features. From the cliffs are awesome vistas up and down the Trail Creek drainage, a tributary of Tom Miner Creek.

Driving directions: From Livingston at the I-90 and Highway 89 junction (Exit 333), drive 37 miles south on Highway 89 to the signed Tom Miner Basin turnoff on the right (west) between mile markers 16 and 17. Drive 0.4 miles on Tom Miner Creek Road—crossing a bridge over the Yellowstone River—to a junction. Turn left on Old Yellowstone Trail, and go 0.7 miles to a Y-fork. Veer right on Tom Miner Creek Road. At 7.4 miles, follow the campground sign, bearing left at a road fork. (The B-Bar Ranch bears right.) Continue on the narrow road to a road split at 11 miles. Curve right, entering the Tom Miner Campground, and drive 0.7 miles to the upper (west) end of the campground to the signed trailhead. A campground parking fee is required.

The Tom Miner Basin turnoff is 15 miles south of Emigrant and 16 miles north of Gardiner.

Hiking directions: Head west past the trailhead gate, paralleling Trail Creek through the grassy meadow fringed with aspen and evergreen trees. At a quarter mile is a signed junction. The left fork heads west along Trail Creek to Buffalo Horn Pass (Hike 90). Take the right fork up the meadow on the west side of a dry, rocky creekbed. Continue northwest beneath the extraordinary lava rock formations and caves. The trail leads uphill through the forest past massive lava rocks. Switchback up the south-facing mountain, passing petrified stumps to the sculpted cliffs and caves seen from below. Each cave has an interpretive station that explains the surrounding geology. After exploring the area, return along the same route. ■

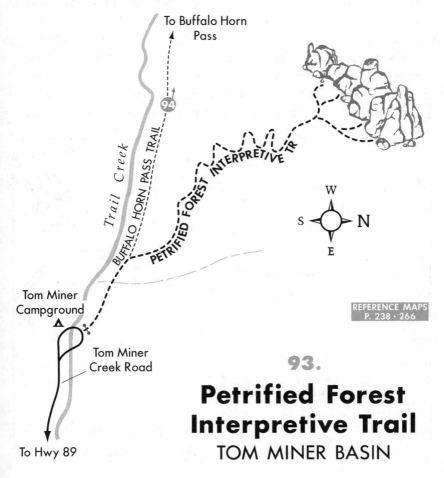

93.

Petrified Forest Interpretive Trail
TOM MINER BASIN

94. Buffalo Horn Pass

TOM MINER BASIN

GALLATIN RANGE from PARADISE VALLEY

Hiking distance: 4.6 miles round trip
Hiking time: 2.5 hours
Elevation gain: 1,450 feet
Maps: U.S.G.S. Ramshorn Peak
U.S.F.S. Gallatin National Forest: East Half

Summary of hike: Buffalo Horn Pass straddles the Gallatin Range Divide between the Yellowstone and Gallatin Rivers. The pass lies near the northwest corner of Yellowstone National Park and Ramshorn Peak in the 26,000-acre Gallatin Petrified Forest. Millions of years ago, volcanic mud flows smothered and preserved ancient tropical forests in this fascinating area. Exposed by erosion, petrified stumps and logs are abundant throughout the landscape. The hike begins from Tom Miner Campground and parallels Trail Creek, continuing past the creek's headwaters

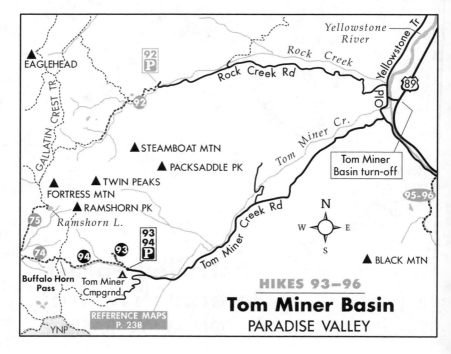

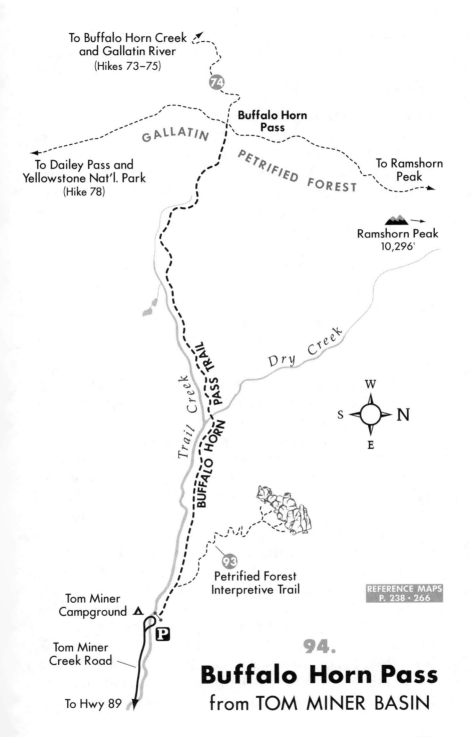

To Buffalo Horn Creek
and Gallatin River
(Hikes 73–75)

74

**Buffalo Horn
Pass**

GALLATIN

PETRIFIED FOREST

To Dailey Pass and
Yellowstone Nat'l. Park
(Hike 78)

To Ramshorn
Peak

Ramshorn Peak
10,296'

Dry Creek

Trail Creek

BUFFALO HORN PASS TRAIL

W

S · N

E

93

Petrified Forest
Interpretive Trail

REFERENCE MAPS
P. 238 · 266

Tom Miner
Campground △

P

Tom Miner
Creek Road

To Hwy 89

94.

Buffalo Horn Pass
from TOM MINER BASIN

to a circular meadow at the 8,523-foot summit of Buffalo Horn Pass. Atop the ridge is the petrified forest and a 4-way junction, with connections to the Gallatin Canyon, Ramshorn Peak, and Yellowstone National Park.

Driving directions: From Livingston at the I-90 and Highway 89 junction (Exit 333), drive 37 miles south on Highway 89 to the signed Tom Miner Basin turnoff on the right (west) between mile markers 16 and 17. Drive 0.4 miles on Tom Miner Creek Road—crossing a bridge over the Yellowstone River—to a junction. Turn left on Old Yellowstone Trail, and go 0.7 miles to a Y-fork. Veer right on Tom Miner Creek Road. At 7.4 miles, follow the camp-ground sign, bearing left at a road fork. (The B-Bar Ranch bears right.) Continue on the narrow road to a road split at 11 miles. Curve right, entering the Tom Miner Campground, and drive 0.7 miles to the upper (west) end of the campground to the signed trailhead. A campground parking fee is required.

The Tom Miner Basin turnoff is 15 miles south of Emigrant and 16 miles north of Gardiner.

Hiking directions: Head west through the trailhead gate on the Buffalo Horn Pass Trail. Parallel Trail Creek through the grassy meadow fringed with aspen and evergreen trees. At a quarter mile, cross a dry streambed to a signed junction with the Petrified Forest Interpretive Trail (Hike 93). Stay to the left, heading west up the sloping meadow. Traverse the edge of the hillside above the creek, alternating between shady forest and open meadows. To the east are great views of the majestic Absaroka Range. At 0.8 miles, rock-hop across Dry Creek and begin a steep quarter-mile ascent. The path remains on the north side of Trail Creek. At two miles, curve around the bowl at the Trail Creek headwaters to the meadow at Buffalo Horn Pass. Atop the Gallatin Divide is a 4-way junction, the turn-around spot for this hike.

To hike farther, the left fork heads south into Yellowstone National Park at Daly Pass (Hike 78), 2.5 miles ahead. The right fork heads 2 miles north to Ramshorn Peak. Straight ahead (west), the route descends along Buffalo Horn Creek to the Gallatin River by the 320 Guest Ranch, 7 miles from the pass (Hikes 73–75). ■

95. Yankee Jim Canyon Historic Route
GALLATIN RANGE from PARADISE VALLEY

Hiking distance: 1.7 miles round trip
(0.7 miles wheelchair accessible)
Hiking time: 1 hour
Elevation gain: Level
Maps: U.S.G.S. Dome Mountain and Miner
Trailhead kiosk map

map
page 272

Summary of hike: The Yellowstone River has been a transportation route for over 7,000 years. Before broadening out into Paradise Valley, the river squeezes through a narrow drainage known as Yankee Jim Canyon. Native Americans used the ancient pathway along the south side of the canyon to reach obsidian quarries. In the mid 1800s, prospectors used this route in search of gold and silver. It was during this era that Jim George, better known as Yankee Jim, built and operated a wagon toll road through the canyon. In the late 1800s, the Northern Pacific railroad built a line into Yellowstone National Park along the same route. From the early 1900s through 1920, when the current highway was completed, this was also the auto route that connected the midwest from St. Paul, Minnesota, to the Pacific Ocean at Seattle, Washington. (The Old Yellowstone Trail, on the south side of the river, is part of this original auto route to Yellowstone.)

The Yankee Jim Canyon Historic Route is a short, partially paved interpretive trail on a bench above the Yellowstone River along the south side of Yankee Jim Canyon. The wheelchair-accessible trail follows a short section of the scenic Old Yellowstone Trail.

Driving directions: From Livingston at the I-90 and Highway 89 junction (Exit 333), drive 37 miles south on Highway 89 to the signed Tom Miner Basin turnoff on the right (west) between mile markers 16 and 17. Drive 0.4 miles on Tom Miner Creek Road—crossing a bridge over the Yellowstone River—to a junction. Turn left on Old Yellowstone Trail, and go 0.7 miles to a Y-fork. Tom Miner Creek Road goes to the right (Hikes 93—94). For this hike, veer left, staying on the Old Yellowstone Trail. Drive 2.8 miles, parallel to the Yellowstone River, to the posted Sphinx Creek Trailhead parking area on the right.

The Tom Miner Basin turnoff is 15 miles south of Emigrant and 16 miles north of Gardiner.

Hiking directions: Cross the Old Yellowstone Trail to the paved path. Walk 20 yards to a signed fork. Begin by continuing straight ahead to the northwest on the paved path. Cross over Sphinx Creek, and follow the grassy bluff to a series of interpretive panels. The trail ends at 0.35 miles by a panel and an overlook of the river and canyon.

Return to the junction. Take the natural path a couple hundred yards to another overlook on the edge of the cliffs, with views up Yankee Jim Canyon and the Yellowstone River. Follow the open, grassy bluff southeast. The path fades in and out until it rejoins the Old Yellowstone Trail. Cross the road and walk up an unpaved road to another panel. This narrow dirt road, blocked to vehicles by rocks, is the original road to Yellowstone. Climb the slope among granite boulders and pine trees, passing numerous overlooks. At the next panel is a large rock with a painted ad for Yellowstone souvenirs dating back to 1914. Continue past the painted rock to the final overlook. Descend past a rock wall, also built around 1914 by incarcerated convicts from Deer Lodge. A short distance ahead, the trail rejoins the Old Yellowstone Trail. Return along the dirt road or retrace your steps. ■

96. Sphinx Creek Trail
YANKEE JIM CANYON
GALLATIN RANGE from PARADISE VALLEY

Hiking distance: 4.5 miles round trip
Hiking time: 2.5 hours
Elevation gain: 1,100 feet

map
page 273

Maps: U.S.G.S. Dome Mountain and Miner
U.S.D.A. Gallatin National Forest East Half map
Beartooth Publishing: Bozeman, Big Sky, West Yellowstone

Summary of hike: Sphinx Creek drops into the Yellowstone River on the south side of Yankee Jim Canyon, where the Yellowstone narrows through the vertical-walled canyon. The creek forms from outlet streams of Yankee Jim Lake and Twin Lakes on the slope of Sphinx Mountain. The Sphinx Creek Trail begins at the Yellowstone River along the steep walls of Yankee Jim Canyon. The scenic path weaves up the lush canyon to a large grassland meadow beneath Sphinx Mountain. The trail crosses the creek five times and climbs through pockets of aspen, Douglas fir, and spruce.

Driving directions: From Livingston at the I-90 and Highway 89 junction (Exit 333), drive 37 miles south on Highway 89 to the signed Tom Miner Basin turnoff on the right (west) between mile markers 16 and 17. Drive 0.4 miles on Tom Miner Creek Road—crossing a bridge over the Yellowstone River—to a junction. Turn left on Old Yellowstone Trail, and go 0.7 miles to a Y-fork. Tom Miner Creek Road goes to the right (Hikes 93—94). For this hike, veer left, staying on the Old Yellowstone Trail. Drive 2.8 miles, parallel to the Yellowstone River, to the posted Sphinx Creek Trailhead parking area on the right.

The Tom Miner Basin turnoff is 15 miles south of Emigrant and 16 miles north of Gardiner.

Hiking directions: From the Sphinx Creek kiosk, head west through the grassland to the mouth of the vertical-walled canyon. Ascend the east canyon slope through a mixed evergreen forest.

Follow the banks of Sphinx Creek, and cross over to the west bank. Pass through a trail gate at a half mile Stay creekside as the trail alternates from climbing to leveling out. At 0.9 miles, cross back to the east side of the creek to a meadow surrounded by mountains. Stroll through the scenic area dotted with a few stands of spruce and aspen. Carefully cross a small boggy area, then hop over Sphinx Creek back to the west side. Cross the creek a fourth time at its confluence with the outlet stream from Twin Lakes and Yankee Jim Lake. Leave the main fork of Sphinx Creek, and continue along the outlet stream to a meadow. Near the top of the meadow, curve left and cross the stream, emerging to an imposing, direct view of Sphinx Mountain. A short distance ahead, the trail ends by the remains of an old log cabin on the edge of a large wetland meadow at the southwest foot of Sphinx Mountain.

To extend the hike, an unmaintained path climbs the slope to Yankee Jim Lake and Twin Lakes. ■

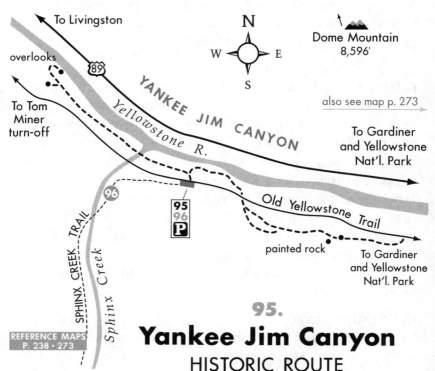

95.
Yankee Jim Canyon
HISTORIC ROUTE

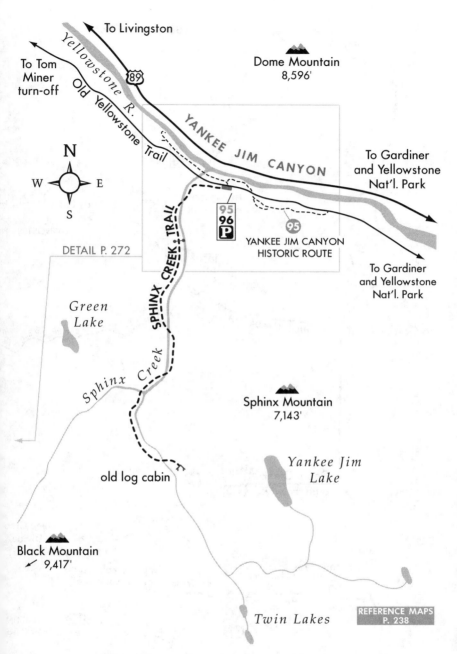

To Livingston

Yellowstone R.

Old Yellowstone Trail

To Tom Miner turn-off

Dome Mountain
8,596'

YANKEE JIM CANYON

To Gardiner and Yellowstone Nat'l. Park

N
W E
S

DETAIL P. 272

SPHINX CREEK TRAIL

95
96
P

YANKEE JIM CANYON
HISTORIC ROUTE

95

To Gardiner and Yellowstone Nat'l. Park

Green Lake

Sphinx Creek

Sphinx Mountain
7,143'

Yankee Jim Lake

old log cabin

Black Mountain
9,417'

Twin Lakes

REFERENCE MAPS
P. 238

96. Sphinx Creek Trail
YANKEE JIM CANYON

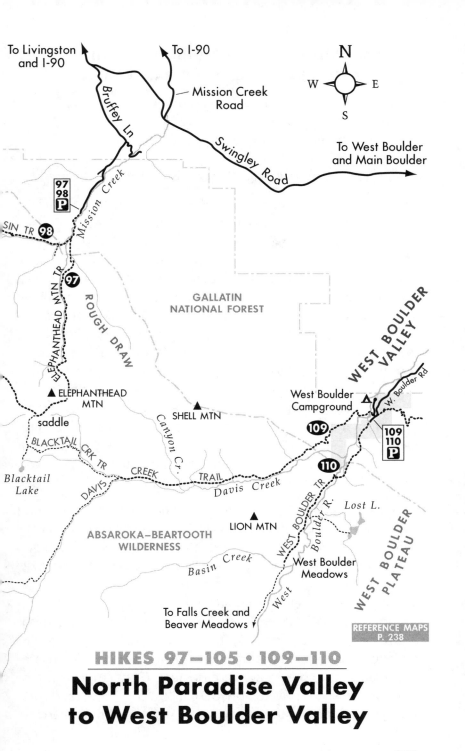

To Livingston and I-90

To I-90

Mission Creek Road

Bruffey Ln

Swingley Road

To West Boulder and Main Boulder

N
W E
S

97 98 P

SIN TR 98

ELEPHANTHEAD MTN TR 97

Mission Creek

ROUGH DRAW

GALLATIN NATIONAL FOREST

WEST BOULDER VALLEY

W. Boulder Rd

West Boulder Campground

▲ ELEPHANTHEAD MTN

saddle

BLACKTAIL CRK TR

Blacktail Lake

DAVIS

CREEK

Canyon Cr.

▲ SHELL MTN

TRAIL

Davis Creek

109

110

109 110 P

ABSAROKA–BEARTOOTH WILDERNESS

▲ LION MTN

WEST BOULDER TR

Boulder R.

Lost L.

WEST BOULDER PLATEAU

Basin Creek

West Boulder Meadows

West

To Falls Creek and Beaver Meadows

REFERENCE MAPS
P. 238

HIKES 97–105 • 109–110

North Paradise Valley to West Boulder Valley

97. Elephanthead Mountain Trail
ABSAROKA RANGE from PARADISE VALLEY

Hiking distance: 7.5 miles round trip
Hiking time: 4.5 hours
Elevation gain: 3,200 feet
Maps: U.S.G.S. Livingston Peak
Beartooth Publishing: Absaroka Beartooth Wilderness

Summary of hike: Elephanthead Mountain, in the Absaroka Beartooth Wilderness, rises along the northern edge of the Absaroka Range on the outskirts of Livingston. The sheer limestone cliffs at the southern head of the mountain are dramatic. There are several accesses to Elephanthead Mountain. This trail strenuously climbs along the eastern base of the mountain beneath the limestone walls. It follows the watercourse of Mission Creek from the mouth of the canyon to a saddle past its headwaters. (Mission Creek was the infamous location where John Bozeman was killed by the Blackfoot Indians.) En route, the trail passes through dense forest, grassy streamside meadows, and expansive alpine tundra with scenic panoramas in every direction. From the 8,900-foot ridge at the head of the canyon are views into Canyon Creek Canyon, Blacktail Creek Canyon, and across three layers of ridges and plateaus in the Boulder River Canyon. The views are worth the steep climb.

Driving directions: From I-90, there are three exits into the town of Livingston—Exit 330, Exit 333, and Exit 337. From Exit 333, drive 3.9 miles northeast on Park Street (Highway 89) through downtown Livingston to Swingley Road on the right. From Exit 337, on the east edge of Livingston, drive 1.3 miles west towards downtown to Swingley Road on the left.

Turn south on Swingley Road, and continue 7 miles to signed Bruffey Lane on the right. Turn right and go 1.7 miles to the 63 Ranch entrance on the right. Turn right, entering the private ranch land on a forest service easement. (Stay strictly on the road, as the land is private.) Drive 0.6 miles to a signed road fork just before reaching the ranch house. Veer left on the narrow

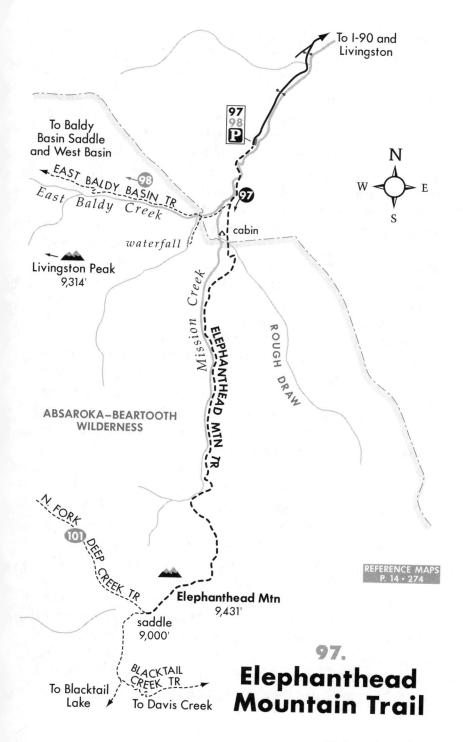

To I-90 and
Livingston

97
98
P

To Baldy
Basin Saddle
and West Basin

EAST BALDY BASIN TR **98**

East Baldy Creek

97

cabin

waterfall

▲▲ Livingston Peak
9,314'

Mission Creek

ELEPHANTHEAD MTN TR

ROUGH DRAW

ABSAROKA–BEARTOOTH
WILDERNESS

N. FORK
101
DEEP CREEK TR

▲▲ **Elephanthead Mtn**
9,431'

REFERENCE MAPS
P. 14 · 274

saddle
9,000'

BLACKTAIL
CREEK TR

To Blacktail
Lake

To Davis Creek

N
W E
S

97.
**Elephanthead
Mountain Trail**

road for one mile—following the national forest access sign—to the trailhead parking area at the end of the road. En route, pass through forest service gates at 0.1 mile and 0.4 miles.

Hiking directions: Walk past the trailhead kiosk, and head south into the forest. Follow the west side of Mission Creek on a gentle uphill grade. At 0.3 miles, rock-hop over Mission Creek to a Y-fork marked with a cairn. The right fork crosses Mission Creek and climbs up East Baldy Basin (Hike 98). Stay on the Elephanthead Mountain Trail, and pass an old cabin. Enter the Absaroka-Beartooth Wilderness at 0.9 miles, and cross Rough Draw Creek. Weave up the lush drainage, with periodic views of Livingston Peak to the west, Shell Mountain to the east, and Elephanthead Mountain to the south. Traverse the east wall of Mission Creek Canyon high above the creek. Pass through the burn area from the Rough Draw Fire and a sloping, wildflower-filled meadow with skeleton trees. In August, this stretch is abundant with thimbleberries, huckleberries, elderberries, and raspberries. Cross a small tributary stream and a talus field. Zigzag up the hillside, following the cascading creek. The view down canyon spans across Shields Valley to the Crazy Mountains. Enter a pine forest and keep ascending the canyon to a grassy knoll surrounded by mountains. Meander through a tree-rimmed meadow with large granite outcrops. Climb up the open tundra landscape, following cairns to the 9,040-foot saddle at the head of the canyon and the vertical rock cliffs. This is our turn-around spot.

To extend the hike, bear right and follow the edge of the steep cliffs and dolomite boulders, with awesome views of the world-class topography. Skirt the southern rock-face of Elephanthead Mountain, and traverse the steep slope on a downhill grade. When the trail fades, cairns mark the route. Ascend the hill to a 9,000-foot grassy saddle, and descend to a signed junction. The left fork heads 0.9 miles downhill to Blacktail Lake, a 4-acre lake surrounded by timber. To the east, the trail connects to the Davis Creek Trail and the West Boulder drainage (Hike 109). The North Fork Deep Creek Trail (Hike 101) goes to the right (east) and follows the rim of the creek-fed canyon 5.5 miles to Paradise Valley. ■

98. East Baldy Basin Trail
from the Elephanthead Mountain Trailhead
ABSAROKA RANGE from PARADISE VALLEY

Hiking distance: 7 miles round trip
Hiking time: 4 hours
Elevation gain: 2,550 feet
Maps: U.S.G.S. Livingston Peak

      Beartooth Publishing: Absaroka Beartooth Wilderness

map
page 282

Summary of hike: Baldy Basin is a narrow stream-fed canyon along the northern base of Livingston Peak. The area is located in the Absaroka Range on the outskirts of Livingston. At the head of the basin is Baldy Basin Saddle, lying a thousand feet below Livingston Peak at an elevation of 8,300 feet. The alpine saddle divides West Baldy Basin from East Baldy Basin. Hikes 98 and 99 climb up to the saddle from opposite directions. This hike begins at the eastern trailhead from the Elephanthead Mountain Trail in the Mission Creek drainage. The trail follows Mission Creek a short distance, then veers west into East Baldy Basin, entering the Absaroka Beartooth Wilderness. The hike passes a waterfall and weaves through wildflower-covered meadows, steadily climbing towards the saddle. From the summit are sweeping vistas of Livingston Peak, Elephanthead Mountain, Shell Mountain, and the West Boulder Divide.

Driving directions: From I-90, there are three exits into the town of Livingston—Exit 330, Exit 333, and Exit 337. From Exit 333, drive 3.9 miles northeast on Park Street (Highway 89) through downtown Livingston to Swingley Road on the right. From Exit 337, on the east edge of Livingston, drive 1.3 miles west towards downtown to Swingley Road on the left.

Turn south on Swingley Road, and continue 7 miles to signed Bruffey Lane on the right. Turn right and go 1.7 miles to the 63 Ranch entrance on the right. Turn right, entering the private ranch land on a forest service easement. (Stay strictly on the road, as the land is private.) Drive 0.6 miles to a signed road fork just before reaching the ranch house. Veer left on the narrow road for one mile—following the national forest access sign—to the trailhead parking area at the end of the road. En route, pass through forest service gates at 0.1 mile and 0.4 miles.

Hiking directions: Walk past the trailhead kiosk, and head south into the forest on the Elephanthead Mountain Trail. Follow the west side of Mission Creek on a gentle uphill grade. At 0.3 miles, rock-hop over Mission Creek to a Y-fork marked with a cairn. The left fork, straight ahead, continues up to the head of the canyon and the southern base of Elephanthead Mountain (Hike 97). Veer right on the East Baldy Basin Trail, and rock-hop back over Mission Creek to the Absaroka-Beartooth Wilderness and a trail split at East Baldy Creek. Detour left on an unnamed path, and follow a tributary stream 0.2 miles to a beautiful 100-foot cascading waterfall.

Return to the junction and cross East Baldy Creek. Follow the north edge of the creek for nearly a quarter mile, then ascend the hillside, climbing high above the creek. The trail is fairly easy to follow, but may be overgrown with vegetation. Pass through a small flower-filled meadow, and climb up two switchbacks. Continue west, weaving across the hillside on the north flank of the canyon. Cross through another meadow, with a view of Livingston Peak, and return to the forest. Pass a couple of 3-foot cairns, and cross East Baldy Creek two times near its headwaters. Steeply climb to a 4-foot cairn on the edge of a boulder field and a view of the saddle separating the East and West Baldy drainages. Walk through a log fence and make the final steep ascent, passing three tall cairns to the Baldy Basin Saddle at 8,300 feet, just below Livingston Peak. This is our turn-around spot.

To extend the hike, the West Baldy Basin Trail continues downhill along West Baldy Creek. The trail follows the north rim of Lost Creek Canyon to the Livingston Peak Trailhead to the west (Hike 99) and the Suce Creek Trailhead in Paradise Valley to the south (Hike 100). ■

99. West Baldy Basin Trail
from the Livingston Peak Trailhead
ABSAROKA RANGE from PARADISE VALLEY

Hiking distance: 6.4 miles round trip
Hiking time: 3.5 hours
Elevation gain: 2,100 feet

map
page 282

Maps: U.S.G.S. Brisbin and Livingston Peak
      Beartooth Publishing: Absaroka Beartooth Wilderness

Summary of hike: Baldy Basin is a narrow stream-fed canyon along the northern base of Livingston Peak. The area is located in the Absaroka Range on the outskirts of Livingston. At the head of the basin is Baldy Basin Saddle, lying a thousand feet below Livingston Peak at an elevation of 8,300 feet. The alpine saddle divides West Baldy Basin from East Baldy Basin. Hikes 98 and 99 climb up to the saddle from opposite directions. This hike begins from the western end at the upper Livingston Peak Trailhead in Paradise Valley. The trail enters the Absaroka Beartooth Wilderness (via the Livingston Peak Tie Trail), overlooking Lost Creek Canyon, Suce Creek Canyon, Paradise Valley, and the Gallatin Range. The steep path traverses weather-carved cliffs, passes through lush meadows, and tops out on Baldy Basin Saddle. The sweeping vistas include Livingston Peak, Elephanthead Mountain, Shell Mountain, and the West Boulder Divide.

Driving directions: From I-90, there are three exits into the town of Livingston—Exit 330, Exit 333, and Exit 337. From Exit 333, drive 3.9 miles northeast on Park Street (Highway 89) through downtown Livingston to Swingley Road on the right. From Exit 337, on the east edge of Livingston, drive 1.3 miles west towards downtown to Swingley Road on the left.

    Turn south on Swingley Road, and continue 2.3 miles to the signed Forest Service Road 2532 on the right. Turn right on the dirt road, and go 0.7 miles to a fork. Veer left, staying on Forest Service Road 2532. Drive 6.6 miles, winding up the mountain road to the signed Livingston Peak Trailhead at the end of the road.

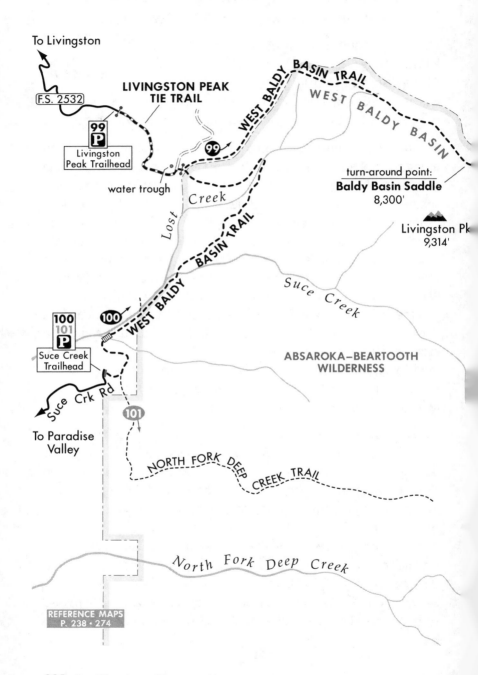

To Livingston

F.S. 2532

99 P
Livingston
Peak Trailhead

water trough

**LIVINGSTON PEAK
TIE TRAIL**

99

WEST BALDY BASIN TRAIL

WEST BALDY BASIN

turn-around point:
Baldy Basin Saddle
8,300'

Livingston Pk
9,314'

Lost   Creek

WEST BALDY BASIN TRAIL

Suce   Creek

100

100
101 P
Suce Creek
Trailhead

WEST BALDY

Suce   Crk   Rd

**ABSAROKA–BEARTOOTH
WILDERNESS**

To Paradise
Valley

101

NORTH FORK DEEP CREEK TRAIL

North   Fork   Deep   Creek

REFERENCE MAPS
P. 238 • 274

282 – Day Hikes Around Bozeman, Montana

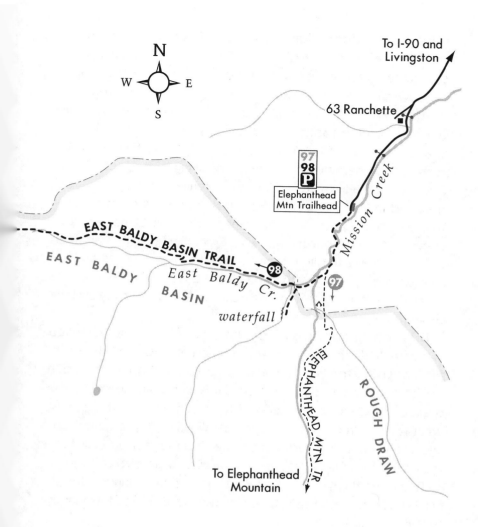

To I-90 and Livingston

63 Ranchette

N
W E
S

97
98
P
Elephanthead Mtn Trailhead

Mission Creek

EAST BALDY BASIN TRAIL

EAST BALDY

EAST BALDY BASIN

East Baldy Cr.

98

97

waterfall

ELEPHANTHEAD MTN TR

ROUGH DRAW

To Elephanthead Mountain

98. **East Baldy Basin Trail**
from Elephanthead Mountain Trailhead

99. **West Baldy Basin Trail**
from Livingston Peak Trailhead

100. **West Baldy Basin Trail**
from Suce Creek Trailhead

Hiking directions: Walk past the trail gate on the Livingston Peak Tie Trail, a 2-track dirt road. Follow the road through the open pine forest. Make a wide U-bend to the left, with a straight-on view of pyramid-shaped Livingston Peak. At the far end of the bend is a horse watering trough and a trail sign at a half mile. Bear right on the footpath and go 80 yards to a gate, located at a junction with the West Baldy Basin Trail and the Absaroka-Beartooth Wilderness on a ridge overlooking Suce Creek Canyon. The right fork—Hike 100—descends 3 miles to the Suce Creek Trailhead in Paradise Valley. Bear left on the West Baldy Basin Trail, skirting the outside edge of the wilderness. Climb at a moderate grade to the north rim of Lost Creek Canyon. The trail levels out and follows the lip of the forested canyon. Livingston Peak looms close by, along with vistas across Lost Creek Canyon, Suce Creek Canyon, and far-reaching views of Paradise Valley and the Gallatin Range.

Drop down and cross a tributary stream in a flower-filled meadow. Walk through the tree-rimmed meadow on the north flank of Livingston Peak. Begin a steep ascent through the open forest. Cross a saddle into West Baldy Basin, and traverse the basin cliffs. Climb to the head of the basin beneath the craggy, weather-sculpted cliffs. Cross and parallel the rock-strewn drainage at a very steep grade. Cross the stream again, and climb to the 8,300-foot Baldy Basin Saddle, marked with two cairns.

To extend the hike, the East Baldy Basin Trail continues downhill, parallel to East Baldy Creek to the Elephanthead Mountain trailhead (Hike 98). ▪

100. West Baldy Basin Trail from the Suce Creek Trailhead
ABSAROKA RANGE from PARADISE VALLEY

Hiking distance: 6 miles round trip

Hiking time: 3 hours

Elevation gain: 900 feet

Maps: U.S.G.S. Brisbon and Livingston Peak
Beartooth Publishing: Absaroka Beartooth Wilderness

map
page 282

Summary of hike: Baldy Basin is a narrow stream-fed canyon along the northern base of Livingston Peak in the Absaroka Range. At the head of the basin is Baldy Basin Saddle, lying a thousand feet below Livingston Peak at an elevation of 8,300 feet. The alpine saddle divides West Baldy Basin from East Baldy Basin.

Baldy Basin Saddle is accessed from three trailheads. Hikes 98 and 99 climb up to the saddle from opposite directions in the Baldy Basin Canyon. The third route up to the saddle—this hike—begins from the Suce Creek Trailhead in Paradise Valley. The hike follows the beginning of the West Baldy Basin Trail for 3 miles to the upper trailhead. The trail parallels and crosses both Suce Creek and Lost Creek in the Absaroka-Beartooth Wilderness. En route are beautiful views of the Gallatin Range and Paradise Valley. After the junction to the upper trailhead, the hike may be continued 2.7 miles up to the Baldy Basin Saddle (Hike 99).

Driving directions: From Livingston at the I-90 and Highway 89 junction (Exit 333), drive 3.1 miles south on Highway 89 to East River Road (Highway 540). Turn left and drive 2.7 miles to Suce Creek Road on the left. Turn left and continue 3 miles—following the trailhead signs—to the Suce Creek Trailhead at the end of the road. Park in the spaces on the right.

Hiking directions: Pass the trailhead kiosk, and veer to the right up the meadow. Enter the shade of the forest to a posted junction at a quarter mile. The North Fork Deep Creek Trail—Hike 101—heads south and leads to Elephanthead Mountain. For this hike, continue straight on the left fork of the West Baldy Basin

Trail. Descend into a large meadow with a picture-perfect view of the Gallatin Mountains. Cross a single-log bridge over a tributary of Suce Creek. Veer right and parallel Suce Creek upstream to a trail split at the creek. Stay on the main (right) fork and ascend the slope. Pass through a meadow, returning to Suce Creek. At just over one mile, wade across the creek or use downfall logs. Gently gain elevation through the forest to Lost Creek. Parallel Lost Creek 0.3 miles and cross over it. Switchback to the left and traverse the north slope of the canyon, with views down Suce Creek Canyon. At 3 miles, the trail levels out at a posted junction on a ridge with sweeping vistas.

The Livingston Peak Tie Trail descends to the left for a half mile to the Livingston Peak Trailhead (Hike 99). Continue with Hike 99 to extend the hike on the West Baldy Basin Trail to the saddle on the divide between West and East Baldy Basins. ∎

101. North Fork Deep Creek Trail to Elephanthead Mountain
ABSAROKA RANGE from PARADISE VALLEY

Hiking distance: 11 miles round trip
Hiking time: 6 hours
Elevation gain: 3,400 feet
Maps: U.S.G.S. Brisbon and Livingston Peak
       Beartooth Publishing: Absaroka Beartooth Wilderness

Summary of hike: The North Fork Deep Creek Trail begins from the Suce Creek Trailhead in Paradise Valley. The trail follows the north rim of the forested, creek-fed canyon to the head of Elephanthead Mountain and its dramatic rock cliffs at the edge of the open tundra. The strenuous route never comes near the creek, but it leads to spectacular backcountry. The trail heads into the Absaroka-Beartooth Wilderness through mixed forests and flower-laden meadows, traveling eastward to overlooks of the weather-sculpted rock formations, the surrounding mountain peaks, and the expansive valleys. Just south of Elephanthead Mountain is Blacktail Lake, with a connecting trail to Davis Creek and the West Boulder drainage.

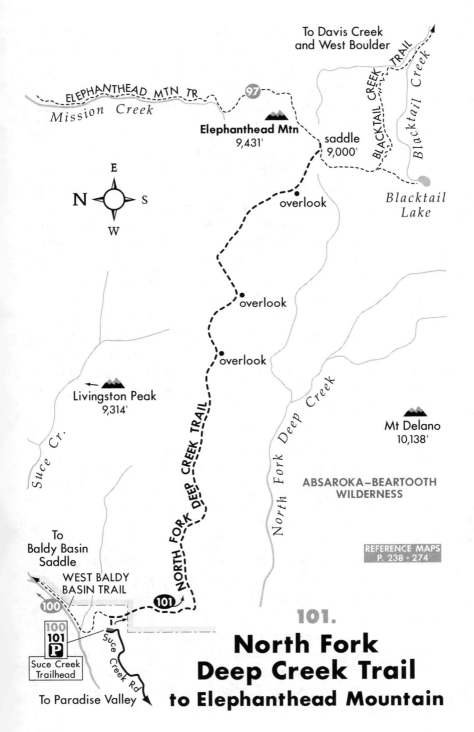

To Davis Creek
and West Boulder

ELEPHANTHEAD MTN TR

Mission Creek

97

Elephanthead Mtn
9,431'

saddle
9,000'

BLACKTAIL CREEK TRAIL

Blacktail Creek

overlook

*Blacktail
Lake*

N E S W

overlook

overlook

NORTH FORK DEEP CREEK TRAIL

Livingston Peak
9,314'

North Fork Deep Creek

Suce Cr.

Mt Delano
10,138'

**ABSAROKA–BEARTOOTH
WILDERNESS**

To
Baldy Basin
Saddle

**WEST BALDY
BASIN TRAIL**

100

100
101
P
Suce Creek
Trailhead

101

REFERENCE MAPS
P. 238 · 274

Suce Creek Rd

To Paradise Valley

101.
North Fork
Deep Creek Trail
to Elephanthead Mountain

Driving directions: From Livingston at the I-90 and Highway 89 junction (Exit 333), drive 3.1 miles south on Highway 89 to East River Road (Highway 540). Turn left and drive 2.7 miles to Suce Creek Road on the left. Turn left and continue 3 miles—following the trailhead signs—to the Suce Creek Trailhead at the end of the road. Park in the spaces on the right.

Hiking directions: Pass the trailhead kiosk, and veer to the right up the meadow. Enter the forest to a posted junction at a quarter mile. The West Baldy Basin Trail continues straight (Hike 100). Take the right fork on the North Fork Deep Creek Trail and head south. Enter the Absaroka-Beartooth Wilderness, and climb to the north rim of the forested North Fork Deep Creek Canyon at one mile. Curve left and follow the ridge east, steadily climbing through a lodgepole pine forest. Stroll through the dense forest as the steep grade temporarily eases up. Continue up to a tree-obscured overlook into the Blacktail Creek drainage at 2.5 miles. Descend through a meadow while enjoying a grand view of Elephanthead Mountain and its tilted rock cliffs. Continue downhill through a mix of forest and meadows, then climb again to an overlook beneath jagged, weather-sculpted formations. The views extend to a cirque of mountain peaks, from Mount Delano on the south horizon to Lyon Mountain in the West Boulder drainage.

Cross a trickling branch of the North Fork Deep Creek in a meadow. Follow the easy rolling terrain to another overlook of Elephanthead Mountain. Drop down and cross the open, tree-dotted expanse. Make the final ascent and top the ridge to the open tundra and a posted junction. The right fork leads 0.9 miles down to Blacktail Lake, a 4-acre lake surrounded by timber. The left fork climbs 100 yards to the 9,000-foot saddle overlooking the rock face of Elephanthead Mountain, Canyon Creek Canyon, Blacktail Creek Canyon, and three layers of ridges and plateaus in the Boulder Canyon drainage. This is our turn-around spot.

To extend the hike, follow the cairns across the head of Blacktail Creek Canyon. Traverse the rocky north canyon wall, steadily climbing to the southern base of Elephanthead Mountain to the top of Mission Creek Canyon (Hike 97), located a half mile from the saddle. ■

102. South Fork Deep Creek Trail
ABSAROKA RANGE from PARADISE VALLEY

Hiking distance: 8 miles round trip to cirque
10 miles round trip to Deep Creek Divide
Hiking time: 4 to 6 hours
Elevation gain: 2,150 (to cirque)
3,570 feet (to divide)

**map
page 291**

Maps: U.S.G.S. Brisbin and Livingston Peak
Beartooth Publishing: Absaroka Beartooth Wilderness

Summary of hike: The South Fork Deep Creek Trail follows a narrow, stream-fed canyon to the Deep Creek Divide, a pass between Paradise Valley and the West Boulder drainage. This remote, backcountry hike in the Absaroka-Beartooth Wilderness leads through the deep canyon between Mount Delano and Mount McKnight. After dropping down to the canyon floor, the path crosses and follows the South Fork Deep Creek to the Amphitheater of the South Fork, a spectacular mountain cirque. Beyond the cirque, the trail climbs up the steep valley wall to the Deep Creek Divide, where you are rewarded with spectacular views from high above Deep Creek.

Driving directions: From Livingston at the I-90 and Highway 89 junction (Exit 333), drive 3.1 miles south on Highway 89 to East River Road (Highway 540). Turn left and drive 5.5 miles south to Deep Creek South Fork Road on the left. Turn left and continue 1.6 miles to the signed trailhead. Park in the spaces on the left.

Hiking directions: From the trailhead are sweeping views across Paradise Valley and the Yellowstone River to the Gallatin Range. After enjoying the views, go through the trailhead gate and head east up the grassy slope. Pass through another gate at 0.3 miles and continue ascending, gaining 500 feet to the ridge and treeline. Cross the ridge and drop down to the South Fork Deep Creek at one mile. Walk upstream a short distance to the log bridge. Cross over the cascading creek, and head up the lush canyon above the creek. Rock-hop over a feeder stream, and steadily gain elevation at a moderate grade. Climb through an open lodgepole pine forest a hundred feet above the creek. Gently descend and enter the Absaroka-Beartooth Wilderness. Return to and follow the tumbling whitewater of the South Fork Deep Creek at the southwest foot of Mount Delano. Climb the north wall of the forested canyon, and cross a tributary stream formed on the upper slope of the mountain. Cross a couple of seasonal drainages beneath the massive, vertical rock wall. Stroll through a 7,000-foot flat below craggy rock formations At 4 miles, enter the Upper Amphitheater of the South Fork, a cirque of mountains that includes Mount McKnight towering more than 2,000 feet above the trail. The South Fork Deep Creek veers south, while the trail continues east. This is a good turn-around spot.

To extend the hike to the 9,112-foot Deep Creek Divide, which is visible to the east, enter the forest again. Head up the mountain, leaving the South Fork Deep Creek. Zigzag up the steep path, gaining 1,450 feet over the next 1.2 miles. The trail levels out near the saddle. From the saddle are sweeping vistas down into the Davis Creek drainage and across the West Boulder Valley and beyond. The Davis Creek Trail (Hike 109) descends and follows Davis Creek 8.7 miles to the West Boulder trailheads. ▪

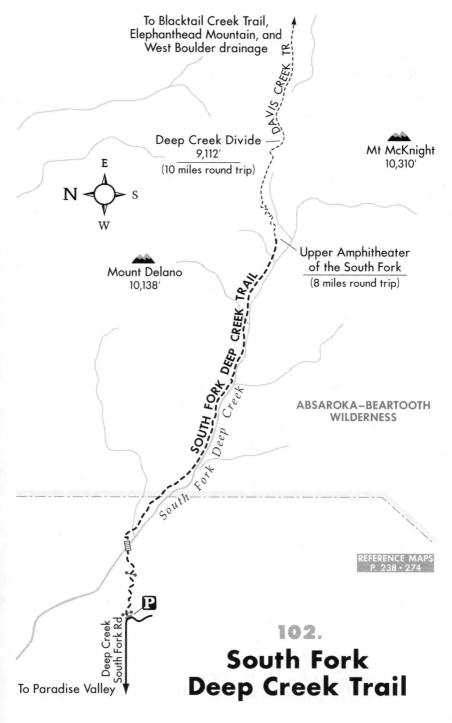

To Blacktail Creek Trail,
Elephanthead Mountain, and
West Boulder drainage

DAVIS CREEK TR.

Deep Creek Divide
9,112'
(10 miles round trip)

Mt McKnight
10,310'

N E S W

Mount Delano
10,138'

SOUTH FORK DEEP CREEK TRAIL

Upper Amphitheater
of the South Fork
(8 miles round trip)

ABSAROKA–BEARTOOTH
WILDERNESS

South Fork Deep Creek

REFERENCE MAPS
P. 238 • 274

P

Deep Creek
South Fork Rd

To Paradise Valley

102.
South Fork
Deep Creek Trail

103. Pine Creek Falls
ABSAROKA RANGE from PARADISE VALLEY

Hiking distance: 2.2 miles round trip
Hiking time: 1 hour
Elevation gain: 350 feet
Maps: U.S.G.S. Dexter Point
Beartooth Publishing: Absaroka Beartooth Wilderness

map
page 294

Summary of hike: Pine Creek Falls is a tall and narrow, double-tier cataract that fans out as it plunges over a large rock outcrop. The headwaters of Pine Creek form at Black Mountain in the Absaroka–Beartooth Wilderness. The creek fills Pine Creek Lake as it cascades 3,000 feet down the east wall of Paradise Valley to the valley floor. The Pine Creek Trail is a 5-mile-long trail that climbs 3,100 feet to Pine Creek Lake (Hike 104). This hike follows the first mile of the trail along the cascading creek to the magnificent falls. The path meanders through a spruce, fir, aspen, and maple forest en route to the base of the falls.

Driving directions: From Livingston at the I-90 and Highway 89 junction, drive 9.6 miles south on Highway 89 to Pine Creek Road on the left, between mile markers 43 and 44. Turn left and continue 2.4 miles (crossing over the Yellowstone River) to East River Road. Turn right and drive 0.7 miles to Luccock Park Road on the left. A sign is posted for the Pine Creek Campground. Turn left (east) on Luccock Park Road, and wind 3.1 miles up the foothills to the trailhead parking area at road's end (0.6 miles past the George Lake turnoff).

Hiking directions: Take the posted trail from the far end of the parking area. Immediately enter a deep, lush forest to a junction. Stay to the right on the Pine Creek Trail. At a quarter mile, pass a junction to the George Lake Trail (Hike 105) on the right. Cross a bridge over Pine Creek at 0.5 miles, and enter the Absaroka–Beartooth Wilderness. Continue along the north side of the cascading creek to a second bridge over Pine Creek at just over 1.1 mile. From the bridge is a dramatic view of towering Pine Creek Falls. Thirty yards beyond the bridge is a side shoot of the waterfall. Several unmaintained trails access the upper chute of the falls.

To hike farther, the trail continues to Pine Creek Lake, 4 miles ahead and 3,000 feet up—Hike 104. The pristine alpine lake sits in a glacial cirque high above Paradise Valley. ■

104. Pine Creek Lake
ABSAROKA RANGE from PARADISE VALLEY

Hiking distance: 10 miles round trip
Hiking time: 6 hours
Elevation gain: 3,400 feet
Maps: U.S.G.S. Dexter Point and Mount Cowen
       Rocky Mountain: Surveys Mt. Cowen Area

map
page 294

Summary of hike: Pine Creek Lake is a pristine alpine lake in a huge, 9,032-foot basin high above Paradise Valley. The lake sits in the glacial cirque on the north slope of Black Mountain, towering 900 feet above the lake in the Absaroka-Beartooth Wilderness. The strenuous but well-defined trail climbs past a series of spectacular waterfalls (including Pine Creek Falls) and a couple of smaller lakes to Pine Creek Lake. En route are vistas across Paradise Valley to the Gallatin Range.

Driving directions: From Livingston at the I-90 and Highway 89 junction, drive 9.6 miles south on Highway 89 to Pine Creek Road on the left, between mile markers 43 and 44. Turn left and continue 2.4 miles (crossing over the Yellowstone River) to East River Road. Turn right and drive 0.7 miles to Luccock Park Road on the left. A sign is posted for the Pine Creek Campground. Turn left (east) on Luccock Park Road, and wind 3.1 miles up the foothills to the trailhead parking area at road's end (0.6 miles past the George Lake turnoff).

Hiking directions: Take the posted trail from the far end of the parking area. Immediately enter a deep, lush forest to a junction. Stay to the right on the Pine Creek Trail. At a quarter mile, pass a junction to the George Lake Trail (Hike 105) on the right. Cross a bridge over Pine Creek at 0.5 miles, and enter the Absaroka-

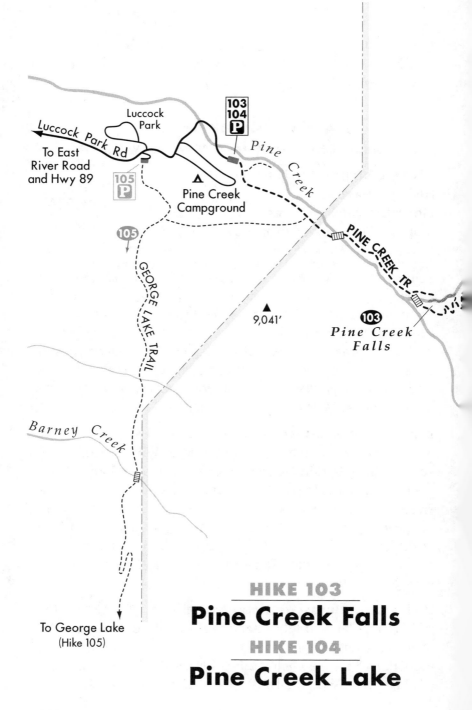

Luccock Park Rd

To East
River Road
and Hwy 89

Luccock
Park

105
P

103
104
P

Pine Creek
Campground

Pine Creek

GEORGE LAKE TRAIL

105

9,041'

PINE CREEK TR

103
*Pine Creek
Falls*

Barney Creek

To George Lake
(Hike 105)

HIKE 103
Pine Creek Falls
HIKE 104
Pine Creek Lake

N
W E
S

PINE CREEK TRAIL

waterfall

104

Mount McKnight
10,310'

waterfall *Jewell L.*

ABSAROKA–BEARTOOTH
WILDERNESS

104
*Pine Creek
Lake*

S. Fork Pine Cr.

Black Mtn
10,941'

REFERENCE MAPS
P. 238 • 274

Beartooth Wilderness. Continue along the north side of the cascading creek to a second bridge over Pine Creek at just over 1.1 mile. From the bridge is a dramatic view of towering Pine Creek Falls. Thirty yards beyond the bridge is a side shoot of the waterfall. Several unmaintained trails access the upper chute of the falls.

Continue on the main trail past the bridge, and cross downfall logs over the south channel of the creek. Zigzag up the hillside to a view down canyon of Paradise Valley. A side path on the left leads 30 yards to the brink of the falls at the narrow rock chute. The main trail follows the cascading creek, steadily climbing past huge granite boulders. The rock-embedded path leads to the creek at just under 2 miles, with a view of a 200-foot waterfall upstream.

Carefully cross the creek on downfall logs and rocks to the north side of Pine Creek. Curve left, away from the creek. Loop around the mountainside, crossing a northern tributary of the creek. Climb more switchbacks beneath the jagged spires on the north canyon wall. Return to Pine Creek and a waterfall. Follow the cascading whitewater past a series of falls. Curve away from the slope, and zigzag up the rocky slope through a scree field. Skirt the edge of a vertical rock wall beneath the crowns of Mount McKnight and Black Mountain. Top the slope and enter a forested cirque with another 200-foot waterfall. Descend to the creek and follow it upstream. A side path on the right leads to a campsite by a small lake and a full view of the waterfall.

Veer left and climb five switchbacks to another view of the falls and the lake below the rock-walled bowl. At the top of the rock face, the trail overlooks Jewel Lake and the cascade feeding the tarn. Descend to the end of Jewel Lake. Follow the west shore and cross the outlet creek 20 yards upstream from the falls. Bear left and continue past the lake, climbing out of the bowl. Pass two waterfalls filling a pool just above Jewel Lake. Above the falls, the trail reaches broad slabs of granite rock that line the north shore of gorgeous Pine Creek Lake. Another waterfall feeds the south end of the lake. After enjoying the views and well-earned rest, return along the same route. ■

105. George Lake

ABSAROKA RANGE from PARADISE VALLEY

Hiking distance: 11 miles round trip
Hiking time: 6 hours
Elevation gain: 2,500 feet
Maps: U.S.G.S. Dexter Point
       Beartooth Publishing: Absaroka Beartooth Wilderness

map
page 298

Summary of hike: George Lake (also known as Shorthill Lake) is a high-alpine lake that sits in a depression on the lower west slope of Black Mountain. The tree-lined lake has a rocky shoreline and a towering rock wall to the east that rises 1,600 feet above the lake. The trail traverses the western slope of the Absaroka Range just outside of the Absaroka-Beartooth Wilderness, with vast views overlooking Paradise Valley, the Yellowstone River, and the east face of the Gallatin Range. En route, the trail crosses Barney Creek and Cascade Creek.

Driving directions: From Livingston at the I-90 and Highway 89 junction, drive 9.6 miles south on Highway 89 to Pine Creek Road on the left, between mile markers 43 and 44. Turn left and continue 2.4 miles (crossing over the Yellowstone River) to East River Road. Turn right and drive 0.7 miles to Luccock Park Road on the left. A sign is posted for the Pine Creek Campground. Turn left (east) and wind 2.5 miles up the foothills to the posted George Lake Trailhead on the right. Veer right on the gravel road 0.15 miles to the parking area.

    Pine Creek Road is 12.3 miles north of Emigrant and 42 miles north of Gardiner.

Hiking directions: Walk up the grassy slope beneath the majestic peaks of Mount McKnight and Black Mountain. Weave through the pine forest to a posted junction at a half mile. The left fork connects with the Pine Creek Trail (Hikes 103—104). Bear right up the mountain slope as views open of Paradise Valley, the Gallatin Range, and the Yellowstone River. Cross a trickling stream in a small grotto with ferns and moss-covered rocks at just under 2 miles. Traverse the hillside along the mountain contours, and cross a small log bridge over Barney Creek at 2.5 miles. Zigzag over a talus slope, with sweeping vistas of the valley, and cross a bridge over a fern-filled drainage at 3 miles.

Descend 0.6 miles into the vast Cascade Creek canyon on a series of nine rock-strewn switchbacks. At the creek, walk a short distance downstream, and rock-hop or cross downfall logs over Cascade Creek. Wind through the riparian vegetation, and ascend the south canyon slope. Leave the drainage, continuing through a lodgepole pine forest. Begin a steep half-mile climb that levels out near George Lake. The faint path is marked with a few cairns as it descends to the north shore of the lake. After enjoying a well-earned rest, return along the same path. ■

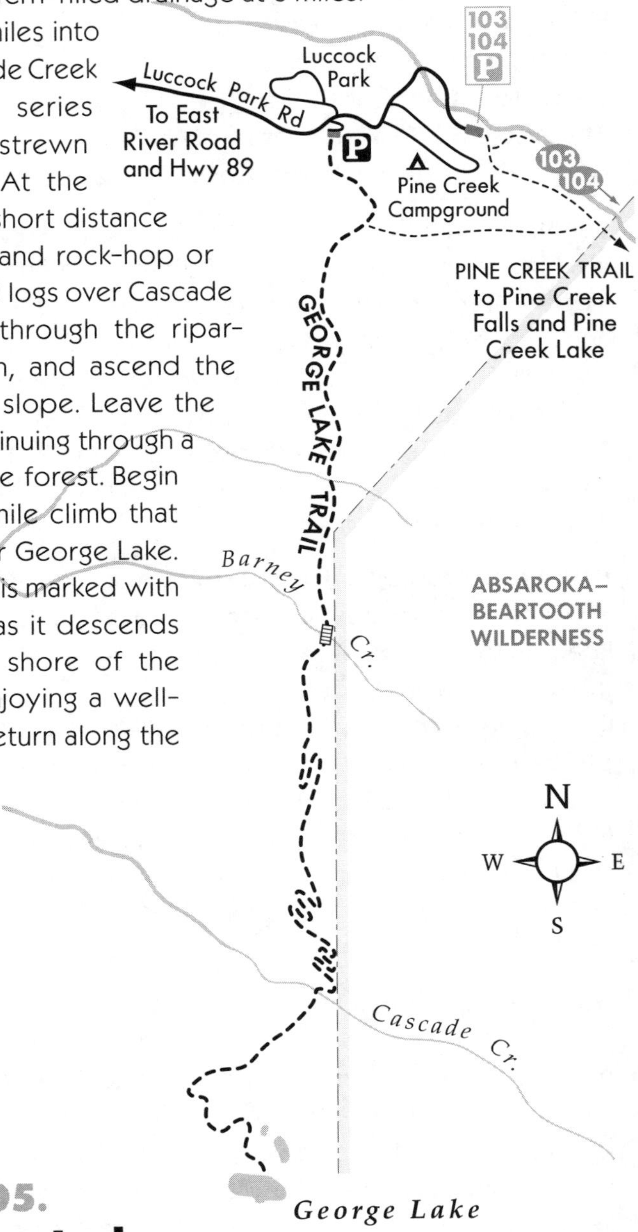

103
104
P

Luccock
Park

Luccock Park Rd

To East
River Road
and Hwy 89

P

▲
Pine Creek
Campground

103
104

PINE CREEK TRAIL
to Pine Creek
Falls and Pine
Creek Lake

GEORGE LAKE TRAIL

Barney

Cr.

ABSAROKA–
BEARTOOTH
WILDERNESS

N
W E
S

Cascade Cr.

REFERENCE MAPS
P. 238 · 274

George Lake

105.
George Lake

106. East Fork Mill Creek
ABSAROKA RANGE from PARADISE VALLEY

Hiking distance: 3 to 24 (overnight) miles round trip
Hiking time: 1.5 to 14 hours
Elevation gain: 300 to 3,900 feet
Maps: U.S.G.S. Knowles Peak and The Pyramid
       Rocky Mountain Surveys: Mt. Cowen Area
       Beartooth Publishing: Absaroka Beartooth Wilderness

map
page 301

Summary of hike: The East Fork of Mill Creek forms near Silver Pass, tumbling down from the upper reaches of Boulder Mountain at the Paradise Valley–Boulder River divide. The East Fork Mill Creek Trail stretches 12 miles eastward to Silver Pass, located on the ridge between Boulder Mountain and The Pyramid. The trail continuously follows the creek in the Absaroka-Beartooth Wilderness, steadily passing through flower–filled meadows and limestone cliffs. Atop the divide, the trail connects with the Fourmile Creek Trail and descends to the Boulder River. At the lower end of the trail is a connection with the Elbow Lake Trail, the main access route to 11,212-foot Mount Cowen, the highest peak in the Absaroka Range. This hike follows the lower end of the East Fork Mill Creek Trail along the watercourse and forested canyon floor. You may turn around at any point along the creek-side trail.

Driving directions: From Livingston at the I-90 and Highway 89 junction, drive 15.7 miles south on Highway 89 to Mill Creek Road on the left, between mile markers 37 and 38. Turn left (southeast) and continue 9.2 miles to the posted East Fork Mill Creek Road. Turn left and follow the creek 1.5 miles upstream to the posted trailhead parking area on the right.

Mill Creek Road is 6.2 miles north of Emigrant and 36 miles north of Gardiner.

Hiking directions: From the east end of the parking area, enter the dense pine forest on the posted trail. Follow the south side of the creek, skirting the Snowy Range Ranch. Traverse the hillside and loop around a small drainage to a posted trail junction at a quarter mile. The Highland Trail veers right on the east flank of Knowles Peak, connecting with the Anderson Ridge Trail and Mill Creek. Stay left, looping through a quiet side canyon and crossing a small feeder stream. Return to the main canyon, with a view of bald Arrow Peak. Continue east on the cliffside path. Zigzag up four switchbacks and enter the Absaroka-Beartooth Wilderness. Drop down and cross a wooden bridge over East Fork Mill Creek to a posted junction with the Elbow Lake Trail. The left fork follows Upper Sage Creek to Elbow Lake for 6 miles, located at the southern foot of Mount Cowen. Stay to the right on the East Fork Mill Creek Trail, following the north side of the creek. The trail steadily gains elevation for 12 miles en route to Silver Pass. Choose your own turn-around spot. ■

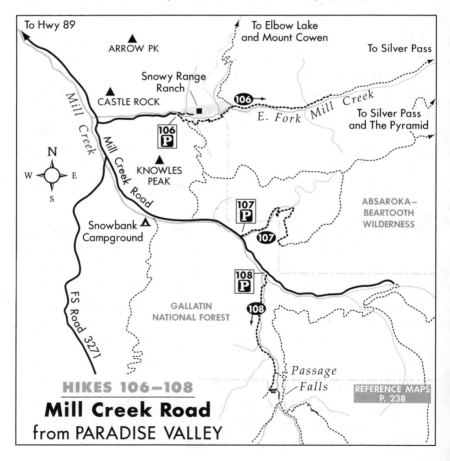

HIKES 106–108

Mill Creek Road
from PARADISE VALLEY

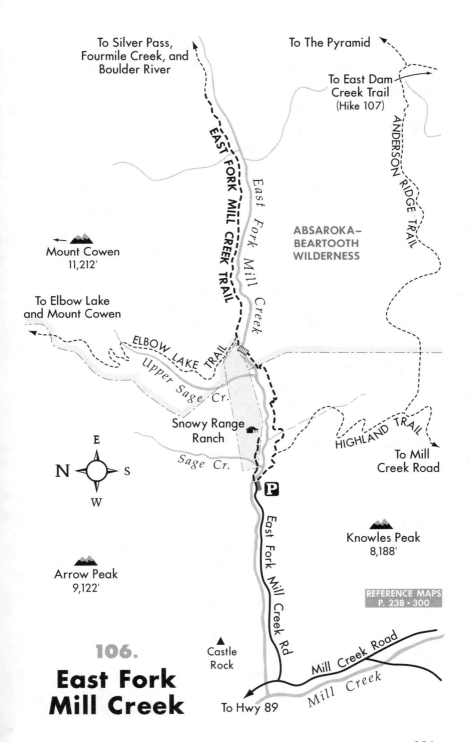

To Silver Pass,
Fourmile Creek, and
Boulder River

To The Pyramid

To East Dam
Creek Trail
(Hike 107)

East Fork Mill Creek

EAST FORK MILL CREEK TRAIL

ANDERSON RIDGE TRAIL

Mount Cowen
11,212'

ABSAROKA–
BEARTOOTH
WILDERNESS

To Elbow Lake
and Mount Cowen

ELBOW LAKE TRAIL

Upper Sage Cr.

Snowy Range
Ranch

Sage Cr.

HIGHLAND TRAIL

To Mill
Creek Road

E
N S
W

P

East Fork Mill Creek Rd

Knowles Peak
8,188'

REFERENCE MAPS
P. 238 · 300

Arrow Peak
9,122'

106.
East Fork
Mill Creek

Castle
Rock

Mill Creek Road

Mill Creek

To Hwy 89

107. East Dam Creek Trail
ABSAROKA RANGE from PARADISE VALLEY

Hiking distance: 3 miles to 9 miles round trip (for a loop)
Hiking time: 1.5 to 6 hours
Elevation gain: 900 to 2,500 feet
Maps: U.S.G.S. Knowles Peak and The Pyramid
Rocky Mountain Surveys: Mt. Cowen Area
Beartooth Publishing: Absaroka Beartooth Wilderness

Summary of hike: East Dam Creek is a small tributary of Mill Creek. The creek trickles through a narrow side canyon between Mill Creek and The Pyramid. It is also a horsepacking route and cross-country ski trail. This hike follows the lower creekside portion of the trail to open meadows and overlooks. The trail makes connections with the Anderson Ridge Trail, East Fork Mill Creek, and the Moose Park Trail along the western base of The Pyramid.

Driving directions: From Livingston at the I-90 and Highway 89 junction, drive 15.7 miles south on Highway 89 to Mill Creek Road on the left, between mile markers 37 and 38. Turn left (southeast) and continue 13.3 miles to the signed East Dam Creek Trailhead turnoff. Turn left and drive 100 yards to the trailhead and parking area on the right.

Mill Creek Road is 6.2 miles north of Emigrant and 36 miles north of Gardiner.

Hiking directions: Head east into the forest on a steady but easy incline. Follow the north side of East Dam Creek in the narrow canyon, passing talus slopes and small meadows. Meander through the riparian habitat with moss-covered rocks, crossing the trickling stream four times. Enter the Absaroka-Beartooth Wilderness. Continue through a lush meadow rimmed with conifers and backed by forested mountains and jagged rocky cliffs. Cross over the creek and loop around the upper end of the meadow at one mile. Traverse the hillside and curve left on a horseshoe bend. Climb to the south wall of the East Dam Creek drainage, overlooking the meadow and the canyon below.

Continue into a large mountain cirque and curve right, skirting the base of the upper mountains. Leave the East Dam Creek canyon, heading south. Curve along the contours of the mountain while steadily gaining elevation. Choose your own turn-around spot.

To extend the hike, the trail continues 3 more miles to the Anderson Ridge Trail, gaining an additional 1,600 feet. The Anderson Ridge Trail loops westward, joining with the Highland Trail for a 9-mile loop. To the east, the trail heads up to The Pyramid. ∎

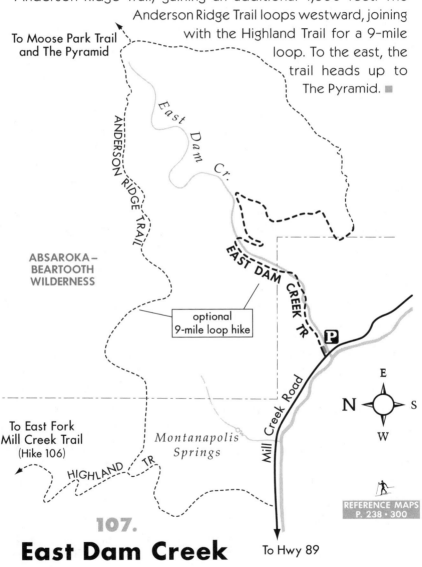

To Moose Park Trail and The Pyramid

ANDERSON RIDGE TRAIL

East Dam Cr.

ABSAROKA–
BEARTOOTH
WILDERNESS

optional
9-mile loop hike

EAST DAM CREEK TR.

P

To East Fork
Mill Creek Trail
(Hike 106)

Montanapolis
Springs

Mill Creek Road

HIGHLAND TR.

N E S W

REFERENCE MAPS
P. 238 · 300

107.
East Dam Creek

To Hwy 89

108. Passage Falls
ABSAROKA RANGE from PARADISE VALLEY

Hiking distance: 4.2 miles round trip
Hiking time: 2.5 hours
Elevation gain: 480 feet
Maps: U.S.G.S. Knowles Peak, The Pyramid, Mount Wallace
U.S.F.S. Gallatin National Forest: East Half
Beartooth Publishing: Absaroka Beartooth Wilderness

Summary of hike: Passage Falls is a massive, powerful waterfall that leaps over moss-covered rocks and plunges straight down to the narrow, rocky canyon floor. The waterfall is located in the Mill Creek watershed beneath Mount Wallace, just outside the Absaroka-Beartooth Wilderness in the Gallatin National Forest. The trail parallels Passage Creek on the Wallace Creek Trail. The falls is located just below the confluence of Wallace Creek and Passage Creek.

Driving directions: From Livingston at the I-90 and Highway 89 junction, drive 15.7 miles south on Highway 89 to Mill Creek Road on the left, between mile markers 37 and 38. Turn left (southeast) and drive 14 miles up Mill Creek Road to the Wallace Creek trailhead parking area on the right.

Mill Creek Road is 6.2 miles north of Emigrant and 36 miles north of Gardiner.

Hiking directions: The trail begins at the bridge by the confluence of Mill Creek and Passage Creek. Once over Mill Creek, continue south to another bridge crossing over Passage Creek. At one mile, cross a stream by a small waterfall and cascade. After a second stream crossing, the forested trail emerges into a small meadow, then ducks back into the forest canopy. At 1.6 miles the path forks just before a bridge on the left. Take the right branch to Passage Falls. Climb up the short, steep hill to a slope. From the slope are views overlooking a large meadow on private land. Take the trail to the left, and descend the eight switchbacks to Passage Falls. After enjoying the falls, return along the same route.

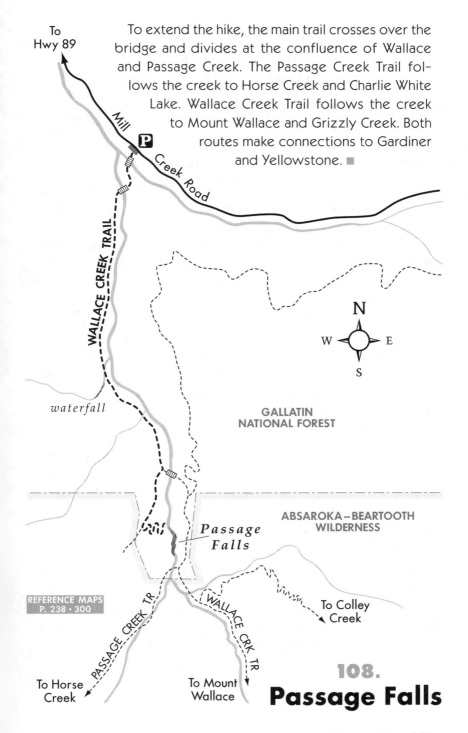

To extend the hike, the main trail crosses over the bridge and divides at the confluence of Wallace and Passage Creek. The Passage Creek Trail follows the creek to Horse Creek and Charlie White Lake. Wallace Creek Trail follows the creek to Mount Wallace and Grizzly Creek. Both routes make connections to Gardiner and Yellowstone. ■

To Hwy 89

Mill Creek Road

P

WALLACE CREEK TRAIL

waterfall

N
W E
S

GALLATIN NATIONAL FOREST

Passage Falls

ABSAROKA–BEARTOOTH WILDERNESS

To Colley Creek

REFERENCE MAPS
P. 238 · 300

PASSAGE CREEK TR.

WALLACE CRK TR

To Horse Creek

To Mount Wallace

108.
Passage Falls

109. Davis Creek Trail to Blacktail Creek

ABSAROKA RANGE from WEST BOULDER VALLEY

Hiking distance: 10 miles round trip
Hiking time: 6 hours
Elevation gain: 1,000 feet
Maps: U.S.G.S. Mount Rae and Livingston Peak
Beartooth Publishing: Absaroka Beartooth Wilderness

map
page 308

Summary of hike: The Boulder River Valley is the next drainage east from Paradise Valley. The West Boulder River forms on the northeast slope of 11,212-foot Mount Cowen at the northwest end of the main Boulder Valley. The Davis Creek Trail heads west out of the West Boulder Valley towards Elephanthead Mountain and Mount Delano, connecting with trails to Paradise Valley. The trail begins from the West Boulder Campground, crosses Davis Creek on a footbridge, then parallels the west side of the wide creek below Shell Mountain and Lion Mountain for 10 miles to the Deep Creek Divide. This hike follows the first five miles of the trail to Blacktail Creek at its confluence with Davis Creek. The remote path weaves through intermittent timber, open meadows, and a quarter mile of private ranch land.

Driving directions: From I-90, there are two exits into the town of Big Timber—Exit 367 and Exit 370. From Exit 367, drive one mile to McLeod Street (Highway 298). From Exit 370, drive 2.4 miles to McLeod Street (Highway 298). Turn south on McLeod Street, passing through downtown and over I-90.

Continuing south on Highway 298, drive 16.7 miles south into the Boulder River Valley to the posted West Boulder Road on the right. The turnoff is located 0.6 miles past the town of McLeod. Turn right and continue 7.4 miles to a posted junction. Bear left, staying on West Boulder Road, and drive 6 miles to a Y-fork at the West Boulder Campground. Stay to the left and park 100 yards ahead in the large trailhead parking area.

Hiking directions: Walk 100 yards back to the campground road fork. Veer left 50 yards into the camp to another fork. Stay left and pass through the gate by the West Boulder forest service cabin. Curve right, passing the rental cabin to Davis Creek. Cross the Davis Creek Bridge and bear left past the trail sign. Head west, traversing the grassy hillside above and parallel to the scenic creek. Bear right, leaving the old road, and head up the hill. About 50 yards ahead, make a horseshoe left bend and continue traversing the hill to what appears as the end of the trail by tall brush. Switchback to the right and follow the mountain slope above the Burnt Leather Ranch, with far-reaching vistas into the West Boulder Valley. Pass a trail gate and enter a quarter-mile easement through the ranch land. Pass through another gate, returning to the national forest.

Stroll through the forest at an easy grade, staying on the Davis Creek Trail past a couple of signed forks. Cross the gently rolling terrain, skirting the base of Shell Mountain, to Crystal Creek at 2 miles. Cross the small stream to an overlook of the tumbling waters of Davis Creek. Pass through another gate to the edge of Davis Creek. Follow the creek upstream a short distance, and enter a lodgepole pine forest. Meander through the dense forest for nearly a mile. Cross a small meadow, with a view of Shell Mountain to the northwest and Lyon Mountain across Davis Creek. Descend and rock hop over an unnamed stream, then drop into a large meadow under the shadow of Mount Delano. Reenter the forest to Canyon Creek at 4 miles. Cross the creek on rocks and continue one mile west to Blacktail Creek. This is our turn-around spot.

To extend the hike, cross the creek to a signed junction. The Davis Creek Trail continues to the left and heads southwest. The trail parallels Davis Creek for 3.7 miles to the 9,112-foot Deep Creek Divide, connecting with the South Fork Deep Creek Trail and Paradise Valley (Hikes 101—102). The Blacktail Creek Trail bears right, leading 2.5 miles to Blacktail Lake and 2.8 miles to Elephanthead Mountain (Hike 97). ▪

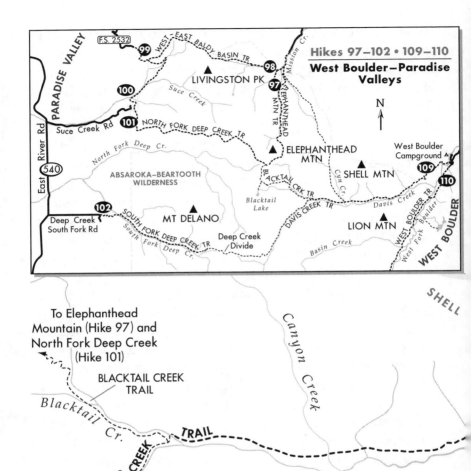

West Boulder Valley

HIKE 109
Davis Creek Trail to Blacktail Creek

HIKE 110
West Boulder Trail to West Boulder Meadows

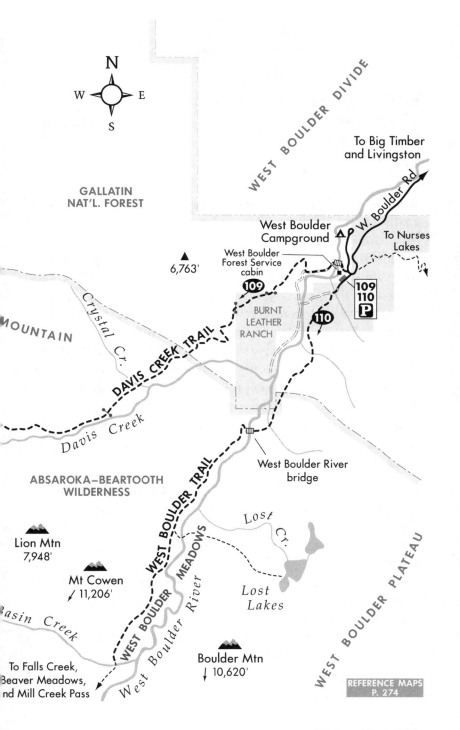

N

W   E

S

GALLATIN
NAT'L. FOREST

6,763'

WEST BOULDER DIVIDE

To Big Timber
and Livingston

W. Boulder Rd

West Boulder
Campground

To Nurses
Lakes

West Boulder
Forest Service
cabin

109

BURNT
LEATHER
RANCH

109
110
P

110

Crystal Cr.

MOUNTAIN

DAVIS CREEK TRAIL

Davis Creek

West Boulder River
bridge

ABSAROKA–BEARTOOTH
WILDERNESS

WEST BOULDER TRAIL

Lion Mtn
7,948'

Mt Cowen
↙ 11,206'

WEST BOULDER MEADOWS

West Boulder River

Lost Cr.

Lost
Lakes

WEST BOULDER PLATEAU

Basin Creek

To Falls Creek,
Beaver Meadows,
and Mill Creek Pass

West Boulder River

Boulder Mtn
↓ 10,620'

REFERENCE MAPS
P. 274

110. West Boulder Trail to West Boulder Meadows

WEST BOULDER VALLEY

Hiking distance: 7 miles round trip
Hiking time: 3.5 hours
Elevation gain: 350 feet
Maps: U.S.G.S. Mount Rae
Beartooth Publishing: Absaroka Beartooth Wilderness

map
page 309

Summary of hike: The West Boulder River forms on the northeast slope of 11,212-foot Mount Cowen, the highest peak in the Absaroka Range, and the snowfields atop 10,620-foot Boulder Mountain. The West Boulder Trail, a portal into the Absaroka-Beartooth Wilderness, extends 16 miles up the glacially carved mountain valley, passing the river's headwaters and skirting the eastern base of Mount Cowen to Mill Creek Pass. This hike follows the first 3.5 miles of the trail to West Boulder Meadows. The vast mountain meadow sits at the eastern foot of 7,948-foot Lion Mountain. Rivulets of the river lace through the lush meadow grasses. The scenic trail follows the river at a gentle grade through meadows and intermittent forests of aspen and mixed pine. Throughout the hike are great views of the West Boulder River, the forested hillsides, and the surrounding snow-capped mountains.

Driving directions: From I-90, there are two exits into the town of Big Timber—Exit 367 and Exit 370. From Exit 367, drive one mile to McLeod Street (Highway 298). From Exit 370, drive 2.4 miles to McLeod Street (Highway 298). Turn south on McLeod Street, passing through downtown and over I-90.

Continuing south on Highway 298, drive 16.7 miles south into the Boulder River Valley to the posted West Boulder Road on the right. The turnoff is located 0.6 miles past the town of McLeod. Turn right and continue 7.4 miles to a posted junction. Bear left, staying on West Boulder Road, and drive 6 miles to a Y-fork at the West Boulder Campground. Stay to the left and park 100 yards ahead in the large trailhead parking area.

Hiking directions: From the far (south) end of the parking area, cross the cattle guard and walk 160 yards south on the dirt road. Leave the road and veer left on the signed West Boulder Trail. Climb the forested hillside, and pass a couple of small flower-covered meadows surrounded by mountains. Pass through a trail gate at 0.3 miles, and enter the Gallatin National Forest. Cross the hillside on the undulating path. Pass through the burn area from the Derby Fire of 2006. Enter the Absaroka-Beartooth Wilderness, and continue to the West Boulder River Bridge at one mile. Cross the wooden bridge over the river, and curve right a short distance downstream. Zigzag up three switchbacks and traverse the mountainside, passing a private entrance to the Burnt Leather Ranch. Head south high above the river, with a great vista up the West Boulder Canyon to Mount Cowen. At 1.8 miles, gradually descend to the north end of lush West Boulder Meadows. Side paths on the left lead down to the meandering river, and fishermen trails follow the river upstream. The West Boulder Trail follows the hillside between the grass-filled meadow and the steep east cliffs of Lion Mountain, pock-marked with caves. Stroll through the mountain meadow, dotted with boulders and a few skeleton trees from the fire. Drop down and cross a stream to a metal gate. Go through the gate, top a small rise, and descend to cascading Basin Creek. This is our turn-around spot.

To extend the hike, rock-hop over the creek and continue through the meadow. Parallel the west side of the river, reaching a junction with the Falls Creek Trail at 7.8 miles. Another 2.6 miles past Falls Creek is Beaver Meadows. ▪

DAY HIKE BOOKS

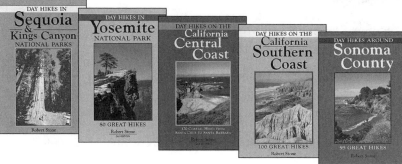

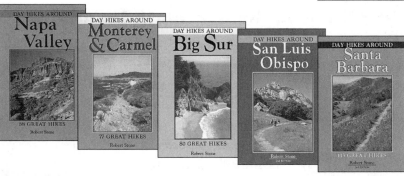

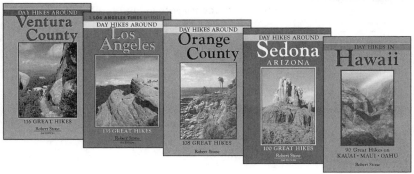

Day Hikes In Yellowstone National Park

Yellowstone National Park is a magnificent area with beautiful, dramatic scenery and incredible hydro-thermal features. Within it 2.2-million acres lies some of the earth's greatest natural treasures.

Day Hikes In Yellowstone National Park includes a thorough cross-section of 82 hikes throughout the park. Now in its fourth edition, the guide includes all of the park's most popular hikes as well as a wide assortment of secluded backcountry trails. Highlights include thundering waterfalls, unusual thermal features, expansive meadows, alpine lakes, the Grand Canyon of the Yellowstone, geysers, hot springs, and 360-degree vistas of the park.

184 pages • 82 hikes • 4th Edition 2005 • ISBN 978-1-57342-054-9

Day Hikes In the Beartooth Mountains

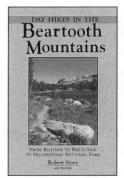

The rugged Beartooth Mountains are Montana's highest mountain range. This beautiful range in the Rocky Mountains rises dramatically from the plains in south-central Montana and stretches to the northern reaches of Yellowstone National Park.

Day Hikes In the Beartooth Mountains includes an extensive collection of hikes within this mountain range and the adjacent foothills and plains. The 87 hikes range from 11,000-foot alpine plateaus to treks along the Yellowstone River as it begins its journey through the arid plains. A wide range of scenery and ecosystems accommodates all levels of hiking, from relaxing creekside strolls to all-day, high-elevation outings. Includes many hikes along the Beartooth Highway and 16 hikes in the Billings area.

208 pages • 87 hikes • 4th Edition 2006 • ISBN 978-1-57342-052-5

LINDA STONE

About the Author

Since 1991, Robert Stone has been writer, photographer, and publisher of Day Hike Books. He is a Los Angeles Times Best Selling Author and an award-winning journalist of Rocky Mountain Outdoor Writers and Photographers, the Outdoor Writers Association of California, the Northwest Outdoor Writers Association, and the Bay Area Travel Writers.

Robert has hiked every trail in the Day Hike Book series. With 23 hiking guides in the series, many in their third and fourth editions, he has hiked thousands of miles of trails throughout the western United States and Hawaii. When Robert is not hiking, he researches, writes, and maps the hikes before returning to the trails. He spends summers in the Rocky Mountains of Montana and winters on the California Central Coast.